Designs and Anthropologies

School for Advanced Research Advanced Seminar Series
Michael F. Brown
General Editor

Since 1970 the School for Advanced Research (formerly the School of American Research) and SAR Press have published over one hundred volumes in the Advanced Seminar series. These volumes arise from seminars held on SAR's Santa Fe campus that bring together small groups of experts to explore a single issue. Participants assess recent innovations in theory and methods, appraise ongoing research, and share data relevant to problems of significance in anthropology and related disciplines. The resulting volumes reflect SAR's commitment to the development of new ideas and to scholarship of the highest caliber. The complete Advanced Seminar series can be found at www.sarweb.org.

Also available in the School for Advanced Research Advanced Seminar Series:

Trumpism, Mexican America, and the Struggle for Latinx Citizenship edited by Phillip B. Gonzales, Renato Rosaldo and Mary Louise Pratt

Archaeologies of Empire: Local Participants and Imperial Trajectories edited by Anna L. Boozer, Bleda S. Düring, and Bradley J. Parker

Walling In and Walling Out: Why Are We Building New Barriers to Divide Us? edited by Laura McAtackney and Randall H. McGuire

How Nature Works: Rethinking Labor on a Troubled Planet edited by Sarah Besky and Alex Blanchette

The Psychology of Women under Patriarchy edited by Holly F. Mathews and Adriana M. Manago

Governing Gifts: Faith, Charity, and the Security State edited by Erica Caple James

Negotiating Structural Vulnerability in Cancer Control: Contemporary Challenges for Applied Anthropology edited by Julie Armin, Nancy Burke, and Laura Eichelberger

Puebloan Societies: Homology and Heterogeneity in Time and Space edited by Peter Whiteley

New Geospatial Approaches to the Anthropological Sciences edited by Robert L. Anemone and Glenn C. Conroy

Seduced and Betrayed: Exposing the Contemporary Microfinance Phenomenon edited by Milford Bateman and Kate Maclean

For additional titles in the School for Advanced Research Advanced Seminar Series, please visit unmpress.com.

Designs and Anthropologies

FRICTIONS AND AFFINITIES

Edited by Keith M. Murphy and Eitan Y. Wilf

Afterword by Arturo Escobar

SCHOOL FOR ADVANCED RESEARCH PRESS • SANTA FE

UNIVERSITY OF NEW MEXICO PRESS • ALBUQUERQUE

Library of Congress Cataloging-in-
Publication Data
Names: Murphy, Keith M., editor. | Wilf,
    Eitan Y., editor. | Escobar, Arturo, 1951–
    writer of afterword.
Title: Designs and anthropologies: frictions
    and affinities / edited by Keith M. Murphy
    and Eitan Wilf with an afterword by
    Arturo Escobar.
Other titles: School for Advanced Research
    advanced seminar series.
Description: Santa Fe: School for Advanced
    Research Press; Albuquerque: University
    of New Mexico Press, 2021. | Series:
    School for Advanced Research advanced
    seminar series | Includes bibliographical
    references and index.
Identifiers: LCCN 2021020074 (print) | LCCN
    2021020075 (e-book) |
    ISBN 9780826362780 (paperback) |
    ISBN 9780826362797 (e-book)
Subjects: LCSH: Design — Anthropological
    aspects. | Design — Human factors.
    | Anthropology — Methodology. |
    Ethnology.
Classification: LCC NK1520. D48 2021 (print)
    | LCC NK1520 (e-book) |
    DDC 745.2 — dc23
LC record available at https://lccn.loc.
    gov/2021020074
LC e-book record available at https://lccn.loc.
    gov/2021020075

Founded in 1889, the University of New Mexico sits on the traditional homelands of the Pueblo of Sandia. The original peoples of New Mexico — Pueblo, Navajo, and Apache — since time immemorial have deep connections to the land and have made significant contributions to the broader community statewide. We honor the land itself and those who remain stewards of this land throughout the generations and also acknowledge our committed relationship to Indigenous peoples. We gratefully recognize our history.

Cover photograph: Adapted from photograph by Albert Vincent Wu on Unsplash
Designed by Felicia Cedillos
Composed in Minion Pro 10/14

The seminar from which this book resulted was made possible by the generous support of the Annenberg Conversations Endowment.

Of Three Configurations

KEITH M. MURPHY AND EITAN Y. WILF

The recent coalescence of design anthropology as a distinct subfield of inter-disciplinary research, appearing most prominently in the form of several edited volumes (Clarke 2017b; Gunn and Donovan 2012; Gunn, Otto, and Smith 2013; Akama et al. 2018; Smith et al. 2016), is a strong indicator that the decades-long alignment of design and anthropology is evolving. From at least the 1990s onward, "design ethnography" (Salvador et al. 1999; see also Graffam 2010)—typically figured as the use of ethnographic research methods in corporate set-tings—was the dominant form of the alignment of anthropology and design. Since about 2010, however, a number of new arrangements between these two fields have emerged, including more anthropologists heeding Lucy Suchman's (2011, 3) call to develop "a critical anthropology *of* design," as well as a turn to design pedagogy and practice as resources for transforming the fundamentals of ethnographic fieldwork more generally (Rabinow et al. 2008). Anthropo-logical research in these veins has highlighted, for instance, the ways in which ethnographic methods have been both productively incorporated into and problematically reified within a number of different design arenas, while other endeavors have attempted to clarify the potential benefits of design methods and pedagogy for a transformed and updated anthropological toolkit.

This volume is both a continuation of and a deviation from this emergent line of inquiry, probing the possibilities and pitfalls underlying interactions between anthropology and design. The anthropologists we originally assem-bled for this project all vary in how they relate to design. Some have trained and worked as designers, some ethnographically studied designers or people in design-adjacent fields, and still others have somehow been influenced by design in their work without ever having dealt with it directly. The basic atti-tudes toward design we all held vary, too, ranging from celebratory to skeptical, with a tremendous amount of complexity in between. The clarion call orga-nizing us was constrained, but also relatively free: participants were asked to explore the design-and-anthropology relationship in whatever way they saw fit, so long as it loosely fell under Keith Murphy's (2016b) articulation of three different configurations—anthropology *for* design, in which anthropological methods and concepts are mobilized in the design process; anthropology *of* design, in which design is positioned as an object of ethnographic inquiry and critique; and design *for* anthropology, in which anthropologists borrow concepts and practices from design to enhance traditional ethnographic forms.[1] The results of these explorations, including a week of intense deliberation at the School for Advanced Research (SAR) in Santa Fe and many writerly revisions in the months that followed, are what we present in this book.[2]

Frictions and Affinities

But a basic question remains: Why ought anthropologists care about design in the first place? There are plenty of answers to this question, of course, several of which are demonstrated in the chapters that follow, but perhaps the most obvious answer is that design is ubiquitous in human life, and in the many guises it adopts it has powerful effects. Yet, until recently, anthropologists have mostly ceded the responsibility for exploring design to scholars from other disciplines. Take, for instance, the Design Research Society. This is the largest international body supporting interdisciplinary research in design, founded in the United Kingdom in 1966 in the context of a general turn in the postwar era toward developing a coherent "design methodology" for large-scale problem-solving efforts. During World War II such efforts had been typically handled by scientists and engineers (N. Cross 2007). Indeed, before this period, neither industry nor academy had paid much special attention to design, outside of architecture (Dilnot 1984). Then starting in the late 1960s, a new generation of thinkers, inspired by both the dawn of the space age and the emergence of new computational technologies, began touting design as a new and flexible framework to complement existing problem-solving models inherited from engineering. But within this growing field of design research there were few to any anthropological voices advocating a critical excavation of design and design practice (this also being the start of the practice theory era). Instead, design research came to be dominated by two distinct agendas, one from engineering (and eventually computer science) that promoted design as a *technical* discipline, and the other from art history that focused more on design as a generator of *aesthetic* products and that was largely steered by the great man theory. When social science did eventually enter the fray, it was in the guise of cognitive psychology — with some notable exceptions, such as the early work of Lucy Suchman and her colleagues — and largely in the service of improving or developing different design practices, rather than critically analyzing them from a broader social or political point of view, or using ethnography as a central methodology.

Beginning in the early to mid-2010s, a range of projects and practical collaborations began addressing the paucity of anthropological attention to design, clustering under a set of almost interchangeable terms such as design anthropology, design ethnography, and ethnographic design, predominantly in Europe (especially Scandinavia), North America, and Australia. In some respects this move reflected anthropology's essential instinct to explore any and all worldly domains touched by human hands, and at the time design and "design thinking" were very much in the air, bolstered by the publication of several influential books, most notably *Change by Design* by Tim Brown of the design firm IDEO (Brown 2009). But rather than merely filling a gap in anthropological knowledge, many of these projects also seemed to succumb to a kind of inchoate allure swaying between design and anthropology, in which practitioners from both fields were seduced by the methodological and concept-building capacities that their counterparts possessed. In a word, anthropology and design were caught in the throes of a mutual attraction.

Squirreled away in a number of Max Weber's writings is the concept of "elective affinities," a partially developed theoretical construct he borrowed from eighteenth-century chemistry — by way of Goethe (see Goethe 1978) — to explain why different sorts of things in the social world seem to "naturally" bind together, even though there may be no real material contiguity between them. The most well-known example of this in Weber's work is the elective affinities that bind Calvinism with capitalism (Weber 2002), but more broadly, elective affinities can hold between all sorts of social and cultural formations. Perhaps the most interesting aspect of this concept is that it productively relies on what one scholar described as "an obvious absurdity" (Howe 1978, 310–71): the seeming contradiction between the free choice of "election" and the naturalness implied by "affinities" both combined into a single idea. However, what Weber was trying to get at is how people find plausible links between different things in the world and then argue that those links are "real" or "natural." Sometimes these bonds are strong and do not require much argumentation at all because they plainly seem to belong together. Other times they are weak, which means more effort is required for making the case that the things brought together properly "fit."

"Design" and "anthropology" are two terms that refer to phenomena out in the world with elective affinities holding between them, features that both anthropologists and designers are choosing to bring together because their links seem to provide benefit to both fields. The earlier iteration of "design ethnography" was a mostly unrequited relationship in which anthropological methods were seen as providing textured insight into what might otherwise be considered shallow research and development processes. As Tony Salvador, Genevieve Bell, and Ken Anderson argued (1999, 36), "A basic assumption of design ethnography is that people here, there, or anywhere are not just consumers. They are social beings, people with desires, wishes, needs, wants—some articulated, some unrecognized." In this early version, anthropology had a lot to give design in terms of concepts, methods, and styles of argument, but anything that design gave back to anthropology was strictly incidental.

Design anthropology in its contemporary form is not as narrowly focused as the earlier incarnation of design ethnography, and as such it predicates a much richer relationship between anthropology and design. Given that elective affinities tend not to align in only one direction, but *mutually correspond*, design anthropology assumes within its scope that if ethnography can be useful for design, then perhaps design can be useful for ethnography. With that in mind, some anthropologists have tried to introduce specific studio practices derived from design pedagogy into how they teach, talk about, and think about ethnography as well as anthropology more broadly (see, e.g., Murphy and Marcus 2013). One premise underlying this move is that ethnographic norms and traditions are stale and often ill-suited for the kinds of twenty-first-century social worlds that anthropologists tend to find themselves studying; design practice is generally really good at stimulating imagination and encouraging problem-oriented thinking. Perhaps using design to "reimagine" ethnography—just as ethnography has been used to reimagine design—can help transform the very possibilities of what ethnographic practice can be.

As it stands, the mutual attractions between anthropology and design are, essentially, instrumentalist exploitations of their identified elective affinities—what can anthropology do for design, and what can design do for anthropology? Indeed, as Christina Wasson (2000) described it, when anthropology was first introduced to design, it originally took on a form much reduced from its traditional conceptualization, notably marked by shorter periods of ethnographic fieldwork and very little theoretical scaffolding. In some domains this situation is changing, but in general only very specific features of ethnography have been selected as usefully correspondent to design, and to be sure, the same is true the other way around: only very specific features of design are treated as usefully correspondent to ethnography. What this means is that design and anthropology function as aspirational figures of salvation for each other, each seemingly offering some missing piece that the other lacks, or a jolt of ameliorative sense or structure. Anthropology, so the logic goes, can make design somehow more "context-sensitive," and design can make anthropology somehow more "relevant."

Contending with Frictions and Multiplicities

Thus far in the development of design anthropology the elective affinities that scholars and practitioners have exploited have by and large—although not exclusively—been methodological and practical, chiefly concerned with the mechanics of conceiving and carrying out the work of each of the broader contributing disciplines. There has also been a growing number of more or less traditional ethnographic studies of different design practices, with an eye toward critically evaluating the positions and conditions of design in particular cultural contexts. Some of the chapters in this volume continue along this path, highlighting in various ways the elective affinities between anthropology and design. Others, though, adopt a different stance, calling into question or even outright challenging the very grounds for elective affinities between design and anthropology in the first place. Indeed, what all of these essays demonstrate, in one way or another, is a critical probing of the "border," to use Suchman's term, between these two seemingly mutually attracted disciplines.

We titled the original SAR seminar "Designs and Anthropologies" as a subtle acknowledgment that while both "design" and "anthropology" are terms typically used in the singular, they both actually refer to a very wide range of things. This is quite obvious with design, which covers phenomena as distinct as creating software interfaces and planning entire cities, but also applies to anthropology, a category ecumenical enough to encompass almost any research centered on humans and their lifeworlds. Indeed, because both terms cover such variable ranges, it is tempting to proclaim that any single "design anthropology" is all but impossible to build. And perhaps it really is impossible to build, at least a design anthropology that incorporates the critiques of each of its constituent parts but still has something useful to say. One of the outcomes of our collective discussions in Santa Fe is that if we commit to the reality that both design and anthropology are unstable signifiers with constantly shifting referents, rather than two coherent facts with consistent elective affinities (as design anthropology has heretofore operated), then we are very much left with the trouble of dealing head-on with the messiness of both design and anthropology.

But then again, perhaps that is the point. Perhaps laying out the troubles that come with aligning design and anthropology directly alongside the virtues reveals pertinent matters that might otherwise remain subdued or undiscussed. We originally chose to explore the three configurations of design and anthropology together, rather than focusing on just one (such as "anthropology of design"), because, despite different commitments and priorities, new and ongoing work in areas roughly covered by those configurations provides valuable perspectives on a shared set of concepts, questions, methods, and implications for both anthropology and design as human-centered disciplines. We posed a set of motivating questions that cut across the configurations—for instance, What is the position of design as a pervasive mode of intervention in human lives? How are the politics (and ethics) of this intervention handled? How do design and anthropology identify and construct "problems" in the social world—and how does each work toward "solving" them? In what ways is creativity conditioned, mediated, and given value by institutions (such as corporations, legal regimes, markets)? And how does design recursively redistribute those processes for users?

In the pieces that emerged from our efforts, some of these questions were addressed, others weren't, and still new ones were raised and worked through. Each of us, in our own ways, was committed to unpacking, critiquing, interpreting, and reassembling the emergent, and timely, alignments of design and anthropology. While the original three configurations remained throughout, the texture and tenor of those configurations shifted away from what we'd originally conceived to become something different. Our guiding agenda in exploring anthropology for design, of design, and design for anthropology was not to abolish the friction between the two modes of scholarship and practice—either by censoring one or the other mode of practice or by ensuring that they align with one another in every dimension—but rather to make sure that whatever friction their collaboration creates remains generative rather than constraining.

Configuration One: Anthropology for Design

Valuable partnerships between ethnographers and designers have long char-
acterized the work of corporate ethnography (Urban and Koh 2013, 147–149),
but the publication of Alison J. Clarke's volume *Design Anthropology: Object
Culture in the 21st Century* (Clarke 2010; cf. 2017b) gave a useful title to this
style of collaboration—or at least a version that specifically placed design at its
center. With its list of contributors spanning a number of areas of expertise, the
work outlined a constellation of differently positioned stakeholders in the field.
Two more volumes soon followed (Gunn and Donovan 2012; Gunn, Otto, and
Smith 2013), which helped further entrench design anthropology as a distinct
and recognizable area of research, with a notable focus among the contributions on integrating anthropology into designing contexts. One central feature
that distinguishes this iteration of design anthropology from earlier versions of
design ethnography is an emphasis on not just ethnographic methods but also
anthropological concepts and dispositions as they relate to design practice and
theory. Many design anthropologists work directly alongside designers in the
design process, helping to transform what is often considered "user research"—
in which "user" is a blunt category defined tautologically as the kinds of people
who will use some designed product—into a rich and textured investigation
into the lifeworlds of the actual people for whom designers are creating objects
(or spaces, interfaces, etc.). In this respect design anthropology has often contributed to the enhancement of design through the introduction of anthropological insights and methods into situated design processes, rather than as a
stage of research that precedes actual design work.

However, as Lucy Suchman points out in her chapter, anthropology's potential contribution to design has often been hindered by the desire to leave out
anthropology's critical and self-reflexive sensibilities. Between the years 1980
and 2000—that is, precisely when anthropology was beginning to develop a
self-reflexive understanding of itself as a critically engaged form of scholarship—key strands of design became institutionalized in technoscientific and
corporate settings such as those that are characteristic of Silicon Valley–style
capitalism, in which questions about the politics of design and corporate
research, as well as the critical analysis of the world economy and financial markets, were discouraged and framed as insubordination and betrayal. Her chapter demonstrates how specific locations constrain and afford the very possibility
of anthropology for design. Anthropology for design should consequently be

understood not as a decontextualized form of productive synergy but as a mode of cooperation that is always already multiply determined and whose impact can therefore be unpredictable. For there to be a viable anthropology for professional design, design ought to undergo the same processes of decolonialization that anthropology experienced in the 1980s and 1990s. Suchman surveys a number of recent books that explore the multiplicities and ambivalent politics of design practices and that suggest that such critical self-reflection is currently taking place.

The potential contribution of anthropology to design practices has also been hindered by the subordination of anthropology's methods of data collection and analysis—which are anchored in relatively slow production norms that reflect the discipline's emphasis on context-sensitivity—to the much faster production norms that prevail in contemporary post-Fordist business settings. As Eitan Wilf argues in his chapter, the contemporary post-Fordist environment requires business organizations to have up-to-date information and to make swift decisions as a prerequisite for survival, if not for success. Pressured by their clients' demand to generate input that is both context-sensitive and instantaneous, designers have transformed anthropology's methods of data collection and analysis into methods of fast data collection and analysis. Those methods entail the streamlining, standardization, and acceleration of ethnography and of the analysis of the data collected by means of it. In so doing, designers endorse a rhetoric of emergence and context-sensitivity, which they operationalize by means of practices that greatly predetermine the end results of their research. Anthropological methods have thus become reified practices that connote context-sensitivity in theory but are stripped of it in practice.

Configuration Two: Anthropology of Design

Ruminations on, or direct analyses of, design and designing from an explicitly anthropological point of view are still comparatively few in number (e.g., Appadurai 2013; Murphy 2015; Wilf 2016, 2019; Yarrow 2019), including some that explore what could be considered the shadow side of designed objects (Jain 2006; Schüll 2012). Nonetheless there has been a marked uptick in studies of various phenomena that critically address design as a cultural practice, or in some way consider design as a relevant context for understanding the ways in which certain phenomena are conceived, shaped, and given meaning.

The central object of inquiry for an anthropology of design cannot be well defined because, as stated above, "design" itself is a rather slippery term. "Design" can refer to things, or sets of things; to a style, such as "modernist" or "socialist modernist" (see Fehérváry 2013); to a process of creation, in which things of all kinds are given form (what we could call "designing"); and to something "value-added," as in "designer" products or objects crafted with a particular attention to aesthetic detail, such as Apple computers and phones. Design traverses multiple scales and multiple phenomena, from the smallest details of printed letterforms to the planned contours of megacities or even completely new forms of human habitation (see Olson 2018, chap. 4). Design holds strong elective affinities with a number of long-standing recipients of anthropological attention, including art, architecture, and craft. In some of these contexts design can be a relatively observable feature, especially within ethnographic studies of advertising (Shankar 2015), urban and suburban development (Low 2003), fashion (Luvaas 2012), and even infrastructure (Larkin 2013). In others—for instance, in population planning (Greenhalgh 2003) and the design of novel artistic styles (Wilf 2013)—design elements may be less obvious. Recent anthropological analyses of brands and marketing (Nakassis 2012) reveal the complex sensitivities that subsist between objects, messages about those objects, and the ways those objects circulate, much of which is explicitly designed by a host of graphic designers, advertisers, and marketers. Indeed, an attention to the features and details of things (Chumley 2013) is a central characteristic of almost every kind of design or designing.

However, as Lilly Irani argues in her chapter, despite the complexity of design as a form of situated action that involves an assemblage of agents and a variety of designed objects, the increased professionalization of design and its increased embeddedness in market capitalism have made many design settings sites in which new forms of social hierarchies are produced and old forms of hierarchies are reproduced, and these changes have transformed design into an invasive mode of intervention in the social world. Irani shows how human-centered design has been eagerly adopted in the field of philanthropy and development because it promises to reconcile and even happily marry top-down development efforts, which have received a bad reputation, and bottom-up feedback, ideas, and autonomy. However, although human-centered design seems to offer the magic formula of a universal best practice—a set of abstract, rule-governed recipes—that is attuned to communal, local, and affective life, its deployment in practice reproduces hierarchies of innovation, where the human-centered designer is conceptualized as the bearer of a higher-level kind of knowledge that can help society transform itself, whereas the local individual is seen as a repository of "ingenious ideas" that represent unsystematic improvisation and short-term, unsustainable solutions in response to disasters or crises. The local individual is thus valorized only on the surface. In practice he or she remains a subject in need of assistance. Ultimately, designers search for needs that might justify intervention into people's lives. Instead of humanizing technology, human-centered design ends up euphemizing old patriarchal practices of management for the creation of new markets for commodities in the developing world.

Configuration Three: Design for Anthropology

Stemming partly from a growing sense that traditional ethnographic forms and norms are incompatible with the worlds anthropologists now study, and partly from the perceived homology between the respective projects of design and anthropology mentioned above (Murphy and Marcus 2013), a number of anthropologists have recently turned to design as a model for productively reconfiguring the possibilities of ethnographic methods and anthropological theorizing. Both Alberto Corsín Jiménez (2014) and George Marcus (2014), for instance, have proposed design "prototypes" as models for developing experimental modes of anthropological engagement that assume, rather than avoid, provisionality, incompleteness, and failure in how fieldwork and theorizing are done. And drawing on the idea that the pedagogical models that underpin architecture and design education help train students to think in certain ways and to work creatively and collaboratively, some anthropologists (Rabinow et al. 2008; Murphy and Marcus 2013) have proposed experimenting with the introduction of design elements into anthropological training and practice in order to push anthropological work in new directions. Finally, a recent book by Arturo Escobar (2018b) advances the possibilities that design holds for anthropology beyond a methodological or instrumental borrowing of tactics. In *Designs for the Pluriverse: Radical Interdependence, Autonomy, and the Making of Worlds*, Escobar draws from the traditions of participatory design and design for social innovation, and he merges some of their most significant strengths with indigenous anticapitalist and anticolonial theories of autonomy to create what he calls a theory of "autonomous design." In effect, what Escobar is offering in his book is a demonstration of how certain bodies of design thought and practice can be used to help structure anthropological theorizing, especially in ways that respect many of the communities that anthropologists work with. In the afterword to this volume, Escobar offers further reflection on these ideas, in light of some of the material the authors have presented in their chapters.

Alberto Corsín Jiménez's chapter draws on his fieldwork with free-culture activists in Madrid, who are focused on developing an urban ecology based on a cross-pollination between hackers, urban activists, and artists and who are driven by histories of autonomy and libertarian socialism. One of Corsín Jiménez's key arguments is that his work with those activists who are committed to building a culture of design for the liberation of urban space can inspire the liberation of anthropological designs. For example, those activists emphasized the importance of documenting every step in the process of prototyping the solutions they devised to specific urban problems in order to facilitate future replications, as well as the need to archive and make public and openly available all documents that result from the documentation. When Corsín Jiménez began working with free-culture communities he soon realized that to gain the trust of his interlocutors he would need to develop his own practices of documentation, archiving, and reportage. The need to reconfigure his own anthropological theorizing and writing and to align them with the design practices of his interlocutors has inspired him to think about his own anthropological practice as an *anthropology with* rather than as an *anthropology for* and about the relationship between himself and his interlocutors as one of epistemic partnership. Most crucially, his exposure to the culture of free activism and its design practices has prompted him to consider how anthropology's practices, which are currently predicated on secrecy of data, nonreplicability of results, and the cult of the individual anthropologist, might be refashioned along the same lines.

George Marcus's chapter points to the potential of design practices, especially scenography, to reconfigure entrenched anthropological methods and assumptions that make anthropology increasingly out of synch with many of the subjects that anthropologists now study. Marcus specifically targets the resistance in anthropology to experiments in aesthetic or design intervention that rearrange or set the stage for the conditions of life that the anthropologist is supposed to study. Based on his work with scenographers, Marcus argues that intentionally enclosing the scenes of ethnographic research without isolating them from their context is crucial as a condition of possibility for the kind of multisited ethnography that many anthropologists need to do today in order to fully account for the phenomena they study. Anthropologists should draw from scenic design principles or, better still, work directly with scenographers as part of their fieldwork in order to produce insights in the different locales that are relevant to their study. For example, an installation of a family motel room that he built together with scenographers for a charity banquet concerning families living in derelict motels in Orange County was displayed in different sites throughout the county (see Cantarella et al. 2019). Although the installation was first conceived as an addendum to the actual fieldwork, it quickly became its core in that it functioned as a mode of ethnographic investigation into the attitudes and notions of charity among Orange County's wealthy middle class. The installation thus performed the role of a moving enclosure that elicited vital ethnographic data in the form of the responses of the audience that confronted it.

Keith Murphy's chapter takes a half step back from the practicalities of designing in action to focus instead on how specific concepts that tacitly motivate design's very existence might be useful for deliberating, with some care, within anthropology's own metaconceptual ambit. The core of his argument is relatively simple. Design of almost all types is figured by its practitioners as form-giving—that is, as centered on practices in which interested social actors "give"—and this giving is, of course, an unpacked black box perfect for anthropological inspection. These are forms of different kinds to the things they produce, but also to the users of those things, and thus to the social worlds those things inhabit. Building from anthropology's own complicated engagements with both "form" and "giving" across decades of social theory, Murphy uses design to shift the framing of these concepts to offer a distinct analytic in which design is only one manifestation of a more general set of social practices of form-giving in which specific social actors "give"—again, an always-unpackable term—forms of various kinds to other social actors in their particular social worlds. Take, for example, governance as a kind of form-giving. When politicians in the United States have passed TRAP (Targeted Regulation of Abortion Providers) laws, which severely restrict or even eliminate the number of abortion clinics in a state, they have essentially given very specific form to the social landscape (Murphy 2016a). And critical to this more general formulation of form-giving is a notion of morality. Through a close analysis of how form-giving and morality play out in several design disciplines, Murphy argues that all instances in which humans intervene in the lives of other humans by means of form-giving—whether though obvious cases of design, or less obvious cases, like legislating—hinge on questions of ethics. Here (as anywhere, really), it is important to note that morality is inherently concerned not only with "the good," but with relative goodness and badness, or relative rightness and wrongness, and how groups of people understand these relative relations. From Murphy's point of view, the idea of form-giving in design is useful for anthropological theorizing because its logic, flexibility, and scalability all quite evenly align with the goals of contemporary ways of exploring human worlds.

In some respects, Douglas Holmes's contribution is itself illustrative of the kind of nonobvious form-giving that Murphy delineates in his chapter. Working with a similar inspiration, Holmes draws on a notion of design to explore the creation of a very specific social form: monetary regimes, which are steered by central bankers, shaped through language, and followed closely by the eye of a critically engaged ethnographer. Parallel to the move recently made by Escobar (2018b), Holmes attempts in his chapter to reevaluate his own previous anthropological work within an adapted design idiom. Monetary regimes are, of course, complex forms. They are composed of a range of heterogenous elements, such as policies, rhetoric, numbers, human beings (both individuals and aggregates), and so much more. Some of these elements are subject to direct human control, while others, though they may originate from human actions, operate beyond the immediate grasp of human intervention. Still others are essentially epiphenomenal to the workings and interworkings of everything else in the system. Holmes interprets the construction and maintenance of monetary regimes as a kind of form-giving on a massive scale and with dire consequences, a process in which a small group of experts—central bankers and allied economists—work like designers by probing, prototyping, and playing with form in order to engineer economic systems into being.

Emergent Themes That Lie Beyond

As useful as the three prepositionally arranged configurations of design and anthropology have been for exploring the possibilities produced by their alignment, they are also not the only alternatives. Inevitably, other perspectives emerged during the seminar. Perhaps the strongest of these is a questioning or probing of the "border" itself between design and anthropology. The distinction between the three configurations is problematic in at least two ways. First, as Suchman argues, the distinction between anthropology of design and anthropology for design is based on a false dichotomy between distanced critique and engaged participation. Anthropologists and designers should strive to enact both engaged participation that is also critical and a critique that also engages with, and participates in, that which it critiques. Second, we should discard the reference to either anthropology or design and instead examine how different forms of design and of anthropology are enacted in specific historical moments and geographical, political, and economic locations. The different perspectives on design and anthropology, which participants presented during the seminar, and the tensions that emerged between those perspectives clarified the plurality of our objects of study. The design/anthropology relationship was sometimes treated as a methodological issue, sometimes as a conceptual issue, sometimes as a moral issue, thus demonstrating that there is uncertainty not just about the status of design, but also about the status of anthropology.

The discussions that took place during the seminar highlighted the need to acknowledge and explore the varieties of design. First, while cautiously celebrating design as a quasi-democratic human practice that is found everywhere, we should also explore design as a historically specific profession, as well as understand who mobilizes it as a legible social form and to what ends. Who designates who is a designer, and who defines what design is to begin with? Second, we need to probe beneath professional design's self-portrayal as a form of practice that democratically takes into account human needs. We should ask, What is being celebrated in design as a form of making, and what are its others? For example, what kind of hierarchy does the distinction between designing and manufacturing reproduce? How has design solidified a hierarchy between different kinds of agency that are superimposed on different social groups? Furthermore, many strands of design presuppose the idea of someone doing something for another from the vantage point of that someone's better understanding of another's needs and the solutions to them. What kind of power relations enable this presupposition, and how does this presupposition reproduce those power relations? How has empathy—a crucial human-centered design term—enabled and naturalized injurious design solutions such as more addictive forms of computer interface? How has the professionalization of design naturalized forms of hierarchy between different kinds of designers?

Perhaps the fact that design both intensely attracted and repelled the seminar participants, who are all professional anthropologists, stemmed from their ambivalence toward their own professional practice, which design provoked because of the strong elective affinities between design and anthropology. Although they tended to probe the question "What is design?" and to leave unspoken the question "What is anthropology?" their questions about design can be easily translated to questions about anthropology. Anthropologists have long debated the different hierarchies that underlie anthropology's self-portrayal as a critical and socially concerned form of scholarship and intervention. Most of these debates focused on the anthropologist's patronizing stance and presumed higher-level knowledge vis-à-vis her interlocutors, as well as the power relations that enable the anthropological gaze to begin with. But the debates around design provoke further questions about anthropology. For example, how has the professionalization of anthropology in academia naturalized forms of hierarchy between different kinds of anthropologists, such as between anthropologists who focus on research and anthropologists who focus on teaching, or between anthropologists who work in academia and anthropologists who work in the corporate world? Who designates who is an anthropologist, and who defines what anthropology is to begin with? How has the transformation of academia into a site of knowledge production that is informed by models of management and by production norms that are anchored in the business world impacted anthropological work and its core normative ideals? What kinds of moral parochialism and double standards has anthropologists' obsession with always performing the moral high ground—such that everything they do is, ultimately, informed by notions of rightness or wrongness—produced and reproduced? Who are the academic anthropologist's others? What kinds of divisions of labor currently exist in academic anthropology akin to that between design and manufacturing? Who among the anthropologists is in charge of "high theory," and who among them is left with "implementation" of this theory or with providing raw data on the basis of which such theory can be built? How are those divisions geographically distributed not only globally (the West versus the rest) but within the North American and European contexts too? What kinds of technologies of engagement with one's interlocutors are theoretically productive or ethically problematic?

These are some of the questions that the current volume addresses and provokes. That the answers to these questions that the seminar's participants provided are highly diverse and far from conclusive is a reflection of one of the book's key insights—namely, the existence of a plurality of anthropologies and of designs whose elective affinities make each of them a productive site for the critique of the other.

Notes

1.   There was nothing particularly dogmatic about this formulation. It was meant to capture the contours of actually existing and generally possible work at the

borders of design and anthropology (cf. Gunn and Donovan 2012 for what is basically the same scheme); if participants deviated (which they did!), they were not taken to task for it.

2. All of the contributors to this volume were present at the seminar in Santa Fe except Arturo Escobar, whom we later asked to contribute to the project. In addition, Natasha Dow Schüll was invited but unable to attend, and Lily Chumley and Lochlann Jain attended the seminar, but were unable to contribute to the volume.

CHAPTER ONE

Border Thinking about Anthropologies/Designs

LUCY SUCHMAN

Debate over relations between any two things presupposes the previous question of how the entities being considered are (separately) constituted in the first place. Our engagement in this collection with questions of design and anthropology is no exception—a situation signaled (and also mitigated) by the use of the plural form in the framing of our topic as "designs and anthropologies." Taking the multiplicity of these entities as our starting place is helpful, as it invites us to state more explicitly just which designs and which anthropologies we are engaging as we go. It encourages a shift from general references to either anthropology or design in favor of an examination of how each is figured and enacted in specific historical moments and geographical, political, and economic locations. That shift, in turn, underscores the ways in which our discussion is itself part of the becoming of the entities in question. The stakes of the debate are not an "academic exercise" in the pejorative sense of that phrase, in other words, but rather have consequences for how we imagine and enact the entities and relations in question as part of our ongoing onto-epistemic practices.

In what follows I start from the distinction between what Keith Murphy (2016b) characterizes as three "configurations" of the anthropology/design relation. Understood as configurations, these phrases denote alternate figures of anthropology and design, along with associated implications for how we conceive their conjunctions. Beginning with the difference between an anthropology of design and an anthropology for design, my aim is to articulate both some differences that I believe matter and also what is in my view a false dichotomy—between distanced critique and engaged participation—that haunts the distinction. To trouble this ghost of anthropologies past, I offer a brief recapitulation of the grounds on which I myself have mobilized the of/for distinction, most directly in "Anthropological Relocations and the Limits of Design" (Suchman 2011; see also Suchman 2013). This involves a précis of my own long-standing engagement with particular design worlds and my associated concerns regarding the inseparability of anthropology or design from commitments, histories, and regimes of value. With that as background, I propose some border thinking (following Mignolo 2012) inspired by recent writings that in my view exemplify the undoing of the of/for dichotomy, and I suggest what seems to be a generative reconfiguration for the future of anthropology/ design relations. My primary references are recent writings (A. Chan 2013; Irani 2019; Escobar 2018b; Pérez-Bustos et al. 2019; Corsín Jiménez this volume) that reframe the question to this one: If we understand the two elements of the anthropology/design relation as multiple, what are the design histories and emerging tendencies that carry affinity with an anthropology committed to decolonizing practices of knowledge and world-making?

Respecifying Anthropology/Design

Murphy (2016b) outlines three alternate configurations of anthropology and design: an anthropology of design, an anthropology for design, and design for anthropology. The articulation of subjects and objects shifts across these configurations. The first two designate alternate relations between a field of anthropology and a field of design (in the form of the study of or provision for/service to), while the third shifts to a field of design that acts upon (and implicitly transforms) the discipline and practice of anthropology. Murphy's aim is to underscore already existing intersections with design practices within the field of anthropology, while also offering a clearer specification of differently framed relations, as well as associated concerns, at these disciplinary boundaries. In the interest of expanding the frame, Murphy wants to extend the presence and relevance of design to anthropology (435). In his discussion of anthropologies of design, Murphy argues that "even though designed phenomena have received significant anthropological attention since the discipline's earliest days, the basic fact that they are designed has largely been overlooked" (440). But we might pause over this "basic fact," perhaps rephrasing the question as this: How is it that designed things come to be delineated as such? This question acknowledges that "design" is not a self-evident process, its myriad methods and techniques notwithstanding. So the question is, How do practices of making become articulated *as design*, within the multiple, messy processes through which things come to be?

Universalizing "design" to name any and all occasions of the purposeful arrangement of a material environment, the organizing of social relations, or the creation of an artifact risks stripping the term of the meanings and associated values specific to its genealogies. At the same time, the term's cultural and historical implications travel with it. So, while applauding the clarity that Murphy brings to the discussion, I want to focus here on the tricky politics of how the term "design" operates in this context. It is at once a signifier for making, most broadly construed, and for a professional discipline inseparable from and haunted by its colonial/modernist histories, as well as by the politics of its contemporary mobilization within dominant capitalist economic relations. The slippage itself helps reinstitute "the designer" as a kind of everyman, while also installing contemporary design professionals as the logical progression of that figure's development. Without their historical and geopolitical specificity, however, references to "material culture, human behavior, and social values" (Murphy 2016b, 434) could reiterate a kind of universalism that, in turn, underwrites the valuation of the anthropology/design conjunction in contemporary political economies of production. We need to begin, then, with restoration of the specificities.

Anthropology/Design in Silicon Valley, Late Twentieth Century

The aim of my previous writings on the topic of this collection was less as a "warning away" of anthropology from design (Murphy 2016b, 441) than as an invitation to bring concerns that seem too often missing, or at least marginalized, into focus. Key among these is attention to how specific locations enable the possibility of enacting anthropology/design in some ways and not others. This is a necessary part of a discussion that "accounts for moral entanglements as a critical consequence of humans provisioning for one another the conditions of life" (Murphy 2016b, 444). In my own case, the anthropology/design conjunction occurred as a kind of unintended consequence of American anthropology's turn to "studying up" in the context of wider political turns in the 1970s. Drawn to the Silicon Valley in the hope of conducting a critical ethnography of a multinational corporation, I found myself at an internationally renowned site of research in the emerging field of personal computing. In my reflections some thirty years later on what was at once a twenty-year career as a member of the research staff at Xerox's Palo Alto Research Center (PARC) and an extended ethnographic encounter within that world, I try to articulate sites of friction, both generative and constraining. Friction, Anna Tsing reminds us, not only is about slowing things down, but also is a sign of the generative power of interaction (2005, 6).

The frictions arose at the complex intersections of a commitment to anthropology as a mode of critically engaged scholarship and the exigencies of design (and associated modes of research) under specific, and changing, relations of technoscience and corporate capitalism between the years 1980 and 2000. These twenty years involved conditions of intensifying competition in the rapidly elaborating market for computational technologies and an associated intensification, during the 1990s, in the neoliberal embrace of modes of entrepreneurship for which the Silicon Valley was emblematic. As the laboratory of which I and my colleagues were a part developed its own orthodoxies—including the embrace of the social sciences—the space in which to question received assumptions regarding the politics of corporate research (and anthropology within it) progressively diminished. Whereas before I and my colleagues had been enrolled in what was clearly an "agonistic" form of interdisciplinarity (Barry et al. 2008), we were now asked to enact an apparently frictionless solidarity. While the former had been fruitfully negotiated based on partial connections, the latter demanded modes of loyalty that seemed to make our differences increasingly indigestible. Taken together, these conditions radically transformed my experience of the possibilities for anthropology/design as a sustainable field of (corporate-sponsored) research. Most obviously absent from discourses of the research laboratory was any critical discussion of the political economies to which our work was increasingly accountable. As the corporation's performance on Wall Street (a topic of little or no interest to researchers when I arrived at Xerox PARC in the late 1970s) became a constant preoccupation (stock prices and business analyses being discussed at every lab meeting in the late 1990s), there remained a deafening silence regarding any critical analysis of developments in the world economy and financial markets. To engage in such critique was treated as naïve at best, "biting the hand that feeds you" at worst.[1]

Yet during the same period that the space of generative difference that I experienced in my earlier days at Xerox PARC was closing down, the rhetorical embrace of anthropology by industry was expanding. My reflections in "Consuming Anthropology" (Suchman 2013) were an attempt to understand the seeming contradiction between the recurring announcement of anthropology's arrival into sites of (particularly corporate) design and the actual limits on investment in anthropological research by industry. Framed within a wider conversation on interdisciplinarity, I took this as an occasion to diffract my extended engagement in design worlds through the lens of sociologies of the market and the wider emergence of "culture" as a form of symbolic capital.[2] One aim of my argument was to reject the conflation of a move toward "relevance" for the field of anthropology with the monetization of anthropology as a consumable commodity and an asset to industry. Another was to attend closely to the relations and differences between anthropology as figure and anthropology as practice. I closed with a reflection on the messy contingencies of this interdisciplinary commerce and their implications for more radical forms of inventive collaboration.

In her discussion of environmental activism in Indonesia during the 1990s, Anna Tsing characterizes the coalitions that formed there as "awkwardly transcended difference" (2005, 18), a phrase reminiscent of Helen Verran's conceptualizations of working incommensurable knowledge systems together (1998). The rise of tropes of "knowledge" and "practice" at PARC in the 1990s, celebrated as evidence for the success of anthropology's interventions, turned out to be the beginning of the end of the organization's tolerance for our presence. While difference was previously valued as generative friction, the smooth appropriation of these concepts was accompanied by increasing demands for our integration. Insistence on differences that mattered in that context became "resistance to change" and, implicitly, insubordination and betrayal.

Of/For

The title of Victor Margolin's book *The Politics of the Artificial* (2002), the author explains, "plays polemically on Herbert Simon's 'sciences of the artificial,' countering Simon's model of seamless rationalism with that of a contentious struggle to determine the limits of design" (2002, 5). It was an interest in joining that contentious struggle that informed my own intensive, long-term engagement with design cultures and practices. Encounters at Xerox PARC quickly drew me into projects in the design of so-called interactive, intelligent machines, and my dissertation became a critical analysis of what I now would characterize as the imaginaries and technical practices of the cognitive sciences and artificial intelligence, with a focus on the problem of (mutual) intelligibility at the human/computer interface (Suchman 1987). Written with multiple audiences in mind (most directly, my home discipline of anthropology and my host disciplines of computer science and human-computer interaction), the book's generation within the nexus of PARC and its research networks afforded it ready circulation within the fields that were the object of the critique, where it received its widest and most positive reception as a work of anthropology *for* design. It was in part the limits of the argument's circulation within the fields of my own closest affiliation—anthropology and science and technology studies—that led me to expand the frame of the original book twenty years later (Suchman 2007), in hopes that it would be read again and more widely as, inter alia, a work in the anthropology *of* design.

Another encounter during my early years at Xerox PARC further complicated the of/for distinction. Among the visiting researchers to PARC in the early 1980s was a small network of Scandinavian students and more senior academics, who were engaged at the time in developing new (object-oriented) programming languages aligned with those being explored in PARC's Smalltalk group. While it was a common interest in programming and the elaborating graphical user interface that initiated the connection, I learned in conversations that these researchers were conducting their own work in the context of workplace democracy and trade-union activism in Norway, Sweden, and Denmark. Well-resourced trade unions able to invest in their own research in the development of prototype systems conducive to the quality of working life were in close collaboration with my visiting colleagues, and together they were shaping the emerging field of participatory or cooperative design of computer systems (see Ehn 1988; Greenbaum and Kyng 1991; Simonsen and Robertson 2012). This was for me a revelation, opening a space of possibilities not only for critique (however generative) but also for an alternative design practice. Beginning in the 1990s, with a small group of colleagues, I undertook a series of exploratory projects in workplace studies and system codesign, aimed at clarifying what kind of participatory design practice could be enacted within the specific conditions of Xerox PARC (Blomberg et al. 1996; Trigg et al. 1999; Suchman 2002; Suchman et al. 2002).

We could be said to have been performing the "anthropology by means of design" recommended by Caroline Gatt and Tim Ingold (2013), wherein anthropologists, "embracing their own expertise and skills, proceed alongside the people they study, rather than at some remove, intentionally and purposefully leaning into the realities that their presence is already helping to shape" (cited in Murphy 2016b, 442). But this begs the question of whether, and in what ways, the anthropologist is also able to raise more fundamental questions about those realities; this is contingent, in turn, on the political and economic orderings within which our research subjects, and we ourselves, are incorporated. (For a perspicuous account of those orderings in the current moment, see Wilf this volume.) It was the explicit commitment to engaging with the politics of system design that distinguished the discourses and practices of my Scandinavian colleagues from those of PARC and wider US research networks. And it was this mode of engagement, as I have suggested above, that was progressively discouraged as entrepreneurialism gained its ascendency. Rather than valuing anthropology's commitment to "cast a wider net through geography and history" (Bornstein and Redfield 2011, 4), the enactment of an anthropology for design at this moment and under conditions of Silicon Valley–style capitalism required a narrowing of concern and the denial of design's politics. So, while the contingent unfolding of engagement belies the clarity of the of/for distinction, the need to articulate the orderings of that border work intensifies.

Differences within Design

This same period has also seen growing contestation within the field of design research, including most radically recent calls for professional design's decolonization.[3] A review of design historian Victor Margolin's two-volume *World History of Design* (2015) elaborates the problem in terms of the profession's enduring Eurocentrism:

> The books are propelled by a gentle but perceptible gust of teleological thinking, in which the world's material culture leads inexorably to the modern professional designer. A telling moment in this regard occurs right at the outset, when Margolin turns to the *Oxford English Dictionary* and notes that "design, understood as a plan or scheme intended for subsequent execution, does not appear as a term until the middle of the 16th century." Surely Margolin knows that there are many other words in many other languages that approximate (and also, interestingly, differ from) this concept of design, but he does not mention this here or anywhere else, nor does he attempt to ground his analysis in the conceptions of the object or authorship that such languages might capture. (Adamson 2015)

In contrast to Adamson, we might see Margolin's careful attention to the genealogy of "design" as a term, specifically located within sixteenth-century Europe,
as part of a process of decolonizing the histories and geographies of making
practices. This counterreading is particularly relevant as Margolin is unques-
tionably one of the most articulate voices of concern from within the design
field itself, particularly with respect to its professionalization over the course of
the twentieth century. In his critical engagement with the field, Margolin calls
for "a more open conception of design activity that is not preoccupied with
justifying a separate sphere of domain knowledge" (2002, 237). The question of
how to figure design becomes more urgent, Margolin argues, with the surge in
the 1990s of interest in establishing doctoral programs with associated curricula
and modes of knowledge making. He himself urges the inclusion of "history,
theory and criticism" (1989) as central to design pedagogy and practice, where
history and criticism must include examination of the unspoken justification
for rationalist conceptions of design theory. The latter, he argues, have "naturalized the methods of design and embedded them in a technical framework . . .
[that] privileges systems thinking as a means of generating design projects, and
efficiency as a way of judging the effectiveness of design thought" (Margolin
2002, 238). Margolin describes how, after a pivotal symposium at Plymouth in
the United Kingdom in 1967, architect Christopher Alexander renounced the
burgeoning "design methods movement," complaining that "rationality, originally seen as the means to open up the intuition to aspects of life outside the
designer's experience, became, almost overnight, a toolkit of rigid methods
that obliged designers and planners to act like machines, deaf to every human
cry and incapable of laughter" (cited in Margolin 2002, 246). To counter this
tendency, Margolin proposes contextualizing design thinking, "rather than
isolating design from its social situation and theorizing independently about
its processes of invention. By holding design in our vision as a social practice,
we are always obliged to consider and evaluate the situations in which it occurs"
(Margolin 2002, 239).

At the same time that the field of anthropology was engaged in critical
reconsiderations of its colonial past, Victor Papanek, in *Design for the Real
World* (1972), called for a radical redirection of design practice from First World
consumer products to Third World sustainability. Initially rejected by numer-
ous publishers (Fineder and Geisler 2010), the book first appeared in North
America in 1972 and has since gone through fifteen editions and been translated into twenty-three languages. Inspired by environmentalism and contempt

for the profession of industrial design, it became an iconic reference for critical design discourses of the 1980s in North America and Europe. Yet in their biography of the book as a social/cultural object in design history, Fineder and Geisler point to "the ways in which *Design for the Real World* lost its initial reputation as a controversial text of the responsible design movement, and became a historical 'landmark' and 'timeless' classic" (2010). Design worlds, like other fields of modernist self-making, are prone to fetishism and eager to forget their more agonistic histories.

A more recent case in point, exploring the multiplicities and ambivalent politics of humanitarian design after Papanek, is provided in Peter Redfield's reflection on the "fluid technologies" of water purification in Africa (2016). Taking as his provocative object the Zimbabwe Bush Pump "B" type described so lovingly by Marianne de Laet and Annemarie Mol (2000), Redfield sets as its counterpoint the LifeStraw®, designed by Danish company Vestergaard Frandsen. As Redfield points out, the devices' names signal their different positioning—politically, economically, and in relation to post-decolonial thinking. Identified in relation to a nation-state and a "series" of prototypes, the Bush Pump signals a hopeful postcolonial future of infrastructure building as well as a provisional and ongoing process of research and participatory development. The LifeStraw®, in contrast, "points to raw existence combined with the legal protections of trademark" (Redfield 2016, 161), an ambivalent interface of humanitarianism and social entrepreneurship. Redfield's aims include the restoration of an open space of critical questioning in our engagements with design, attentive both to the seduction of that which seems to materialize the values that we hold dear and to the dismissal of possibilities that may be fraught with compromise, but are manifest in the messy realities of projects enacted in the name of care. As Redfield points out, our current condition "is a world where much of the 'technology transfer' from global North to South involves not intentional design but discarded objects, repurposed for a second life in a poorer environment" (176). He cites the story told by Uli Beisel and Tillmann Schneider of a German ambulance that becomes a Ghanaian minibus, an achievement that the authors characterize as "ambivalent" (2012, 643) insofar as the vehicle, while functional, is also highly, and increasingly, dangerous to passengers: "Referring directly to de Laet and Mol's Bush Pump, the authors suggest that technological fluidity can hold danger as well as opportunity. Instead of love they foreground the warier sentiment of ambivalence. Ambivalence and doubt seem well suited for humanitarian design" (Redfield 2016, 176).

Redfield observes that while ambivalence is rarely satisfying, it can in the best case inspire further and deeper inquiry.

Paths to Border Thinking

The benefit of a "design-influenced framework" for anthropology, Murphy suggests, is that it "encourages fieldworkers to expect to intervene and to work reflexively and creatively with that intervention as part of the ethnographic process" (2016b, 442). We might note, however, that problematizing the opposition of ethnography and engagement has a lineage that extends well before and beyond the turn to design.[4] Tsing's suggestion that it is "the messy and surprising features of . . . encounters across difference [that] should inform our models of cultural production" (2005, 3) includes the ethnographer as well as her research subjects and provides a suggestive beginning to our boundary thinking with respect to anthropologies/designs. To elaborate this possibility, I turn to recent works in anthropology/design that undo the of/for distinction, demonstrating the intimate and enabling relation of generative critique and the articulation of resistance and response.

Anita Chan's *Networking Peripheries* (2013) offers a rich ethnography of the tensions between state-sponsored and grassroots innovation in Peru. Hers is one among a growing body of works that are helping to rewrite diffusionist histories of design through a generative combination of critique and the articulation of decolonizing alternatives (see also Philip 2005; Philip et al. 2010; Medina et al. 2014). This research illuminates the ways in which location matters, but not in the sense assumed by the narrative of centers and peripheries that has dominated our understandings of where innovation happens and how it travels. Of the prevailing figure of design Chan writes:

> There is a particular notion of the periphery conjured here, of course, as mere agents of global counterfeit—as sites of replication of a future invented prior and elsewhere. As much as the authoritative role of innovation centers for extending design and invention is rarely questioned, so, too, is the periphery viewed unquestioningly as a zone of diffusion and simple uptake of such designs. But the periphery is hardly so passive or uninventive. (A. Chan 2013, x)

In her introduction to the text Chan does a critical reading of a missive issued by the editors of *Wired* magazine, in the context of an initiative to nominate the Internet for the Nobel Peace Prize in 2010. Her critique points to the ways in which the missive, in the name of inclusiveness and emancipation, effectively anonymizes and decontextualizes the same movements (e.g., the Arab Spring) that it cites as evidence. This rhetoric thus erases the historical and political specificity of political struggles, as well as the differential distributions of risk involved, and it implicitly credits a universalized Internet with inherently emancipatory powers. Resisting what she identifies as "Western and techno-universalist" accounts of design and innovation, Chan traces through her research in the city of Lima and the northern Peruvian village of Chulucanas the effects of a state-sponsored initiative to deploy proprietary "Domain of Origin" certification in rural areas. Imagining the translation of otherwise-marginalized rural populations as a "creative class" producing goods that can travel in the global economic market, she documents with poignant clarity how an initiative launched in the name of preserving traditional craft practices can result instead in the selective, and highly divisive, transformation of social relations and material artifacts. Chulucana ceramicists were urged to remake themselves as entrepreneurial producers with global connections, which in turn necessitated that their artifacts be remade into mass-producible commodities for consumers in the global North.

As well as documenting the forces of resistance emerging from within the Chulucana community, Chan turns to examine how citizen-based "maker" communities in Peru have hacked the One Laptop per Child initiative, in order to transform it from a project in replicating neoliberal subjects to a medium for honoring and reanimating collective modes of creativity. She suggests that these modes of creative resistance and remaking demonstrate the possibilities of what postcolonial- and science-studies scholars have framed as "engaged universals" (citing Chakrabarty 2000 and Tsing 2005). As Chan observes, "Such engaged forms would acknowledge the promise and peril they carry as bodies of 'knowledge that move,' like all universals, across local space, time, and cultures" (2013, 19). With a tentative hopefulness, Chan suggests that "it's here, in such newly forged zones, that the presumed givens and consensus of technology's universalizing future can begin to be unsettled and slowly, perhaps, give way to something altogether unexpected" (195). Inclusiveness within information and communication technologies, Chan observes, offers a "seductive" promise of redress of historical exclusions and new forms of multiply scaled, emancipatory connection (13). Operating within market logics, however, these initiatives further rationalize "the inevitability of civilization's scarcity," naturalizing the differential and unequal distribution of resources and rewards (107).

In *Chasing Innovation: Making Entrepreneurial Citizens in Modern India* (2019; see also this volume), Lilly Irani challenges discourses and practices enacted in the name of "innovation" in contemporary India, as a contribution to a wider body of decolonizing scholarship. Irani introduces the trope of "entrepreneurial citizenship" to deepen and elaborate our understanding of how neoliberalism relies upon, and reproduces, particular figurations of value in labor, social hierarchies, and subject positioning. Irani develops her argument through a close investigation of user-centered design practices as they travel between the Silicon Valley and India as well as other sites in South Asia, through the case of a design studio, pseudonymed DevDesign, based in Delhi. She argues that the figure of the entrepreneur has expanded from its relevance to commercial enterprise to become a model for civic action and the good citizen. At the same time, the figure of the citizen entrepreneur relies upon the reproduction not only of innovators but of innovation's others, those who serve alternately as the devalued labor that makes creative work possible and as the distanced subjects/objects of development. Both are necessary, Irani argues, for innovative entrepreneurship's self-reproduction. Significantly, this process operates even among those entrepreneurs who see themselves as the champions of those not previously recognized as innovators. It is in the act of claiming innovator status, as a way of asserting the value of those so designated, that the privileging of entrepreneurship and innovation is reiterated.

Irani identifies what she calls the "transnational legibility" of innovation practice as an ongoing project of those with investments in sustaining the value of innovation as a good and in securing professional design as its preeminent site. Her focus on class as it manifests in hierarchies of labor and self-identification within India, with particular attention to entrepreneurial citizenship as an aspiration for middle-class Indians, contributes a further analysis of intersections of nationality, gender, and ethnicity in imaginaries and material distributions of entrepreneurial labor. By maintaining as her organizing theme the broad frame of entrepreneurialism and tracing its many and often mutually contradictory locations (from industry to social activism), Irani shows us the seductions of the discourse of entrepreneurial citizenship, while not herself being seduced. The result is that we gain not only a more nuanced understanding of how entrepreneurial citizenship is figured, but also a deeper appreciation for the possibilities that it displaces from consideration.

Irani's further observation is that entrepreneurialism casts social movements, deliberative debate, and even national planning as excessive impediments to the execution of innovators' visions. The implication of her argument is that modes of resistance—of which the book itself is an enunciative example—to the dismissive and depoliticizing effects of entrepreneurialism are an essential condition of possibility for more socially just cultural imaginaries and material practices of commercial and civic life.

In *Designs for the Pluriverse: Radical Interdependence, Autonomy, and the Making of Worlds* (2018b), Arturo Escobar reminds us of the difference between projects in alternative development and more radical initiatives in alternatives *to* development. He turns to discourses of "transition" as a promising alternative to development—one based in a cosmopolitan localism (Manzini 2015) that relies upon the political mobilization of what Escobar names "relational ontologies" by communities and social movements in both the global North and South (Escobar 2017, 101).[5] He provides examples, from Transition Town Initiatives in the United Kingdom focused on degrowth and the rebuilding of sustainable communities, to postdevelopment projects in Latin America based in indigenous struggles in alliance with wider social-change movements. Escobar calls for a transition from design as a central political tool for modernity to, in his words, "designs for the pluriverse" as "a tool for reimagining and reconstructing local worlds" (2017, 4).

An exemplary enactment of designs for the pluriverse is the body of research by Colombian anthropologist Tania Pérez-Bustos and her collaborators within the worlds of feminist textile activism (Pérez-Bustos et al. 2019; Cortés-Rico and Pérez-Bustos 2019).[6] Working with collectives based in both urban and rural locations, these projects emphasize not only the metaphorical power of textile crafts in reimagining social processes but also the relatively neglected material practices that actually comprise ongoing, transformative world-making through this craftwork. Crucially, the possibilities for rethinking human-material-communal relations in these collaborations are found through specific, differentially gendered, racialized, and valued practices of making. To understand those specificities requires taking seriously the pedagogy of making, as ways of analyzing textile activism are explored through the agencies that different textile practices afford at the same time that those practices are reimagined in their conditions of possibility and transformative effects. Crucially, these processes of collective learning are laborious and messy, full of mistakes, of undoing and trying again, of broken threads (Pérez-Bustos 2016).[7] The practice of feminist textile activism also reweaves relations of the domestic and the public spheres. This is the case both insofar as it is through "the intimacy of material textile-making" that political analysis and strategy are generated and in the ways that the artifacts produced within those intimate spaces are made to travel (Pérez-Bustos et al. 2019, 373). At the same time, these projects in conjoining anthropology and design suggest that collaboration itself requires ongoing processes of unraveling and mending disciplinary histories, politics, and onto-epistemic commitments in ways that can be reparative and mutually transformative.

Pérez-Bustos observes that, in the case of research on *calado* embroidery, "the main effect of careful unraveling and mending in the interaction between ethnography and engineering design was modifying . . . the structure embedded in problem solving and prototyping paradigms" (Pérez-Bustos 2017, k). The transformation of prototyping paradigms connects these projects with Alberto Corsín Jiménez's decade-long engagement with free-culture activists in Madrid. Corsín Jiménez (this volume) considers the implications of the trope of *autonomia* for ethnographic practice. "Not just a political or ontological impulse," he writes, "autonomy has been bodied forth in this context as a design and an infrastructure" for a self-determining urban ecology, built upon a culture of culture's liberation (this volume). The site of the latter is the social squat, a physical space in which intersections of making and living, and of making a living together beyond the confines of capital, can be experimentally prototyped. This is a prototyping practice that is radically alternative to the prototype as a claim to invention patented by Silicon Valley entrepreneurs. Rather than the anticipation of a closing down of ownership as an opening to the accumulation of profit, the free-culture prototype is an "opening toward the social" that promises liberation from the injustices of the neoliberal market (Corsín Jiménez this volume). The prototypes in question take the form of operations like the "Contest of Ruins," in which digital maps are created to expose derelict buildings and hold responsible both their owners and the municipal government. Corsín Jiménez examines the possibilities for ethnographic engagement at the intersections of infrastructural hacking, urban activism, and socially engaged artistic practice as well as their implications for anthropology's remaking. It is in this context of free-culture activism in the social squats of Madrid in the mid-2000s and in Madrid's associated spaces (in this case, specifically, Madrid's publicly funded Medialab) that an "anthropology of" becomes problematic, as the intellectual, creative, and critical practices of Corsín Jiménez's interlocutors challenge the relevance of his own. Continued engagement becomes impossible for Corsín Jiménez without committed participation in the open-source culture of self-reflection, documentation, and communication under development by his research subjects/collaborators. The figure of the prototype is remade as well, from a device that materializes the promise of a future commodity to a method of investigating "how to open-source the technical, juridical, and pedagogical dynamics of every sociotechnical assemblage" (Corsín Jiménez this volume; 2014). This is, as Corsín Jiménez summarizes it, "a project in the prototyping of autonomy itself."

The practices that Pérez-Bustos and Corsín Jiménez describe comprise an "anthropology with" (Holmes and Marcus 2012, 129) that emerges from a radically different position than that which I inhabited during my tenure as a member of the research staff at Xerox PARC. This difference highlights another in the commitments of the design practitioners and associated institutions with whom we are engaged. We come in the end, then, to the question of location; specifically, the ways in which *where* we enact our anthropological practice— in relation to whom and to what initiatives, aims, and political or economic conditions—is crucial to the shaping of our ethnographic stance. There is, in other words, no definitive way of articulating a normative position between "of," "for," or "with" in the relations of anthropologies/designs. Rather, these prepositions index the politics of our ethnographic practice, their suspension between "complicity and complexity" (Corsín Jiménez this volume), documentation and aspiration, as inseparable from the specifically situated projects of world-making of which we are a part.

The question that these writings leave us with is this: How can we further an anthropology of design's decolonization and a decolonizing design for anthropology? This requires resisting an anthropology with design that is unable to question design's modern and colonial genealogies as well as design's capture within dominant modes of neoliberal capitalism. Walter Mignolo's (2012) embrace of "border thinking," with genealogies in movements of resistance to the imperial operations and universalist pretenses of colonialism and modernism, as a strategy and practice of decolonization is highly relevant here. Engaged with humility and care, those traditions might inform how we work through and across the colonial and modernist histories of anthropology and design disciplines toward alternate grounds for thought and action. With reference to the "/" in his title, *Local Histories/Global Designs*, Mignolo writes: "The '/' that divides and unites both terms of the title is the space of border thinking" (2012, ix). Border thinking is necessary, Mignolo argues, to make evident modern and colonial logics in ways that clarify their nonviability as grounds for sustainable and just futures. This work of critical ground clearing is crucial, in his view, to the articulation of how it could be otherwise: "Border thinking is the pluriversal (emerging from diverse local experiences through time and around the world, between local Western histories and non-Western local histories) epistemology that interconnects the plurality and diversity of decolonial projects" (xxii). Rather than reiterating the opposition of critique to generative intervention and action, in other words, we need to think inside the "/" of critique/intervention, enacting both as inseparable elements of wider projects of decolonization that can, in turn, set out generative conjoinings of and possibilities for anthropologies/designs.

Murphy (this volume) argues that it is the enduring question of the moral consequences of form-giving, which I read as the reconfiguring of social/ material worlds, that conjoins matters of concern across anthropology and design. That concern also joins discussions of anthropology and design with recent engagements with questions of "humanitarian" intervention within anthropology (Bornstein and Redfield 2011). In their introduction to the SAR volume on relations of anthropology and humanitarianism (2011), Erica Bornstein and Peter Redfield suggest, "Anthropology's gift to the intersection of scholarship and practice lies in its ability to engage ambiguity, to recognize concrete events and forms of action that fall between conceptual divides" (26). Coming back to the multiplicity of the figures that frame this discussion suggests that a crucial starting place needs to be specification of the anthropologies and designs with which each of us is engaged. What are the particular historical moments and geographies that inform our engagements? What method assemblages are we enacting (Law 2004), and what do they make present and absent? What is our stance on the deepening commitment among many in the field of anthropology to contribute to transformations in its theory and practice, in alignment with ongoing efforts of decolonization? What are the historical, professional, and political genealogies of the design worlds that are our referents? And what are the frictions, both constraining and generative, that characterize thinking at the boundary of anthropologies/designs? Design occurs, Margolin observes, "within a social space, and its very contingency is guided by the values and limits that inform particular projects" (2002, 241). Along with whatever insights anthropology and design might have for each other, thinking at the border of anthropology/design insists that our practices take an analysis of their own conditions, and articulation of their own commitments, as integral and inalienable.

Notes

1. In the increasingly rumor-saturated worlds of PARC and Silicon Valley in the late 1990s, I was told that my own position had been characterized in that way by an unnamed commentator, as part of an emerging "problem" attributed to our research group.

2. In the dominant discourses of late twentieth-century management theory, culture is both the basis for explaining how people think, feel, and act and the means for engineering desired forms of behavioral change.

3. See, for example, the agitations of the Decolonising Design collective, posted at http://www.decolonisingdesign.com.

4. For classic examinations of anthropology as critical and relational project, see, for example, Marcus and Fischer (1986); Strathern (1995); Gupta and Ferguson (1997); Marcus (1999).

5. Walter Mignolo distinguishes between "relational ontology," as it has developed in Europe and the Anglo United States, and indigenous relational ontologies, in which "'relationships' are not between objects or events outside myself, as in Western relational ontology; instead, it is *my relation with the world and the world with me* that provides the epistemic foundation" (2012, xvii, emphasis in the original).

6. Most recently this work continues in the project "Remendar lo nuevo / Mending the new"; see http://artesanaltecnologica.org/remendar_lo_nuevo-2.

7. In the case of *calado* embroidery, the decorative technique itself involves the partial unraveling and mending of threads in an existing textile; see also Pérez-Bustos (2017).

CHAPTER TWO

The Wrong Means to Misguided Ends
Corporate-Based Design, Streamlined Insights, and Anthropologists' "Desire for Relevance"

EITAN Y. WILF

"The Unbearable Slowness of Being an Anthropologist Now"

This chapter has a twofold purpose. First, based on fieldwork with business-innovation consultants in the United States, I analyze a specific predicament of some of the consultants that I worked with, as well as how they address it. Second, based on this analysis, I critically engage with recent calls for ethnographic experimentation with design methods whose purpose is to revamp anthropological training and work.

The calls for ethnographic experimentation with design methods have been motivated by the sense that traditional models of anthropological training and work are no longer adequate because of many of the subjects that anthropologists study today (Rabinow et al. 2008). First, anthropologists can no longer pretend to be studying timeless, clearly bounded, and internally coherent "cultures," to which the classic fieldwork methodology might have been appropriate (even if such "cultures" were always more imaginary than real). Anthropologists' primary focus has shifted to emergent and rapidly shifting contemporary social phenomena that are often distributed across many sites and contexts and that involve reflexive experts who are in many ways similar to the anthropologists who study them. Second, in a piece titled "On the Unbearable Slowness of Being an Anthropologist Now," George Marcus (2003, 8) has argued that another challenge is "the near unbearable slowness and belatedness in producing ethnographic knowledge." Such slowness is problematic because today anthropologists are encouraged or forced to complete their research and writing at a faster pace because of institutional constraints (e.g., dwindling graduate funding and stringent tenure considerations). In addition, many of the phenomena they write about change too quickly. This means that their research, which they often address to academics and nonacademics alike, can be ethnographically irrelevant by the time they publish it.

Against this backdrop, "design" has emerged as a model of knowledge production in which anthropologists might find inspiration for how to address these challenges:

> The term "design" refers to both the form fieldwork/inquiry takes and the form of textual presentation to which it might lead. More specifically, it expresses the pedagogical effort to teach students the art of finding the design of research—and of its eventual textualization—in the course of inquiry, to let the field or the particular story or theme that is emerging take over the design. The challenge is to become part of a foreign milieu, to submit to the outside, to get drowned in and carried away by it, while staying alert to the gradual emergence of a theme to which chance encounters, fugitive events, anecdotal observations give rise. In short, the term design emphasizes the significance of long-term research, the need to be sensitive to the singularity of the field site, and the art of not letting one's research and thinking be dominated by well-established theories and/or tacit norms of what fieldwork "is," of what a published monograph should look like. . . . As such, the term design expresses the primacy of inquiry and data over theory. (Rees 2008, 116)

One difficulty I have with this formulation is that it uncritically treats "design" as an abstract set of principles that transcend specific contexts and cultures of knowledge production. To be sure, proponents of the turn to "design" specify that the "design studio" is "a phrase developed with the architectural design studio or lab meetings in the sciences in mind" (Rees 2008, 116). However, they do not unpack in detail the models of knowledge production that prevail in such design contexts; do not address the question of whether the "architectural design studio" and "lab meetings" share the same model of knowledge production; and, finally, do not ask whether the "architectural design studio" and "the lab meetings" denote homogeneous categories to begin with. The same goes for design thinking, which has been mentioned as another design model that can inform anthropological work. Treated in this abstract way, "design" risks becoming a catchall reified notion that promises to provide anthropologists with a solution to many of the discipline's contemporary challenges.

In what follows, I point to the danger of such a reification by drawing on my fieldwork with design and business-innovation consultants in the United States (Wilf 2015, 2016, 2019). As I show, on the surface "design" in the context of business innovation can seem to be an inspiring model for the quick and "timely" production of "an anthropology of the contemporary" (Rabinow et al. 2008). Many of the design and innovation contexts I studied are embedded in corporate settings that mandate the quick production of insights with respect to ever-shifting, market-based phenomena. However, in response to the pressure to produce quick insights, the designers and innovation consultants I worked with endorsed an epistemology of emergence but operationalized it by means of practices that greatly predetermined its end results. To put it in simpler terms, although their design practices seemed to be predicated on sensitivity to the emergent nature of "design" and of its objects, they were based in decontextualization and standardization as conditions of possibility for the fast production of insights. This was the result of my interlocutors' attempt to hold the stick at both ends in light of the contradictory demands made by their clients—namely, to be context-sensitive under tight time constraints. Some of the iconic design practices that anthropologists have recently sought to incorporate into their own work in the hope that these practices might give them an edge in their attempt to be "timely" and to produce ethnographically relevant knowledge played a key role in the kind of decontextualization under the guise of context-sensitivity that I observed during my fieldwork. This chapter thus takes an "anthropology of design" perspective to discuss a "design for anthropology" perspective.

Before proceeding with my analysis, I want to clarify two things. First, if I focus on the recent calls for revamping anthropological work, it is because I find them thought-provoking in relation to some of the real challenges that anthropologists face today. Second, my point is not that there can be no value for anthropologists in seeking inspiration in design practices. Rather, I suggest that some design practices, especially those that are embedded in corporate settings and business innovation, might not be the best source of inspiration, especially now that academic work is under pressure to align itself with corporate and market-based organizational models of knowledge production. Turning to such design practices in an effort to revamp anthropological work might mean succumbing to and legitimizing this pressure instead of critiquing it. Indeed, given the contemporary fetishized status of the design practices that I discuss below—a status they received because of their association with Silicon Valley's discourses and practices of technological innovation, such a move would mean celebrating this pressure and the worldview that animates it.[1] Rather than turning to "design" in an effort to address the challenges that anthropologists of the contemporary face, it might be more advisable to reexamine these challenges in an effort to ascertain if they are real and, if they are, to devise alternative responses to them.

The Unbearable Fastness of Being a Designer Now

Today many design practices take place in institutional settings in which the conditions of possibility for knowledge production are a far cry from the kind of independence from market forces that an iconic research, design, and innovation setting such as Bell Labs enjoyed from 1956 until 1984 as it provided its researchers and designers with the space for free experimentation. The design and innovation consultants I worked with readily acknowledged "the tendency for design firms to skimp on analysis . . . due in part to financial pressures"—that is, their difficulty "to persuade clients to fund adequate labor time for researchers to develop well-grounded interpretations" as well as clients' pressure "for immediate results" (Wasson 2000, 385). As David, a design and innovation consultant, told me in an interview, "It's very hard to get the time to spend with a client to really dig into their life and their world. It's hard to get the time to dig into the world and spend time with users. On both sides people just want results: 'Make it good, make it great, you're really smart.'" He added with visible exasperation: "A lot of people are not willing to really ask: 'Well, why do you want to change? What are you trying to get? What would success look like to you? What else have you tried?' All of this stuff is very personally or intimately related."

Such pressures can be contextualized in companies' overall desire to develop new strategies to further reduce the turnover time of capital in today's business world. The transition to part-time and temporary labor force (Muehlebach and Shoshan 2012; Ho 2009), cheaper manufacturing of goods in small batches and new distribution systems such as just-in-time inventory-flow delivery systems (Elam 1994; Shead 2017), geographical dispersal and mobility (Esser and Hirsch 1994), and the ability to take advantage of up-to-date information through computerization and electronic means of communication (Zaloom 2006;

Holmes and Marcus 2006) are a few manifestations of this trend. This contemporary economic playing field requires organizations to have up-to-date information and make swift decisions in order to survive and be profitable. Indeed, organizations must not only instantaneously respond to but also orchestrate and anticipate future market changes by generating a constant stream of ideas for new products and services (Wilf 2015). This business environment has "spawned a wide array of highly specialized business services and consultancies capable of providing up-to-the-minute information on market trends and the kind of instant data analyses useful in corporate decision-making" (Harvey 1990, 159).

One way in which innovation and design consultants have responded to these market pressures is to come up with the means to generate "fast data"—for example, data "reported instantaneously by consumers via cell phones, Internet blogs, pagers, and so forth—[which] reflect and recreate the new managerial imperative for faster production, management, insights, and innovation that businesses now run" (de Waal Malefyt 2009, 207). This is, in fact, "fast ethnography," whose problems deserve a separate discussion. Below I discuss the ways in which the design and innovation consultants I worked with came up with ways to generate "fast analysis"—that is, to streamline, standardize, predetermine, and thereby accelerate the production of "insights" while maintaining the rhetoric of "emergence" and "context-sensitivity."

Templating the New

My first example is taken from fieldwork I conducted with a design and innovation consultancy that is based in New York City, which I call Newfound (Wilf 2016). Since its foundation in 2012, Newfound has offered innovation corporate training and workshops, as well as contract work with individual companies on specific projects. It has collaborated with companies from the banking, apparel, food, education, and tourism sectors and industries on a wide range of projects. Its founders and facilitators base their expertise in design, business management, and advertising. They trace most of their professional lineage to design thinking, the highly influential method of user-centered design and innovation that is widely associated with the iconic Silicon Valley innovation consultancy IDEO and Stanford's Institute of Design (Brown and Wyatt 2010).

One of Newfound's design and innovation workshops that I attended lasted five weeks. The workshop was structured around a specific problem that was presented by a real client, an educational organization that wanted to redesign and innovate its website to achieve higher retention rates among its target audience. Participants in the workshop came from the start-up sector and the creative industries. By trying to solve the client's problem by means of the innovation strategies inculcated in the workshop, participants hoped to gain hands-on experience and what they considered to be crucial skills in the contemporary marketplace. The client hoped to benefit from the insights generated in the workshop. It consequently was willing to underwrite some of the workshop's costs.

In the third week of the workshop, the participants arrived with notebooks filled with the data they had collected in the previous two weeks by means of interviews with the client's target audience, online search, and experimentation with the client's website (Wilf 2019, 112–14). The workshop facilitators told them that the third week would be dedicated to learning ways to "understand" the data they had collected in the previous two weeks and to developing insights that could lead to innovative solutions to the client's problem (cf. Wasson 2000, 383). At the beginning of the session, Jeffrey, one of the facilitators, defined the goal of this stage of the design process with the following words: "What we are actually doing is moving things around, finding insights, learning something new, and then moving things again, and it's that constant evolution of the data that helps us get to some interesting places. The purpose—and this is extremely important," he emphasized, "is not to nail an insight from the onset. It's not like to beat into all this information and be like—'Oh my god, I have it!' It's going to take time where you will be like: 'This is kind of interesting, not really, but kind of interesting; oh my god, this is getting slightly more interesting, this is starting to make some progress, this is starting to become compelling!'"—he simulated increased excitement. "And then when you make it to the end you'll say: 'Wow, this is something I'm really excited about!' But allow all those steps," he resumed in his usual tone. "Don't put the pressure on yourself to get it from the onset. Allow yourself to move slowly through these steps, and as you do it tonight I think you'll end up getting at something really satisfying and really compelling."

Jeffrey's explanation is almost an exact replica of the idea behind the recent calls to turn to "design" as a source of inspiration for anthropological training and work. To reiterate, these calls are about teaching students of anthropology "the art of finding the design of research—and of its eventual textualization—in the course of inquiry, to let the field or the particular story or theme that is emerging take over the design. The challenge is to become part of a foreign milieu, to submit to the outside, to get drowned in and carried away by it, while staying alert to the gradual emergence of a theme to which chance encounters, fugitive events, anecdotal observations give rise" (Rees 2008, 116).

However, in tandem with their explanation of the "understand" phase, the workshop facilitators distributed to the participants a handout that included a number of readymade templates (Figure 2.1; see Wilf 2016). Jeffrey projected a slide that showed the readymade templates and then said: "We will use these frameworks and abstractions to start to pull out what these things are that we're hearing on a larger scale and what they actually mean. Now," he cautioned, "often in this phase I find people wanting to collect tons of information. They want to complicate this. It's not necessary. When we're going through this, using basic frameworks is going to give you amazing insights and we don't need something crazy with seventeen different lines and eight different compartments and a back door—it's not necessary. And so this is what we are looking for: what is there that is something new? An insight is when you get something and you're like: 'You know what? I never would have guessed this. From the preconceived ideas, the assumptions that I've had, this is telling me a different story and this is a story that I'm excited to tell back to the client.' And an insight can look like a lot of things." He paused and looked at the frameworks again. "Sometimes an insight is just a great framework where people just look and they are like: 'Wow, that means something to me. I can connect with that. That's unexpected. That's interesting.'"

On the one hand, Jeffrey kept emphasizing that the point of "understanding" is to analyze the data and thereby come up with new assumptions that would problematize preconceived ones. On the other hand, he recommended using readymade templates as forms of insights in and of themselves. When he cautioned the participants not to collect "tons of information" and instead to use "basic frameworks" that are "going to give you amazing insights," he inadvertently pointed to the fact that because of the designer's current working conditions, extensive fieldwork and user-centered data collection are not feasible. Against this backdrop, the frameworks, which have become conventional visual templates of what a valid insight might look like, can help the designer or innovator generate insights as fast as possible with little information. These insights will nevertheless have persuasive power over the client because they have the appearance of valid insights. The "unexpected," "emergent," and "new" has thus been standardized and streamlined by means of the reified visual forms that valid insights are expected to have.[2]

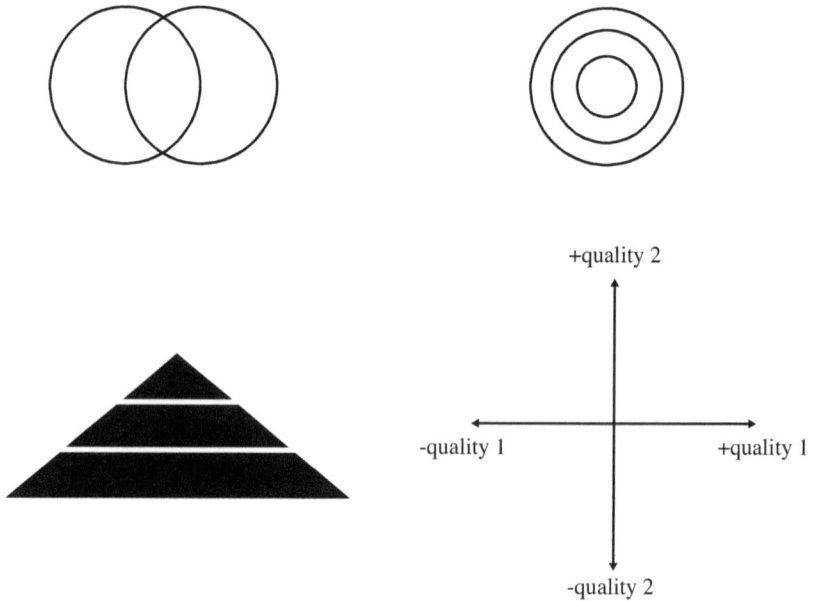

Figure 2.1. Ready-made frameworks for data analysis.

Jeffrey continued his explanation in a way that revealed another form of standardization or streamlining of the "unexpected" in this design context: "Sometimes an insight is something we are sharing out and we need to be able to verbalize it. These are great ones," he pointed to the next slide that he projected on the wall. The slide showed the following lines:

INSIGHT FORMATS
WE THOUGHT . . .
BUT LEARNED . . .
THEREFORE . . .

He then animated the slide:

We thought *that* but we learned *that*—this is expressing a point of tension. This is an assumption that I had coming to this project. We had a fundamental belief that people behave in this way. We went out and we watched them, and we saw something completely different. So normally it's "We *thought* but we *learned*," and then instead of this period it's going to be "*therefore.*" We *thought*, blank; we *learned* something completely different; *therefore* this is what needs to be done. It's dramatically different from what we believed before, and this is something you [i.e., the client] need to take into account as you're building your product.

What Jeffrey is trying to teach the participants is a standardized template of how to verbalize insights to the client in a way that would make these insights appear to be the end result of an emergent form of inquiry. At stake in this verbal template and in the visual templates are conventionalized and rhetorically powerful strategies of templating the new.

When the participants presented their insights to the client's representatives in the workshop's final week, they used these visual and verbal templates. Their celebration of an epistemology of emergence that was operationalized by means of practices that to a great extent standardized and predetermined its end results will remain unexplained as long as we approach "design" abstractly rather than as a culturally and historically specific situated practice. Conversely, if we acknowledge the fact that Jeffrey's design and innovation practice is embedded in contemporary market forces that mandate the fast production of results that should retain the appearance of the unexpected, his practice will begin to make sense.

The Seductions of a Decontextualized, Algorithmically Inferable World

My second example suggests that the simultaneous endorsement of an epistemology of emergence that is operationalized by means of practices that greatly predetermine and standardize its end results may be the very definition of "design" in many of its contemporary market-based formations. The example is taken from my fieldwork with another design and innovation consultancy, which I call Brandnew. Brandnew was founded in 1994. Since its foundation it has collaborated with major companies from different sectors on a vast spectrum of consumer products and services, one of which has become a standard of innovation in the field of consumer electronics. Its facilitators base their expertise in cognitive science and the study of creative problem-solving with a focus on engineering problems, in addition to business management. Participants in its design and innovation workshops and corporate training sessions are senior executives in large, established companies, some of which are

Fortune 500 companies. They are mostly c-level executives (e.g., chief innovation officers) with business management degrees. In addition to fieldwork with Brandnew, I participated in a course on business innovation in one of the top five US business schools, which focused on the core principles of Brandnew's signature innovation strategy.[3] The course was taught by Dan, a man in his late fifties who is an internationally recognized expert in marketing research, new product development, and diffusion of innovation. The course lasted six weeks and was attended by close to seventy students. It is offered a few times a year at this school.

The first point I want to emphasize is that Brandnew's design and innovation strategy promises to help business executives to address the problem of relevance and timing—that is, how to develop products that will cater to "consumer needs" before one's competitors do so. This point situates Brandnew's strategy at the center of the problem of relevance and "timeliness" that the recent calls for ethnographic experimentation with design practices address. Consider the way in which Dan described to his students the futility of market research in the idea-generation stage of new product design and development (Wilf 2019, 95): "Suppose that you just graduated from the MBA program at Yale and you are doing research for Citibank," he began. "And you want to explore the market to come up with new services. But," he continued, "someone else just graduated from NYU and he is working for Chase Manhattan and he's also doing research. So you both learned from the same professors of market research, you are talented in the same way, you use approximately the same budget, you are using the same sample sizes. If this happens—and it happens all the time—then don't be surprised if you come up with the same ideas as that other person. Because you are using needs that have already evolved into the demand." Dan paused and gave his students the time to digest this ominous prospect. "You want the numbers?" he asked. "Ok, I'll give you the numbers. What are the odds, if you have eight competitors, that through market research alone you can be the first?" At this point a few of the students raised their hands and offered their estimates. Dan shook his head. "I'll give you a hint," his voice suddenly assumed a grave tone. "It's not twelve and a half percent. It's less than a half percent! And the bad news is that there are more than eight competitors, because millions of eyes are looking at the market, trying to make easy money by developing an idea, a concept, and then sell it to a company that can introduce it officially to the market. So by market research you cannot find something that your competitors can't find in the same way. It's practically impossible."

Brandnew's solution to this problem is telling. When I met Dan in his office at the business school, I asked him if he could articulate what sets Brandnew's method apart from other design and innovation strategies that are currently popular in the business world (Wilf 2019, 78). "Well, take design thinking," he said. "They begin with the users whereas Brandnew's innovation method begins with the product. The argument is this: you have some kind of a system, service, product, whatever. And these systems evolve. According to what?" he asked rhetorically. "According to their adaptability to the environment. So if there is suddenly some kind of [consumer] need, the system needs to respond. So this is an evolutionary development because there are engineers that adapt the product according to the demands of the environment. A product that doesn't do this will disappear." He went on to explain that it is possible to collect information about how consumer needs develop by investigating the history of a given product's adaptation to those needs: "Inside the product there is a certain movement or move that the product makes according to the demands of the environment. If we can identify the pattern—imagine a regression," he offered. "There are points on a certain line [i.e., on the identified pattern]. If I proceed a little bit ahead, I will be able to know what the next point is before the market even knows. Design thinking needs the market to already know about this unmet need. Brandnew's approach is that the data about the unmet needs can be found not in the market but in the product and that we can predict this data before the market gives off signals. So we can get to the unmet needs sooner." In his course, Dan specified that the backward analysis of the history of a successful product and of the stepwise changes between its past versions can reveal common patterns of change that can be synthesized into "templates." These templates represent "the laws of product evolution." By applying these "laws" or "templates" to existing products, it is possible to predict new products before the consumers' needs for them become active—that is, when the needs are still "unmet" (cf. Suchman et al. [2002, 166] regarding the notion of "latent needs").

Two points are noteworthy. First, this method of new product development takes to the extreme the endorsement of an epistemology of emergence that is operationalized by means of practices that greatly standardize and predetermine its end results. It argues that products and their forms emerge as a result of dynamic evolutionary processes, which have become the epitome of emergence in the modern West. However, it promises to tame the randomness associated with the notion of evolutionary processes by revealing the deep structures that underlie them in the form of "templates." This is an ingenious rhetorical construction. Evolution is associated with chance-based changes that business executives might find unsettling because of the unpredictability they connote. At the same time, the notion of evolution only boosts the appeal of Brandnew's method of innovation because the inventors of this method argue that they have identified the deep structures that underlie "product evolution." Chance or emergence is thereby both retained and tamed by means of predetermined "templates" qua "scripts."

Second, when Dan contrasts Brandnew's method of innovation with design thinking, he emphasizes that the designer does not have to engage with consumers because the "rules" that govern "product evolution" contain information about the pattern of emergence of consumer needs. Because the innovator can infer this information from the history of the evolution of successful products and synthesize it in the form of templates, he or she does not need to engage with consumers to generate ideas for innovative products that will cater to future consumer needs. The innovator can apply the templates to existing products in an algorithmic way and thus predict new products that will cater to "unmet" needs "before the market gives off signals." In this sense, Brandnew's method allows the innovator to "get to the unmet needs sooner"—namely, before the innovator who uses design thinking and who needs to engage with consumers can get to them. One condition of possibility for this framework, of course, is a very specific notion of "consumer needs." Such needs emerge deterministically and unchangingly in that the pattern that determined the emergence of past needs is the same pattern that will determine the emergence of future needs. This framework thus purifies consumer needs from the noise and heterogeneity that typically saturate them. It approaches them as unchanging, universal, transcending contexts, and naturally emerging from consumers, as if mediating cultural and symbolic structures such as marketing did not exist.

The pressure to produce instantaneous results before one's competitors do so while endorsing an epistemology of emergence thus results in an innovation method that foregoes context altogether and replaces it with the fantasy of being able to algorithmically decipher future "consumer needs" before consumers become aware of them and by interacting solely with products. If, according to the recent calls to take design as an inspiration for anthropology, the anthropologist of the contemporary (Rabinow et al. 2008) should strive to remain relevant by publishing at a faster pace that matches the pace of change of the phenomena that he or she is writing about, Brandnew's designers try to remain relevant by producing insights on phenomena (i.e., "consumer needs") that do not even exist yet. More so, they then orchestrate the emergence of these phenomena through advertising that creates consumer needs in what is essentially a performative action that validates their insights. Rather than take such designers as a potential source of inspiration for the timely production of an anthropology of the contemporary, we should approach them as a cautionary tale about the potential repercussions of the battle for ethnographic relevance whose very necessity should be questioned.

Conclusion: The Wrong Means to Misguided Ends

One of the conclusions that can be derived from the two cases I presented above is that if "design" is to function as a source of inspiration for revamping anthropological work, it might be advisable to turn to strands of design that are not embedded (or are only somewhat embedded) in the norms and practices of business innovation. These norms and practices cannot be easily incorporated into anthropological work without either losing their appeal if they are subjected to the production norms of anthropological work, which emphasize careful analysis and context-sensitivity; infusing anthropological work with the production norms and goals that prevail in many contemporary corporate design settings, which emphasize quick "deliverables," often at the expense of context-sensitivity; or becoming reified icons of methodological innovation in anthropology, giving anthropologists the illusion that they (in addition to the knowledge they produce) have become "timely," "relevant," and one with the contemporary zeitgeist of innovation.

The question still remains whether the challenges that have motivated the calls to take design as a source of inspiration for revamping anthropological work are real or not. This question is far more complicated and nuanced for me to be able to answer it here. Consequently, I will only briefly discuss the role played by "relevance," for anthropologists' desire to be "relevant" seems to me to emanate from the same cultural matrix that has bred the design practices I have critiqued above.

Marcus has formulated the problem of relevance with the following example, which I quote in detail:

> Recently, a Chicana graduate student of mine who was seeking a subject for her dissertation fieldwork that addressed life on and across the border of Mexico and the United States discovered the complexity of the used

clothes business as a transnational, transcultural activity with many actors, sites, and diverse cultural codings, unified in a single frame and rationale of business. She was excited about this activity as the focus of dissertation fieldwork. Then she found a brilliant piece featured in a Sunday edition of the *New York Times* that provided a virtuoso treatment of this subject in a few pages. An ethnographic study of the topic could only be an elaboration of what this inspired journalism had already accomplished, with the aid of considerable resources (what I call a writing/research machine), much more concisely and more timely than ethnography is capable of. Placing a high value on originality in her work and considering carefully whether such a duplicate study over a much longer period of time would contribute significantly in the context of media and scholarship that treat the US-Mexican border as well as Chicano culture itself as a kind of social movement, the student decided to abandon her interest in developing dissertation research on this subject, with the idea of perhaps reprising it later as a component of a broader study of objects and symbols that flow across the border. In any case, the situation of this student is typical of many anthropologists in formulating their research today, in particularly scholars who are beginning their careers in the present professional culture for the production of ethnography that I have outlined—a professional culture that highly values recognition and response from outside its own disciplinary community and that has been deeply affected by the desire for relevance that I have described. (Marcus 2015, 151)

This vignette raises a key issue. Why would it be the case that "an ethnographic study of the topic could only be an elaboration of what this inspired journalism had already accomplished . . . much more concisely and more timely than ethnography is capable of"? One would think that the theoretical analysis of the ethnographic material—however diverse this theory's sources of inspiration might be today—could easily be anthropology's unique contribution in comparison with investigative journalism, where theory, if it even exists, takes the form of academic experts qua talking heads who briefly comment on the ethnographic material. The construction of new theoretical tools and the problematization of existing ones rarely exist in investigative journalism precisely because of its different and much faster production norms, as well as its different goals. Because theory is not mentioned at all in Marcus's description of the "desire for relevance," we can only surmise that the meaning of the "originality" in the student's work on which she placed a high value is something like this: being the first to provide an ethnographic description of a given reality, perhaps with the goal of changing this reality by taking part in it rather than by describing it from afar (hence contributing to "Chicano culture . . . as a kind of social movement"). When we define anthropology's telos in this way, we indeed turn it into a kind of investigative journalism, in which case anthropologists would be better off seeking employment in the *New York Times* or the *New Yorker*, where their social impact and wages are likely to be higher than in academia.

Anthropologists' misguided "desire to be relevant" notwithstanding (Marcus 2015, 149), it seems to me that design has emerged as a possible way to satisfy this desire because of the unexamined idea that a number of highly visible and prestigious design strands in the contemporary moment represent a kind of expertise that can generate context-sensitive data at a fast pace. Only a critique of this idea will ensure that the knowledge that social scientists produce and the ways in which they organize themselves to produce it do not become yet another one of Silicon Valley's many contemporary fashionable subsets, offshoots, and, indeed, "spin-offs."

Notes

1. There is evidence that some of the institutional sites of anthropological research that have been established in the model of the design studio in the wake of the calls to revamp anthropological training and work have followed this problematic path. Consider, for example, the initiative entitled "University of California Collaboratory for Ethnographic Design," which "builds on the respective accomplishments of ethnography incubators at six campuses (San Diego, Irvine, Los Angeles, Berkeley, Davis, and Santa Cruz) to establish a UC-wide interdisciplinary hub for innovative ethnographic theory and methodology" (http://sed.ucsd.edu/coled/). The tropes "incubators," "hubs," and "innovative" suggest that these initiatives are heavily informed by Silicon Valley's norms and practices of business innovation.

2. IDEO has disseminated the same visual frameworks in its different publications (cf. IDEO 2011, 101). Its institutionalized prestige is thus responsible for the popularity of these frameworks. This fact points to the reified status of design thinking as a key strand of "design" in the contemporary moment.

3. The school's ranking is based on the *Financial Times*'s "Global MBA Rankings for 2015." See http://rankings.ft.com/businessschoolrankings/global-mba-ranking-2015.

CHAPTER THREE

Feeling, Action, and Speculative Value through Human-Centered Design

LILLY IRANI

In 2013, a *Wired Magazine* journalist asked Paul Farmer, an anthropologist and public-health physician, and Melinda Gates, a former software manager turned head of the Bill and Melinda Gates Foundation (BMGF): "What innovation do you think is changing the most lives in the developing world?" Melinda's answer, presented without equivocation: "Human-centered design." She continued, explaining human-centered design (HCD) as "meeting people where they are and really taking their needs and feedback into account. When you let people participate in the design process, you find that they often have ingenious ideas about what would really help them. And it's not a onetime thing; it's an iterative process" (Roper 2013).

The enthusiasm was not Gates's alone. Farmer added an example of a "design" approach to development practice. He described hospitals in Haiti where patients might wait three days to see a doctor, resting their heads on found objects and waiting without food. "We have to design a health delivery system by actually talking to people and asking, 'What would make this service better for you?'" He continued: "As soon as you start asking, you get a flood of answers." The article, entitled "The Human Element: Melinda Gates and Paul Farmer on Designing Global Health," headlined the promise of human-centered design in the face of development pessimism famously manifest in books such as *Dead Aid* (Moyo 2009) and *White Man's Burden* (Easterly 2006).

The foundation supported the work of several design studios in India, including one I studied extensively through participant observation: DevDesign. The foundation's reach was transnational, linking sites of expertise production and development across the world. The foundation sent DevDesign project members to Kenya to learn from sanitation projects and to share methods. The foundation commissioned California design firm IDEO to develop and disseminate human-centered design (HCD) "toolkits" (worksheets and guidebooks) to NGOs across the world (see Brown and Wyatt 2010, 34). They organized TEDx conferences and funded social-innovation labs to disseminate innovation and HCD. They advocated for "philanthrocapitalism," or charity organized through business (McGoey 2015). They were not alone. The Rockefeller Foundation and Britain's Nesta had also funded the production of toolkits, workbooks, and case studies to train NGO workers, government workers, and social entrepreneurs in HCD techniques for innovation.

These critiques of development made sense to designers and social entrepreneurs, who flocked to these events. Through my fieldwork, I met many who believed that the state ought to design development better. Films such as *Peepli Live* critiqued state and policy elites for addressing human crises—farmer suicides, in the case of the film—with spectacular schemes that failed people in practice. Government officials offered water pumps, but did not ask how recipients would install them. Vivek and Kritika, two designers I worked with, discussed the film on several occasions to talk about the promise of design as providing a "systemic" view that could offer India's poor solutions that "just work."

Yet why did anthropology and development need design? At this moment, anthropology might have been thought to be in its heyday. Farmer, well known as a cofounder of NGO Partners in Health and as a Harvard anthropology professor, stood for culturally and historically informed development in action. His cofounder, Jim Yong Kim, also a Harvard anthropology PhD, was named president of the World Bank in 2009—a highly visible testament to the importance of cultural expertise even as the bank remained dominated by economic reason (Mosse 2011). And BMGF was one of the most powerful philanthropies in the world. In 2018, the foundation was the second biggest contributor to the World Health Organization (Moulds 2020). Researchers observe that the foundation gives at a magnitude that allows it to shape agricultural and health policies in Africa and India (Ignatova 2017).

And yet Gates and Farmer championed design; this invites a question based on the introduction to this book: How do "design and anthropology function as aspirational figures of salvation for each other?" Why does design seem to save both development and anthropology, just as anthropology had been pulled into service of saving development decades earlier? The traffic between design and anthropology renews development. It articulates a field of intervention, a will to improve (Li 2007), and an interest in the unruliness of life. In pursuit of innovation, designers and engineers have taken up some methods of anthropology, not to find patterns of culture or to engage in cultural critique, but to understand the practices of others: those that can be changed, those that cannot, and the opportunity for transformation that lies in knowing the difference.

Design in the context of philanthrocapitalism—the belief that markets and profit can be turned toward philanthropic goals—interweaves care for others in service of the capacities and goals of clients, most often business firms but sometimes governments. This turn to design took place as companies expanded their vision of consumers to include the very poor. In doing so, they sought to make value out of tweaked versions of what they already knew how to make—software, soaps, and other commodities. Human-centered design, I argue, offers a method for finding opportunities and managing risk to these speculative projects of value accumulation.

This chapter traces the work of design for philanthrocapitalism from Delhi, India, as middle-class designers translate a Nehruvian desire to build the nation into projects funded by foundations such as those of Bill and Melinda Gates, Rockefeller, and Ford. "Human-centered design" practices offered ways for entrepreneurial citizens (Irani 2019) to find opportunities for innovation and economic value in the lives of their poorer counterparts. I show the practical work of seeing as a designer: seeking empathy for targets of development, suspending judgment, and eschewing disciplinary knowledge in pursuit of a feel for "opportunity." In scenes of rural fieldwork and expert workshops, I show how designers' practices of ethnographic seeing mobilize affects of empathy and hope in service of innovation that produces legible economic value. These cases illustrate epistemic practices of innovation I observed over fourteen months of ethnographic fieldwork following the work of a design studio DevDesign. I did fieldwork in Hindi and English between 2009 and 2014.

This chapter offers an anthropology *of* design. The practices and projects detailed here are very much built on the history of anthropology in shaping and critiquing the field of development. These design practices come, I argue, to supplant anthropology as a form of knowledge production suited to the needs of speculative capitalist practices that search for value by inserting commodities into new niches of cultural life.

The Value of Design in India

First, the political economy of the case. Delhi at the time of my fieldwork seemed a development boomtown. Since before independence, Delhi has been a center of development planning to modernize what Nehru called a "needy nation" (S. Roy 2007). The central government's preliberalization five-year plans and import controls had given way, after liberalization, to facilitating public-private partnership and the movement of capital investment (Corbridge and Harriss 2000, 120; Kohli 2006; Rajagopal 2011; Jayal 2013). By 2004, Goldman Sachs directed global investors to the potential of emerging markets in BRICs—what management consultants call Brazil, Russia, India, China. Michigan business school professor C. K. Prahalad directed business leaders to seek their fortunes "at the bottom of the pyramid" at the same time that the central government called for "inclusive growth"—the production of economic growth that India's masses could feel. BMGF and those in their orbit of influence called this movement "philanthrocapitalism." Geographer Ananya Roy calls this turn to the poor as debtors, entrepeneurs, and financial profit "poverty capital" (2010). My focal field site, DevDesign, worked in this speculative "dream zone" (J. Cross 2014) as innovation consultants doing user research and design for these emerging markets. They did fieldwork for London global-health start-ups looking for opportunities. They coached Indian college students in design thinking to innovate water distribution. They refined and retooled corporate products to be corporate social-responsibility initiatives.

At the same time, Indian public discourse celebrated "innovation" and "entrepreneurship" as a way of resolving the contradictions of national, community, or even personal identities and global capital. In the face of a service-oriented IT economy, those I worked with saw design and creativity as ways of making more locally relevant and self-expressive commodities. IT grads and village inventors alike could innovate, the common sense went, thus contributing to development, economic growth, and an "authentic" India through the commodification of everyday creativity. These anxieties about mimicking the modernity of elsewhere were not new. What was new as of the mid-2000s was the language of "innovation" as novelty, locality, and profit combined. Policy makers turned to design as one knowledge practice that could promise such profitable novelty. The driving force behind the discursive and policy shift to novelty was the World Intellectual Property Organization's TRIPS agreement and the intellectual property preferences of "advanced economies." India had historically privileged access and wide manufacture of invention over novelty. Since the 1970s, it had enforced "process patents" but not "product patents." It allowed reverse engineering by consequence. The TRIPS agreement forced India to accept product patents, forbidding the production of equivalent goods and thus making the production of novel products a legal and moral imperative (Sunder 2006; Ramanna 2002; Mehrotra 1987). In India, development had not always mandated novelty. Nehru understood the horizon of technoscience as a universal resource; postcolonial nations could produce authentic modernities by drawing on these universal endowments to address national needs. TRIPS criminalized the drawing from these knowledge commons.

Beyond India, entrepreneurship and innovation had more recently become a soft-power project to protect US interests globally. I will say more about this later, but suffice to say for now that the call to innovate through entrepreneurship came not only from the Indian state, software sectors, and pharmaceutical sectors. It also came from the Davos set and trickled into international aid norms. Then–secretary of state Hillary Clinton launched Partners for a New Beginning, a nonprofit organization led by Steve Jobs's biographer Walter Isaacson, former secretary of state Madeleine Albright, and executives of Dow, Intel, Cisco, Exxon, Morgan Stanley, CARE USA, and Interfaith Youth Core (Partners for a New Beginning 2010). Along these lines, USAID's India 2012 strategy declared a shift from seeing India as a recipient of aid to a "peer-to-peer partnership for addressing Indian and global development challenges . . . [with] USAID as convener, accelerator, and broker . . . of innovation and partnerships." The India USAID policy declared, "Innovate. Partner. Go global" (USAID 2012). These mandates will haunt the case study of human-centered design for water provision, to which I now turn.

Within these global geopolitics and public-private developmentalisms, innovation went beyond products. It was an ethos. DevDesign, the studio where I did the bulk of my fieldwork, evangelized design as a model for making Indians into entrepreneurial citizens (see Irani 2019; Chakravartty and Sarkar 2013). They put on an annual festival celebrating "interdisciplinary action"—their words—directed at students, planners, engineers, artists, and development workers. Their festival showed existence proofs of activism, social business models, and even vernacular literary production. They reached wide to elicit what they called "progressive" innovation. They designed software. They designed water filters, films, NGO "toolkits," and even traveling theater for sanitation.

DevDesign's client, a US health technology nonprofit, had hired them to find ways of innovating sanitation technology. The nonprofit had five years of funding from BMGF to design a water filter for the poor.

When the Medical Anthropologist Met the Software Manager

The Bill and Melinda Gates Foundation was one of the many foundations exploring innovation, design, and entrepreneurship as vehicles for organizing development. How did design become such a promising practice for development in trouble? Design at once seemed rational and systematic, yet in touch with human emotions, needs, and desires. Design promised to take a social, contextual, and embodied understanding of people and their practices and turn it into large-scale interventions, systems, and products to transform human life. HCD promised intimate alignment with community life and individual experience in the developing world, and yet paradoxically it appeared a universal best practice for achieving that alignment. It was localization, but as a universal process.

Human-centered design extended and knotted together two genealogies of how the social sciences have been put in service of transforming human life: anthropology's relationship to development, and social science's engagements with computer systems design.

ENGINEERING ACCEPTANCE IN DEVELOPMENT

Colonial and early developmental projects drew on the social sciences to manage top-down projects, including extraction, rule, or infrastructure development. These are the histories that produced concepts of culture (Birla 2009), tradition (Fabian 1983), *adat* (the backbone of customary law and a word that connotes "habit") (Goh 2006; Mamdani 1996).

As colonial people formed formally independent nations, development emerged as a way for American-led capitalist nations to keep people of the poorer nations away from communism (Prashad 2012; Goldman 2006). This was the era of bridges, roads, and institution building.

By the mid-1970s, it became clear that these top-down projects registered poor results, and development agencies turned to participation as a way of enlisting consent and managing resistance (Escobar 1991, 662–63). Though participation emerged in response to social movements and radical demands on development institutions, it withered over the decades from a language of people's "control" to one of people's "influence" over development (Hickey and Mohan 2005; Cornwall 2000).

Gates and Farmer advocated a notion of participation somewhere between top-down and bottom-up strategies in making development more social. Human-centered design, Gates explained, was a way of seeking "ingenious ideas" for helping people from people themselves. Yet the foundation was known for privileging cutting-edge technology and science research, pursuing spectacular last-mile eradication efforts over disease control that affects more lives, and promoting mass-scale "evidence-based" interventions (e.g., mosquito nets) (McGoey 2015).

This turn to the poor for "ingenious ideas" fit a broader shift to what anthropologist Julia Elyachar calls "development after development," in which the poor are seen as repositories of tacit knowledge, "next practices," and opportunities for agencies and corporations alike (2012). Human-centered design rode on the legitimacy of poor people as knowing subjects who ought to have a voice in their future, but translated those voices not into political control but into sources of ideas—the very currency of the TED conference's "ideas that matter."

Further, human-centered design drew on anthropological methods to understand practices, habits, and cognitive biases of those whose lives were to be transformed (World Bank 2015). This aligned with a turn in development to see "culture as an ally"—a set of practices that development interventions can marshal rather than treat as a barrier to change (T. Tufte 2013, 31; Wood 1996).

ENGINEERING ACCEPTANCE IN SOFTWARE PRODUCTION

The human-centered design championed by Gates and Farmer also rode on a second history of top-down projects negotiating bottom-up resistance: the history of the computerization of everyday life.

Bill and Melinda Gates were not just any sorts of philanthropists. They were also software engineers and product managers. While they rarely cite software production as a pedagogy for development, in my fieldwork I found frequent crossings between software engineering and development. BMGF hired program officers with no background in development, but with background in software engineering and design. The Gates-funded NGO employed an ex–software designer for the filter project. That same NGO sponsored human-computer-interaction (HCI) researchers to develop design methods for sanitation interventions. HCI had enough legitimacy to extend and adapt its expertise to noncomputational domains.

Early HCI was a top-down project situated in military and industrial expertise. Early research into "man-machine systems" focused on optimizing the role of humans in airplanes and control systems, primarily on reducing their errors and, later, improving their speed. A second wave focused on improving the speed and usability of computers as they entered the workplace. As technology companies expanded their attention beyond selling to managers to sell to end users, HCI turned toward culture and desirability as aspects of design (Harrison et al. 2011).

One product of this turn to user experience was the operationalization of empathy as a tool for design. Designers described their empathy for users as what distinguished them from engineers whose affections were for technology itself; designers sought to know human difference and bring technology into closer relations with it (Goodman et al. 2011; Patnaik and Mortenson 2009; Suri 2001; Salvador et al. 1999; Segal and Suri 1997; see Taylor 2011 for critiques within HCI). But having empathy did not mean assuming that users knew what was best. It meant only that they felt they knew what was best, and that their feelings determined the success of the product. Empathy did not imply user control (see Beck 2002 for an exception).

These twin trajectories of social sciences in the computing industries and in development work came together as designers looked for opportunities that tapped into local desires, managed local resistances, and promised large-scale developmental "impact" on human life.

Design Ethnography: The Politics of Empathy When Impact Means Scale

With this context on how development came together with HCD, I turn to my first case: the project to produce "clean water" for the poor.

DevDesign had been commissioned by a client to complete a home-placement study of prototype household water filters. The studio would place existing filter designs in homes to learn the limitations and desires that a revised filter would have to address. They then spent several months following up to observe and interview people using the filters.

The client was a reputable global-health NGO based in the United States that I will call HealthWorks. HealthWorks saw the project as a first step to developing a "market out of thin air" for usable, affordable commercial water filters for poor consumers across Asia and Africa. Expanding filter use, the logic went, would curb waterborne illness. HealthWorks recognized the audacity of the project: "How do you begin to get acquainted with four billion people?"

DevDesign's team drove hundreds of kilometers from village to village searching for participants. The imagined study recruit, according to the lead designer, was "fairly poor," getting "water from the dirty river," often ill from waterborne illness, and without a filter. Few matched the HealthWorks image of poverty. What the design researchers found instead were villages where people seemed relatively happy or even proud of their water, claiming that they were acclimated. They boiled water for elderly people, for infants, for sick children, or during the rainy season. Designers found few complaining about illnesses such as diarrhea or parasites. It appeared that designers had a solution without a constituency.

They looked for subtle signs of need. Designers trained in ethnography labeled certain everyday practices "work-arounds"—practices they read as evidence that the person might desire a more designed solution.

JUGAAD AND "WORK-AROUNDS":
DISORDERLY CREATIVITY IN EVERYDAY LIFE

One sweltering afternoon, designers spotted just such a crucial clue hanging on a shaded tree branch outside one family's home. A pair of vessels sat on the ground, wrapped in rough, wet cloth, each secured with some wire. Sushmita, who lived in the house, had soaked the cloth around the vessels, effectively creating an evaporative cooling device with items already available. The wire appeared carefully done; on the pot, it was criss-crossed across the wet cloth. Some of the materials—the cloth and the clay of the pot, for example—were inexpensive and widely available. The plastic bottle, by contrast, had come to village through retail shops that sold privatized water; it found second life as a storage device.

A patent examiner would need schematic drawings to recognize exclusive rights to this invention. Prior examples of cloth-covered vessels would invalidate the claims to an original design. But those questions seemed irrelevant to the work of going on with life; with this "people's solution," Sushmita cooled water using available materials, without spending cash or taking out a loan. This solution failed to build the nation, however; it did not register as economic exchange, let alone national economic metrics. It was made, but not bought or sold. Sushmita's cooling vessels did not replicate a design at scale. Like a Schumpeterian entrepreneur (see Schumpeter 1934), Sushmita's vessels produced use value through new combinations and know-how. Unlike that entrepreneur, her concern was use value, not exchange value.

Designers saw Sushmita's act of making not as a need fulfilled sustainably but as a sign of need. In the weeks that followed, the designers and NGO seized upon this as an opportunity. An American development consultant on the project explained, "People know you get sick from dirty water [but they still don't filter]. But what they really want is cold water and consistent access." They labeled Sushmita's cooling vessel as a "work-around," suggesting that her practice signaled a need incompletely fulfilled—a need to be fulfilled by a properly designed product. They also described the cooling vessel as "inspiration" for their design efforts—a social category that directs our attention to the rush of creativity in the one inspired, rather than the labors of those who produced the inspiration.

The design professions frame these encounters as a participatory alternative to modernist authoritarian planning without feedback (e.g., Scott 1998). Designers saw themselves as drawing in subaltern knowledge so they could humanize technology in turn. In contrast to Sushmita, however, designers could travel across sites, collecting stories and data about many people's practices. On returning to the studio, they could contemplate, synthesize, and posit a proposition for a form that addressed the needs of many across wide spatial scales. Sushmita's solution had no such aspirations; this form would move if someone—a designer or another villager—thought the idea was worth recirculating.

Designers simultaneously saw creativity everywhere and yet consolidated their own status as innovating elites by distinguishing their practices from more everyday forms of creativity. The jug, to the designers, exemplified a Hindi social category of creativity called *jugaad*. "Jugaad" connotes a clever improvisation that achieves a goal in highly constrained situations. As the Indian press debated Indians' capacities to innovate, some marshaled jury-rigged devices such as bullock carts propelled by diesel irrigation pumps as evidence of a recognizably Indian form of innovation (Kaur 2016). Critics of jugaad countered that it stood for shoddy quality and short-term thinking that has hobbled India's development. In India's *BusinessLine*, a "strategy and innovation consultant" wrote that jugaad has no "design element or risk-taking. It is not born of research or from technical mastery—from identifying lacunae in customer needs or a eureka moment in a laboratory" (Chadha 2009). Critics painted jugaad as a form of situational reason—temporally and spatially particular, developed in the heat of the moment, and constrained by the rigors of necessity. One professor at India's prestigious National Insitute of Design explained jugaad to me as a form of *majboori*, translating the concept by way of explanation: "It's helplessness. The constraints are so high that you are pushed up in the corner. Do something with whatever is available!" In these understandings, jugaad mostly reproduces the status quo while finding niches of survival within it. At a University of Pennsylvania conference called "India Innovation," Modi's chief financial advisor and Penn economics professor Arvind Subramanian called jugaad clever, but also "bad or not-so-good innovation"—the sort of innovation that creates a disorderly and unstable India (2014). Even in pop culture, a film titled *Jugaad* (2009) narrated how jugaad stymied entrepreneurship. In the film, an up-and-coming Delhi advertising consultant found his office shut because of a legal mistake. As he pursued proper channels, he found only lazy and corrupt bureaucrats; he spent his days pulling strings, chasing favors, and stepping outside the law to open the doors to his business again. Jugaad was central to Indian imaginations about transformational processes, but it failed to promise orderly progress, an end to corruption, rational planning, or the efficient conversion of Indians' energies into economic growth. Jugaad was what people figured out when their backs were pressed against the wall, not when they had free choices about how to proceed.

When designers presented work-arounds they discovered in the field, including *jugaadoo* solutions, they translated ingenuity and feminized domestic knowledge into evidence of unfulfilled need—a problem that justified design intervention into people's lives.

THE SUBALTERN CAN'T SPEAK. CAN THE USER DESIGN?

These subtle ethnographies of design need aside, the design team *had* found a pervasive but different water problem in a number of villages—this one explicitly voiced by potential users. Even better, those they interviewed—from physicians to farmers to itinerant rickshaw pullers—resoundingly articulated a desire for a solution. Over and over, designers heard Andhra villagers complain of fluorosis. Many villages got their water from bore wells—wells bored deep into the ground to access groundwater. For a variety of reasons—including industrial pollution, dams, and wells dug too deep into mineral deposits—the water had an excess of fluoride. Activists had agitated in the area, asking the government to install fluoride-filtration facilities. The local government had not done much.

The political economy of philanthrocapitalism—expressed as "impact" and "scale"—mediated what designers could hear, interpret, and act on in the project. The NGO commissioning the design team had already decided not to address fluoride early in the project. The reasons were many and overlapping. The NGO had a $17 million grant to develop household water purification. In global-health worlds, "clean water" usually meant diarrhea and waterborne disease; researchers assigned urgency to those diseases in disability-adjusted life years (DALYs). DALYs, in turn, informed philanthropic strategies that sought to fund areas with the largest impact on health. The NGO planned to pilot the filters in Africa, South Asia, and Southeast Asia. Fluorosis, even if it affected millions in India and China, seemed local by comparison. The immediate, present need for fluoride filters was a diversion from the global imaginary of development impact.

Further, addressing fluorosis risked the NGO project timeline. The NGO, one of the lead designers told me, was "on a timeline to prove themselves to [the foundation] so taking the fluoride project is too risky." Existing fluoride filters required electricity; engineering filtration that could work without electricity could take an unknown amount of time. By contrast, the bacterial filters the NGO wanted to market to the poor ran without power and were already being sold at higher price points to wealthier consumers: middle-class Indians and American hikers. The bacterial-filtration mechanism already existed; the NGO sought design, distribution, manufacturing, and financing strategies that would make it desirable.

Ultimately, the design team reinterpreted people's requests for fluoride filtration as a "perception." As a perception, fluoride became yet another aspect of user beliefs that might influence the desires for and expectations of a bacterial water filter. Even if the team could address the fluoride problem, to empathize became to treat overfluoridation as a feeling rather than as knowledge. The feeling that there is too much fluoride in the water became like the feeling that metal was more beautiful than plastic, or the feeling of confusion at which part of the filter contains the processed water. These feelings about materials, about bodies, and about aesthetics were what designers were interested in and needed to generate new products likely to succeed. Embedded in philanthrocapitalist design, empathy became a tool for managing people's perceptions that bacterial filtration was not what they needed.

To design with global reach, designers had to translate the embodied, the voiced, and the local into opportunities with reach, scale, and promise for partners. To innovate was not to address people's declared needs; rather, it was the demand that designers find new ways to sell to the poor what manufacturers knew how to make at scale.

Stakeholder Workshops: Constructing Opportunity, Generating Investments

Once fieldwork, in rural Andhra in the last case, wrapped, designers took their findings to expert workshops to translate stories into knowledge about opportunities. Knowledge here was not something stable and formal, but rather loose and open-ended to support speculation among stakeholders searching for opportunity.

The scene was a workshop at a five-star hotel in Delhi. This project was not for HealthWorks, but the Gates Foundation itself. The foundation tasked DevDesign with studying defecation practices among poorer Indians. The studio conducted a five-city, four-month study in which they interviewed people about where they defecated. They followed people to community toilets and open defecation fields to understand the experience of this basic human activity. At the workshop, they would present this research to the foundation and experts in its network.

The foundation convened the workshop with economists, sociologists, and NGO staff in its network. The workshops were a place where the foundation and the design studio could elicit critiques and generate, as they put it, "buy-in" as the studio developed its research findings. "Buy-in" could mean many things. It could mean that the foundation's partners would accept and speak well of this human-centered design research project. It could mean that NGOs would take up some of the findings and produce experimental sanitation projects. It could also mean that those present co-constructed interpretations of the findings that were mutually plausible to the experts present and those like them.

DevDesign boiled hundreds of hours of fieldwork film and photography into a few key clips meant to transport workshop attendees into homes, fields, and the everyday lives of others. The purpose of these curated stories was to provoke attendees to generate novel approaches to toilet design. These research findings DevDesign produced were qualitative and affective, organized in extensive slide decks featuring portraits, maps, and color-saturated photos of people and place. One of the studio founders was a filmmaker. Such was the priority of photography that the studio trained all new staff members in the basics of documentary photography and film.

    Studio members chose films that generated optimism in the room about the project. They did not accomplish this by producing single-message polemics or calls to action. Instead, they produced films about the intimate and complicated lives of users—bodily surfaces and movements held center stage. Histories of how lives came to take those forms never featured. These moving portraits of the present allowed divergent readings to coexist in parallel. One potent example was a video following a man as he walked through dense walkways between small apartments. The film was sped up, set to a melody undergirded by rapid string strumming. The film depicted the man entering a toilet, and then coming out to wash his body at a communal waterpoint. He soaped his face next to others passing around a hose to wash themselves. As he went to rinse, he grabbed the hose to find that it sprung a water leak. A boy standing near him held the hose to seal the leak. The film was so arresting to attendees that one staffer called this "the heart-wrenching potty video." For studio members, this video was a challenge to individualism, pointing instead to interdependence, shared infrastructure, and conviviality. For the BMGF program officer, however, the video signified human dignity and individual privacy. She explained, "You never see his privates. . . . Like you felt, it was a private thing in a way you shouldn't look at. He still managed to totally still be dignified while doing it."

    These multiple, even contradictory readings of films and photography were valued because they could generate divergent design ideas. Workshop talk was punctuated with what-ifs and maybes: maybe there could be a way to draw on community behaviors to share responsibility for facilities; we could put some kind of sanitizing mat at the exit of the toilets so those leaving stalls don't drag germs to the bathing facility; and so on.

    Staff paired observational slides with interpretations of opportunities or provocations to new design. One of their most provocative findings was that people enjoyed open defecation. They spoke with many people who described the open fields as a place where they could have a smoke, enjoy a beach or grass, and defecate without lines ahead of them or behind them. Community toilets, by contrast, seemed filthy and a hassle of long lines.

    At this workshop, two economists and a sociologist called the studio's findings into question. This was not all that uncommon. I witnessed at several workshops NGO and academic experts question DevDesign's legitimacy as researchers. Some of the studio's findings—such as "clear ownership [of toilets] drives responsibility"—were old hat in development circles, one economist told them. An Indian sociologist asked them if they could bring a trained anthropologist on the team, critiquing them for not studying any neighbor-hoods in India's contentious northeast region. Another development economist questioned whether open defecation could really be desirable, or whether it is the last resort of desperate people.

The gender and health activist advised the group on the power of well-researched truths that compelled powerful actors to "own" the truths as their own and publicize them. As an activist, she had produced social-science studies characterizing and quantifying domestic violence in India. The data itself was so compelling, she argued, that she found industrialists, police, and filmmakers clamoring to help. The filmmaker made a documentary; the industrialist went to TV stations and had them put film spots on for free; the inspector general of the police introduced the findings into police training. Good data could become powerful people's truth, she argued. Positivism could become the public's truth.

The Gates Foundation program officer, Erica, cut in to explain how she saw DevDesign's expertise. She had seen DevDesign's work on a prior NGO project; she told workshop attendees how in that project DevDesign had shown how poorer Indians thought about water filters as short-term durables rather than long-term household investments. That finding had jarred the program officer into a different way of imagining filter design and sales, and it was that gen-erative jarring toward a "user-experience" perspective that she hoped the team would produce today.

"ERRING ON THE SIDE OF INNOVATION": THE GENERATIVITY OF NAÏVETÉ

The director of the foundation, the funder of each person in the room, inter-vened as well. "I think the tension you're hearing," he began, "is that we would actually rather at this point you err on the side of innovation. There is just not enough of that sort of thinking where people are open minded and start from a user's perspective. . . . So we're—I guess we're not as eager to come up with the direct solution now as we are to have a process that would seed a bunch of ideas that might eventually come up."

This conflictual assembly of competing epistemologies—the gender activ-ist and the economist, for example—was not a planning mistake. Workshops like these were designed to generate both dissonant feedback—information to inform the search for solutions—and buy-in. Such forms of communication and production are common in research organizations—organizations char-acterized not by mass production but by collaborative search for opportunities amid multiple possible orders of worth (Stark 2009, xvii–xviii). The sorts of tensions the director marked and managed were common features of such gatherings. The challenge was to make sure that arguments about *what is* did not get in the way of arguments about *what could be*. The client and studio members considered the studio's lack of specific expertise in existing research an advantage to generate innovation.

After the workshop, Mukta, Kritika, and Vivek griped over drinks about the attendees who called on them to read the existing literature: "No, we didn't cite your research. We started fresh. . . . Seeing the reports is scary! You think, 'Oh, all that has been done!' It's like designing when you've been staring at pretty things. Then you think, 'Oh, how do I make something that is as nice?' It's scary. It's better to just spit it out. . . . Collectively, all of us are myopic. We have a different myopia than their myopia, which is why they come to us. [The foundation] comes to us because three hundred people have done it and none of it has worked." If they had done all of their homework to read the extant literature and studies, they would begin to inhabit the point of view of the people already working on the sanitation problem—approaches that, Mukta added, had not worked anyway. Then, what fresh perspective would they bring?

The program officer independently echoed Mukta's assessment in an interview with me after the workshop. The program officer had a PhD in development and understood the academics' unease about the rigor of DevDesign's research, yet she reinforced the value of their research:

> They're not coming at it through an academic discipline. Their naïveté is an upside to an extent. You just have to calibrate that right. Their naïveté helps them ask questions and get answers to them that might—someone who is saying I have a model of human behavior and that's gonna be my lens—they might miss something. . . . You could have had an anthropologist do this. . . . You know, they would have come at this with a particular worldview. I think these guys are kind of worldview free. I don't think they're coming at this with a worldview except that people are customers and consumers—they're not just passive beneficiaries.

To see people as consumers was a very historically specific but widespread form of naïveté—a generalized kind of social category upon which hinged middle-class discourses about Indian citizenship, private industry expertise, and transnational development practice. Many anthropologists and sociologists would have come ready to critique this formation, bringing to bear analyses of neoliberalism, marketization, privatization, and individuation of subject. These critiques call for structural change, not the design of new products.

Mukta and the program officer shared a rationale for naïveté. It allowed designers to discern newly relevant features of the situation that suggested promising paths on which to proceed. Their professional vision, and here I am invoking Charles Goodwin (1994), was to notice what others had not noticed about everyday life. Epistemic cohesion was not a virtue here, for it diminished the lines of speculative flight that generated innovative, investable experiments. An undisciplined perception—or perhaps perception disciplined differently—was to sense the possibilities imminent in the present that might be ignored by others. What anthropologist Eitan Wilf calls the "routinization" of creativity (2019) called on designers not only to diagram, sketch, and shuffle Post-its, but to sense and make sense of the everyday naïvely. This was more than simply bringing a fresh perspective by outsiders to development.

This naïveté was a common feature of design education, both in the Silicon Valley strains of human-centered design and in the strains that DevDesign staff taught. A guidebook on human-centered design produced by Palo Alto design firm IDEO (funded by BMGF) called on people to interpret their observations without reference to "prior experience." Instead, it instructed designers to cultivate a peaceful mind that attuned to the present, letting go of ego, rank, and abstractions. This way of being present to possibility draws on Zen writings from the San Francisco Bay Area, particularly Shunryu Suzuki's *Zen Mind, Beginner's Mind* (1970). It aligned with cybernetics understandings of systems as already embodying their history; thus agency within the system required action and feedback, not historical knowledge (Bowker 2005). Prior research and knowledge of failures—history, the literature review, the patterns of politics—threatened the beginner's mind.

New-age ways of knowing overlay canonical business knowledge. Recall Mukta describing "seeing reports" as "scary" impediments to entrepreneurial action. Beginning in the early 1980s, McKinsey consultants Tom Peters and Robert Waterman wrote on how to manage corporations in the face of the failures of rational, predictive, linear models. The world, they argued, was one of complexity and rapid change. They advised that managers ought to quickly research, implement, experiment, and learn rather than run into "analysis paralysis." They advised, instead, a "bias to action" and experiment through learning. Understanding needs on the ground completely was less important than drawing out *likely* lines of opportunity and risk. Design could find the contours of an opportunity, and usability tests, market pilots, or randomized controlled trials would follow to evaluate how the speculative project could be better aligned with its target.

PRODUCING INSIGHTS, ELICITING INVESTMENTS

Studio members routinely described their work as that of not only gaining insights to share but also facilitating insight by eliciting and finding ways of addressing the agendas of multiple stakeholders in a process.

In one pitch deck, for example, studio members often depicted three potentially conflicting orders of value: "business," "social," "personal." The three were overlapping circles in a Venn diagram, surrounded by evocative terms: "entrepreneurship," "play," "impact," "sustainability," "community," "innovation." The center of the slide boldly announced how all these could be brought together: "Design is the tool that can facilitate it." In explaining the slide to a group of students, the studio director explained: "It's always a good sign when the designer did not come up with the big idea. . . . The designer's role is that of a facilitator. He's in charge of creating tangible visions for their aspirations and needs and a synergy among the team members." Design here stood for more than a progressive, entrepreneurial ethos. It also was a sensibility and set of techniques for "creating tangible visions" of speculative alternatives with others.

The facilitation role complemented the beginner's mind. If designers approached a problem without expertise, they could facilitate communication among experts, pose questions to them, and attempt to generate design ideas that addressed the desires and constraints elicited. With a beginner's mind, they ought to notice that which others have learned to ignore. This view of design work emerged out of understandings of design as an information-processing task—the challenge of sensing an environment, calculating alternative futures, and choosing a satisfactory course of action. Professional designers were not necessarily makers of things. They were facilitators who found novel ways forward, coupling their naïveté with the knowledge of other kinds of experts.

This view of design as facilitation can be traced at least to the 1950s views of decision theorist Herbert Simon and American designers Ray and Charles Eames. Simon's highly influential account of design as "a science of the artificial" famously argued that "everyone designs who devises courses of action aimed at changing existing situations into preferred ones" (Simon 1996, 111). Despite the putative universality of design, he called for its perfection through mathematics, decision sciences, and artificial intelligences. These were the models of how to optimize for "what ought to be." Notably, these models had to operate as a "bounded rationality," constrained by the temporalities of action rather than perfect calculation. Artificial intelligence would, for him, model the planning problems that designers too needed to solve. His work influenced computer science, management science, political science, and cognitive science. Good design took in as many parameters as possible and made good decisions in reasonable amounts of time. Good design, in other words, judged, mediated, and governed based on varieties of inputs and processes. And it did so in the temporal bounds and manufactured urgencies of clients, institutions, and even crises discourses.

Ray and Charles Eames also saw design as a kind of mediation of complexity. They articulated design as a practice that intervenes in a cybernetic system. To design was to sense a vividly communicative environment and shape it through form, texture, and symbol. In their 1959 film *A Communications Primer*, a film sponsored by IBM for an articulation of these ideas, the narrator explained: "The communication of the total message contains the responsibility of innumerable decisions made again and again, always checking with the total concept through a constant feedback system." Like "erring on the side of innovation," designers sought not correct answers but an ongoing relationship of intervention and adaptation. The film foregrounded Claude Shannon's theory of communication, and the credits cited computer scientists and mathematicians of the day, including Norbert Weiner, John von Neumann, and Claude Shannon, for "ideas, direction, and material." The Ford Foundation actually tasked the Eameses with addressing India as a complex system. Their 1958 *India Report* proposed the designer as a "steering device" to help what they called "a tradition bound society" adapt to rapid changes posed by national independence and changing communication technologies.

DESIGN WHEN HOPE FALTERS

The promise of design was that studio members could bring user voices and their own nation-building aspirations to steer NGOs, foundations, and entrepreneurs. At his most optimistic, one of the studio's founders described this process as like "a Trojan horse." He explained, "We try not to be a sellout but speak their language. . . . We speak their language but they"—the American and European clients, he meant—"definitely can't speak ours."

When the trade-off was between sustaining optimism and making a critical intervention or even refusing, designers always chose optimism. On another project for a UK start-up, a student designer frustratedly told staff coaches Kritika and Mukta that the start-up's product was pointless. Nobody needed a new kind of hand sanitizer, he argued, because everyone is already using soap. Another student expressed doubt that the sanitizer was the most valuable way to improve the lives of those they were interviewing. Kritika laughed and looked at the student sympathetically: "I've been there too. We Indians are a little pessimistic." Vivek broke in: "If you create actual value they can see, or if it has aspirational value, they *will* use it."

Even DevDesign staff's faith flagged at times. This was a state they talked about as being "mindfucked." To be mindfucked was to be drained of inspiration, frustrated by thwarted promises of getting from research to design, or disillusioned about the virtue of the work. Mindfucked designers smoked, snacked, ranted, and clicked; they critiqued themselves, funders, and politicians. During one long studio work session, Kritika once implored Mukta: "If I'm still doing this in five years, slap me!" The videos they produced to enroll partners, they used also to reenroll themselves. Kritika made this explicit to me when admiring a film I had made of a woman washing a staircase to prepare it as a drying rack. As Kritika watched the woman repurpose the staircase, she gasped at the sweeping gesture, telling the rest of the team, "When we get mindfucked over, like coming up with ideas, we can just watch that again and get inspired." Designers, then, not only labored to produce others' enrollment and motivation to pursue opportunity. They also labored to restore their own faith in work that always failed. Films were one way. Hackathons and side projects were other ways of reinvigorating their hope.

They constantly had to restore promise in a milieu where promise generated projects and projects were vehicles for speculative investment and livelihoods. When development was defined as economic growth, then projects were experiments in finding new places to generate exchange value. Companies and venture capitalists required hope as an engine of speculative investment.

Designing a Better Future: Soft Power as the Subsumption of Hope

Human-centered design was one pedagogy in a broader project of rendering development as a set of entrepreneurial projects, recasting citizenship, in turn, as a venturesome practice of doing development, nation-building, and career building all at once (Irani 2019). Human-centered design taught optimism, observation, storytelling, and imagination that some Indians, the innovators, could observe and propose profitable interventions into the lives of others. This is more than just developmental or work practice. It is a formation of soft power in global capitalist geopolitics.

In Cairo in 2009, Barack Obama launched a now-annual Global Entrepreneurship Summit. The summit promoted entrepreneurship—especially high-tech or high-impact entrepreneurship—as a vehicle by which citizens of Muslim-majority countries could find "mutual interest and mutual respect" with the United States (Obama 2009). A year later, Hillary Clinton, then secretary of state, wrote a foreign-policy piece explaining the importance of cultivating global networks of entrepreneurs friendly to American values. She argued that entrepreneurship could mitigate ugly feelings that metastasize into terrorism. Bill Gates and Bill Clinton both testified about their global development activities to the US Congressional Committee on Foreign Relations in 2010. Gates described the power of the Internet to share "living proof" and "heart-rending stories" of the successes of development to convince skeptical, unemployed Americans about the importance of development projects abroad (Building on Success 2010, 44). But to Congress, Clinton made a harder sell: "We cannot kill, jail, or occupy all of our adversaries. We have to build a world with more partners" (Building on Success 2010, 20). These arguments have roots in American economic thought as well. Prominent economist William Baumol argued in 1990 that all countries have some number of enterprising individuals, but those entrepreneurial people might allocate their energies to "productive activities such as innovation and largely unproductive activities such as rent seeking or organized crime" (1990).

I spotted this Rolex ad in the *Economist* in 2013 (Figure 3.1). It promises that "anyone can change everything." Here "anyone" refers, crucially, to people of color rather than familiar white saviors. Social enterprise promises a world without poles, where Global South elites can be presented as grassroots, South–South achievement. Colonial anthropologists worked for companies or states to produce knowledge about difference in service of governmentality and extraction (Philip 2004; Scott 1998). Knowledge constructing tradition, caste, and tribe, for example, helped render *terra incognita* (lands unknown to colonizers) navigable, exploitable, and governable. Today, entrepreneurs appeal to a wider set of patrons—financiers, philanthropies, government agencies, and companies. They too draw on applied anthropology and resource maps. But they also

Figure 3.1. A two-page spread in the *Economist* advertises winners of Rolex's Awards for Enterprise. The ad pictures laureates' faces in different parts of the globe, connected to one another and others through abstracted, globe-spanning networks. (With special thanks to Rolex Awards for Enterprise.)

search themselves, their communities, and their resources to construct opportunity. Entrepreneurial citizens—in this case, children of India's governing classes—appear as another postcolonial resolution. These postcolonial leaders are part of Clinton's strategy of networked, entrepreneur-led development, transforming potential threats into generators of opportunity (Clinton 2010; see also Slaughter 2009).

This call on people to become changemakers, intervening to care at scale, is productively vague. "Change" here is a wide-open signifier available for myriad world-changing fantasies, from environmental activism to medical care. These are the sorts of caring affects that emerge out of histories of social movements that demand limits to mining, limits to exploitative labor, and limits to premature death. The call to make profitable opportunity out of harm or oppression turns channels' affects into enterprise rather than politics. It channels them into optimism about partnerships rather than critiques of ruling classes.

In his work on humanitarian design, anthropologist Peter Redfield explores the humanitarian love that animated Danish company Vestergaard Frand-sen as it retooled its textile business, in the face of flagging sales, to create the LifeStraw—a drinking straw that filters bacteria out of water. The straw, crucially, uses Frandsen's textile manufacturing capacities to create a new line of business (2015), finding the fortune out of retooling for the bottom of the pyramid. DevDesign had worked with Frandsen's LifeStraw in their Andhra Pradesh study for HealthWorks. The LifeStraw, as it happened, tested very poorly compared to less high-tech clay and plastic vessels from Cambodia. At DevDesign, Kritika and others quipped frustratedly about the global, spectacu-lar attention the LifeStraw attracted. "You know the LifeStraw," Kritika com-mented wryly. "Brown child sucking water from a river?" She scorned tropes of humanitarian love and the questions it leaves unanswered. This chapter is not a critique of a particular humanitarian technology design, or even design as a process of mistaking politics for a technical or material intervention. Rather, I want to point out that the LifeStraw's love comes with strings attached—those strings guide humanitarian technologies along the channels of investors' inter-ests and manufacturing processes. If technical solutions brought bureaucra-cies closer to the lives of Lesotho's people in *The Anti-Politics Machine* (1994), here technical solutions bring rural people closer to manufacturing and retail supply chains, while reorienting companies' existing capacities to new mar-kets. Design-thinking methodologies renarrated questions of existing, vested interests as viability, collaboration, and finding solutions at the intersection of stakeholders' interests. Design thinking prefers to love when loving reveals opportunities as a form of "low-hanging fruit"—that chance to make value in ways already aligned with firm capacities, priorities, and brands. Vestergaard Frandsen's LifeStraw venture converted an overcapacity in textiles for malaria needs into a new line of profit as "disease control textiles" (Redfield 2016, 10). HCD is only one pedagogy of entrepreneurial citizenship (Irani 2019), but one with powerful institutions such as BMGF disseminating the ethos as a way of mining love for opportunity and using ethnography to reveal latent practices, infrastructures, and resources to draw upon.

The Rolex ad models this loving openness. Abstracted networks—as pro-ductively vague as a Nike swoosh—connect these agents of change beyond their towns and nation-states. Are they IT networks? Are they retail distribution chains? Are they self-help groups mobilized to sell or educate? (see Elyachar 2010). This entrepreneurial agency attracts, organizes, and channels diverse lifeworlds and social relations into investable opportunities. In other words, it makes civil society an engine of enterprise. The changemakers figured in the ad may have conflicting ontologies (Escobar 2018b)—all the better for generating novel, generative paths of innovation. The ad calls on "anyone" to care, mobilizing their humanitarian or developmental feeling to intervene across wide sets of social relations and material infrastructures.

Along the way hopeful, entrepreneurial citizens will search for investors in their hopes to care, quarantining themselves away from social movements. The figure and ethos of entrepreneurship and, as I've argued in this chapter, human-centered design will sculpt these energies into a particular kind of historical agency—visionaries whose hope is subsumed into capitalist supply lines (Tsing 2015, 301n2).

CHAPTER FOUR

Autonomia Ethnographica

Liberal Designs, Designs for Liberation, and the Liberation of Design

ALBERTO CORSÍN JIMÉNEZ

This chapter develops an argument about the relation between autonomy and ethnography—in particular, about autonomy as an experimental design in political and anthropological praxis. I am interested in what I call *autonomia ethnographica*: the pressures and challenges confronting the mise-en-scènes of anthropological fieldwork today and the sometimes troubled, sometimes conflictive, yet ultimately liberating arrangements in complicity and complexity through which anthropologists construct the conditions for ethnographic practice and description.

The concept of autonomy I am summoning here needs a little unpacking. In some respects, autonomy is undergoing somewhat of a comeback in social and political theory (Nelson and Braun 2017; Luisetti et al. 2015). Most famously deployed by the Italian *operaist* (workers) movement in the 1950s in the context of accelerating and exploitative labor conditions in the automobile industry, "autonomia" was invoked at the time to describe a revolutionary impulse for the ontological self-determination of workers' power—the power, as it was referred to at the time, to "refuse to work" (Virno 1996) and in this capacity to disengage from, and invent novel imaginative alternatives to, the spatial and temporal matrices of the state-capital nexus (Aureli 2008). Throughout the 1970s, however, "autonomia" gradually lost its attachment to workers' power, leaving the factory floor for the street protests of students, feminists, and environmental activists. Thus, a second generation of "diffuse autonomy" was born, a new wave of insurrectional and intersectional politics (Cuninghame 2013), which, in the wake of the alter-globalization movement in the late 1990s, entered also the

Anglophone academy under the liberation aesthetics of networked-mediated multitudes and commons (Hardt and Negri 2005, 2009).

It is not my intention in this chapter to retrace the genealogies of the autonomy complex. From Cornelius Castoriadis (1987) to Henri Lefebvre (2009), autonomy has indeed played a fundamental role in the configuration of critical thought in the second half of the twentieth century. More modestly, here I wish to essay an argument about the ethnographic purchase of autonomy, an argument born from my own fieldwork with free-culture activists in Madrid over the past fifteen years. In particular I draw on the situated history of the entanglement between autonomous collectives, squatted social centers, public art institutions, and free-culture activists to illustrate the dense interdependencies of methods, technologies, and aesthetics that these various actors have mobilized and deployed in bringing forth an autonomous framework for an urban ecology. Not just a political or ontological impulse, autonomy has been bodied forth in this context as a design and an infrastructure for the thick entanglement of complicities and complexities—not unlike, I will suggest, how ethnography itself is often choreographed and arranged.

Autonomia ethnographica emerges in this context as a *tactical climate of methods* wherein the promises, affordances, and constraints of designs are continuously recalibrated as shared systems for grappling with. As such, it offers a lens for reinterpreting the situated entanglements of Keith Murphy's three orientations of design: anthropology for design, design for anthropology, and the critical anthropology of design (Murphy 2016b; see also the introduction). We will see in particular how these are loosely mapped onto historically situated systems of liberation—liberal designs, designs for liberation, and the liberation of design—and how the movements and moments of autonomia ethnographica surface in the interstices and "borders," as Murphy and Wilf point out in the introduction, of their complex and overlapped trajectories.

The view of autonomy as an experimental design of sorts is one that has recently been put forward by Isabelle Stengers and Arturo Escobar. For Stengers, autonomy offers one possible placeholder for the navigational skills demanded by our devastated and catastrophic times (Stengers 2017). Well aware of the concept's distinguished anchorage in a tradition of Italian Marxist and post-Marxist thought, she prefers instead to assay a different ground for the reclamation of autonomy, one that commits to the very positionality of *reclamation* as a commitment to the struggle for "a life *worth living* in the ruins" (Stengers 2017, 388, emphasis in the original). Such a project in the reclamation of autonomy takes as its point of departure the "relaying" of modes of "sensing together" (con-sensus), modes that may meet for the first time in an exchange (a "palaver") of embodied and situated antagonisms, but which in that very encounter signal the loss of, but also the hopes for, autonomy (Stengers 2017, 396, 391). Stengers explains, "I mean to 'stay with the trouble' [after Donna Haraway], characterizing autonomy not in philosophical, conceptual terms but by starting from devastation, from the humiliation, shame, and temptation of cynicism that I take as signals of its destruction" (Stengers 2017, 392). The reclamation of autonomy, then, can only proceed, not as a critical or political project, but as a project in "experimentation," an art of "adventure" oriented toward sounding out the "artifacts" of the autonomous moment, the "fact of the art" (Stengers 2017, 394–95, 398). "Autonomy," she concludes, "is not a flower spontaneously blooming in a devastated, depopulated desert. It needs relayed stories and experiences, the anticipation of testing, difficult choices, a sense of precariousness, the fostering of a taste for experimentation" (Stengers 2017, 399).

For his part, Arturo Escobar has built on the activist experiences of indigenous, peasant, and Afro-descended communities in Latin America to outline an argument for "autonomous design" as a project in the ontological reclamation of worlds (Escobar 2018b). Escobar's approximation to autonomy is inspired not by the philosophical frameworks of post-Marxist autonomy but by the theories of autopoiesis and systemic and self-emergent organization of Humberto Maturana and Francisco Varela. Defending the co-ontogenesis and interdependency of life forms, Escobar turns to the concept of design as a privileged site for understanding how grassroots communities fight for the worlds they wish to bring into existence, worlds whose devastation or disappearance shows the very real ontological menace they are subjected to. In this light, "autonomía is a theory and practice of interexistence and interbeing, a design for the pluriverse" (Escobar 2018b, 175, emphasis removed).

Building on ten years of fieldwork among free-culture collectives in Spain, and following in the steps of Stengers and Escobar, in this chapter I also wish to develop an argument about the struggle for autonomy as a specific struggle for experimentation and design. In addition, I wish to draw attention to the ways such a struggle can double back on the very ecology of practices through which we, as anthropologists, inhabit and navigate our field sites. For an academic discipline whose historical project has traditionally been conceived as the study of culture, the liberation of "culture" that free-culture activists have insistently engaged in since the late 1990s presents some interesting challenges.

At a minimum, it opens up inquiry into the specific legal licenses and arrangements, technical and descriptive materials, and infrastructural resources and assemblages through which anthropology is internally configured as an intellectual and practical operation. In this light, free-culture activism offers an apposite site for thinking about the autonomy of ethnography by way of an ethnography of autonomy.

The origins of the free-culture movement have traditionally been traced back to the networked protests against the expansion of patent and copyright protection to cultural works in the digital age that took place at the turn of the century (Postigo 2012). The story of free culture has been imagined in this context as a "modulation," to use Chris Kelty's term (2008), of the free and open-source software movement and philosophy—a story about the liberal values of hacktivists and their explorations of digital freedom (Coleman 2012) and, more amply, about the libertarian ethic of the Californian ideology (Barbrook and Cameron 1996). In this context, the story of free-culture devices and innovations (open-source software, urban apps, massive open online courses [MOOCs]) has often been taken as a proxy for the predicament of liberal designs.

In this chapter I wish to essay a somewhat different take. I develop an argument about free-culture activism in Madrid as fundamentally an urban social movement and sensibility whose origins harken back to the radical autonomist scene of squatted social centers in the 1980s and 1990s. It was at squatted social centers that the first hacklabs opened and that the first discussions about free licenses and the challenges of intellectual property rights were had. It was at squatted social centers, also, that these conversations met with the housing predicaments and economic precariousness of squatters, that artists and activists first imagined potential extrapolations of the "public domain" and "digital commons" into "public space" and "public infrastructures," and that subtle and intriguing alliances between the institutional art world and squatters were established. It was also amid these conversations between hackers, activists, and curators that a specific culture of techno-political design saw the light: the making of so-called prototypes, where the prototype was at once a model for the continuous open-sourcing of a specific material design and a tentative assembly and assemblage for conviviality and hope.

In this light, my aim in this chapter is threefold. First, I offer a genealogy of free-culture activism as part of a broader movement for urban autonomy and the right to the city—free culture, then, not just as a digital culture but as a specific urban ecology. Second, I situate the designs of free-culture prototypes as part and parcel of a cross-pollinating exchange between hackers, urban activists, and artists. I shall argue that unlike other accounts of technical hacktivism, where the arts and crafts of hackers are strained by the cultural politics of liberalism, the culture of prototyping in Spain has been driven instead by histories of autonomy and libertarian socialism, where the complicities between squatted social centers, public cultural centers, and technical communities have been pivotal. Finally, I reflect on how the aspirations of autonomy of such prototyping communities double back on anthropology itself—how anthropology's inhabiting of an urban culture invested in the liberation of designs and methods inevitably modulates our own ecologies and infrastructures of apprenticeships. In other words, I discuss how a culture of designs for liberation may inspire the liberation of anthropological designs.

Autonomy

The first hacklab in Spain opened at a squatted social center in Madrid in 1997 (Domínguez 2012, 62; see also Sádaba Rodríguez and Roig Domínguez 2004). Then called a "telematics zone" (*área telemática*), it was hosted by The Laboratory, a squatted social center that between 1997 and 2003 became an emblem of the autonomist social movement. The Laboratory opened after a tumultuous period of evictions of squatted social centers in the mid 1990s and, in this context of expulsions and abandonment, was purposefully designed as an experimental venue: a hybrid environment where different sensibilities of squatting activism could meet, from autonomists to ravers, from feminists or environmentalists to neighborhood activists. As participants in the project then put it, The Laboratory aimed for an "apertura a lo social" (opening toward the social) (Domínguez and Padilla 2008), beyond the specific genealogies of different traditions of militant activism (Rubio-Pueyo 2016, 390–91). To better understand the novelty that The Laboratory then represented, it is worth taking a few steps back.

In the late 1960s, Madrid had witnessed a wave of associative effervescence that culminated throughout the 1970s in a number of struggles for housing and urban rights. These were led by neighborhood associations and libertarian workers' movements, which Manuel Castells famously portrayed in *The City and the Grassroots* as "the most powerful and innovative neighborhood movement" of any European capital (Castells 1983, 287). By the time Castells published these lines, however, much of the energy of the movement had already deflated, in the wake of the democratic municipal elections that had put an end to the country's forty-year dictatorship in 1978. When a younger generation of urban activists picked up the relay from their fathers in the late 1980s, it was not their legacy they summoned, however, but the memory of the factory-floor organization and Dadaist resistance of the Italian autonomists. In particular, they were inspired by the "diffused" or "creative autonomy" movement, which in the late 1970s aimed to expand the experience of autonomy beyond the factory floor to incorporate the subaltern consciousness of gay, feminist, and other countercultural and artistic avant-gardes (Cuninghame 2013).

A key referent of the diffused autonomy movement in Italy was the free-radio collective, Radio Alice. One of its founders, Franco "Bifo" Berardi, had been arrested in 1976 after being accused of "morally instigating revolt" in the months preceding the student riots that stormed the streets of Bologna in 1977 (Guattari 1984, 238). The story of Radio Alice was published by Bifo and his collaborators under the provocative title *Alice è Il Diavolo* (Alice Is the Devil) in 1976 (Collettivo A/traverso 1977), and it was translated and published in French a year later. The preface to the French edition was written by Félix Guattari, who spoke with admiration that the "viewpoint of autonomy towards the mass media of communication was that a hundred flowers should blossom, a hundred radio stations should broadcast" (Guattari 1984, 236). As Bifo himself would later reminisce, Guattari had been drawn to the Italian free-radio movement as "a precursor of libertarian cyber culture" (Berardi 2008, 31).

The Spanish translation of *Alice è Il Diavolo* was published as early as 1981 (Collettivo A/traverso 1981), when the exchanges and conversations between Italian, French, and Spanish libertarian groups still lingered from the heydays of urban struggles. It was not, however, this edition but the original Italian that a younger generation of Madrid urban activists picked up in one of a number of trips they made to squatted social centers in Milan and other Italian cities in the early 1990s (Jacobo Rivero, cited in Martínez López and García Bernardos 2014, 206, 209). By then, the scene of the Italian autonomist and squatted social centers had undergone substantial transformations. Inspired by the legacy of diffused autonomy, a "second generation" of squatted social centers had taken root across the urban landscape, aiming deliberately for the "contamination" and "amalgamation" of the "self-management practices" of "autonomists, punks and underground cultures" (Membretti and Mudu 2013, 79). It was this eclectic and plural ecology of practices that the Madrid-based activists imported into their local scene under the aforementioned label of an "opening toward the social."

The 1990s was a period of convulsive political and economic change in Spain. The country had joined the European Union in 1986, and the process of unionization set in motion a series of structural adjustments that had a profound impact on the economy, including the "deregulation and flexibilisation of capital and labor market, control of nominal wage increases, and an accelerated privatization of public enterprises" (Charnock et al. 2014, 66–67). The labor market in particular was hit like no other in the European economy. In 1988 the then-ruling Socialist party presented a proposal for labor reform aiming to introduce flexible contracts popularly known as *contratos basura* (garbage contracts). The project was met with a general strike where "more than 95 percent of the active population stopped working" under the "call to fight 'precarious contracts'" (Casas-Cortés 2014, 208). By 1994, however, the government had succeeded in introducing these and other measures to deregulate the labor market, and the effects were catastrophic, with unemployment reaching a record high of 24.17 percent and youth unemployment peaking at 42.33 percent for the twenty to twenty-four age group (Instituto Nacional de Estadística 1995). It is in this context that student activists first declared their resistance to corporate and transnational globalization—a few years ahead of the alter-globalization protests in Seattle in 1998—by reclaiming the legacy of political autonomy and liberation from the spatial and temporal dictates of capital. It is also in this context that the conceptual framework of "precarity" was first invoked by these young autonomists to make sense of their conditions of disenfranchisement and ruination (Casas-Cortés 2014).

Not unlike movements of disaffection toward neoliberalism elsewhere at the time, the generation of young Spanish precarious activists was also inspired by the Zapatistas' insurgency of 1994. During the late 1990s a few Spanish activists traveled to Chiapas and established contact with the Zapatista Army of National Liberation (EZLN). Whatever relationships the Spanish activists and the Zapatistas established during this time, they were robust enough for The Laboratory to host the Madrid node of the Second Intercontinental Meeting for Humanity and Against Neoliberalism on July 1997, the first international encounter ever to be attended by members of the EZLN (Marcos 1997). The unusual presence of the Zapatistas pulled in a multitudinous crowd of activists from all over Europe. For example, members of the European Counter Network (ECN) attended, an Italian hacker and counterinformation community who only a year later, on June 5–7, 1998, organized the first hackmeeting in that country, which was also attended by members of The Laboratory. The ebb and flow of activists between Italy and Spain weaved a textured network of activist complicities. Thus, when in the summer of 1998 members of The Laboratory decided to set up a free software server to service the counterinformational community in Spain, it was to the ECN that they turned for technical guidance and initial support. The hosting and server project was eventually called sinDominio (NoDomain); over the next decade it would become the preeminent server infrastructure for social movements in the Spanish-speaking world. The machine where the server was first installed, a Pentium II 450MHz 256Mb RAM computer, was jokingly referred to as Fanelli, in homage to the Italian anarchist Giuseppe Fanelli, the emissary sent by Mikhail Bakunin to Spain in 1868 to set up the local branch of the International Working Men's Association (the First International) (sinDominio.net 2004). The joke could hardly be lost: the strong Italian autonomist connection, cultivated over years of visits and exchanges between squatted social centers in both countries, had overseen the rite of passage of the Spanish autonomous movement into the international free-software community.

In sum, when The Laboratory opened in 1997 it did so in part as a response to the global dynamics of neoliberal expulsion and precarity, but also as an expression of the rich and singular history of autonomous designs and exchanges that activists had established with the traditions of Italian social squatting; with the intellectual legacies of cyber-libertarian Dadaism and creative autonomy, as expressed in Radio Alice's explorations of antagonist telematics and affective labor; and finally, in the memory of the grassroots neighborhood movements that had struggled for the right to the city during the years of the dictatorship.

The Copyleft and the (Copy) Right to the City

On November 13–15, 1999, a group of artists took out to the streets in the historic quarter of Lavapiés in Madrid to stage a variety of performative and critical installations denouncing the gentrification of the neighborhood. Under the name Rehabi(li)tar Madrid (Reinhabit/Rehabilitate Madrid), the event partook of the spirit of street and public art interventions that were gaining currency at the time, such as Reclaim the Streets in the United Kingdom (Baena 2013, 58). A number of these interventions were further designed as explicitly participatory and collaborative projects and used The Laboratory as their center of operations. They were articulated around the Red de Lavapiés (Lavapiés Network), a loose coalition of activists, neighborhood associations, educational projects, squat social centers, and art-activist collectives that had been activated by The Laboratory shortly after its opening in 1997 (Carrillo 2009, 194–95, 197). The network embodied the center's agenda for a diffusely autonomous "opening toward the social," as noted above.

One of the art-activist collectives that took part in the antigentrification demonstrations was La Fiambrera Obrera (The Workers' Lunchbox). The collective had a history of critical public art practices in and around public-space and housing issues, and in Madrid they organized a very effective "antiruins" campaign aimed at signaling the ruinous state of certain buildings in the Lavapiés neighborhood. These were buildings whose maintenance had been deliberately neglected by their owners in the hope that the properties would be officially declared structurally damaged and unsuitable for dwelling. Under the law, such declarations enabled owners to evict tenants without compensation as well as to claim substantial municipal subsidies toward the buildings' renovation. However, if the attention of the municipality was drawn to their ruinous state before the buildings underwent a technical inspection, then it was the municipality's legal responsibility to undertake the renovation and subsequently charge and bill the owners for negligence. The "Contest of Ruins" (Concurso de Ruinas) that La Fiambrera organized in the context of the Rehabi(li)tar event successfully mapped many such ruinous properties around the neighborhood. The contest was organized as a festive stroll around the quarter that enabled a "jury" of neighbors and participants to both gain awareness of the gradual deterioration of the area and playfully award different prizes to the most ruinous properties. To this end, as they toured the neighborhood, the march of juries plastered with flamboyant posters and signposts the facades of the ruinous estates they found on their way, calling attention to the specific materials, structures, or roofs that were falling apart. They further produced a map and census of the properties thus identified, which were made available online by hosting them in the recently launched sinDominio server, and they archived the documents (flyers, posters, photographs) of the whole event.[1] Importantly, as a public record of negligence, attended by residents and the media and publicly documented on the Internet, the spectacle succeeded in drawing the municipality's attention.

La Fiambrera's work at the vanguard of artistic collaborations with social movements quickly drew the attention of the institutional art world. In 2000 the Museum of Contemporary Art of Barcelona (MACBA) invited La Fiambrera to curate an unusual experiment in socially engaged art. Known as Las Agencias (the Agencies), the project was designed as a choral residency of artists and social movements aimed at redefining "the art institution as a working space for social activists" (Kolb and Flückiger 2013, 9). Widely praised in the international arts scene, Las Agencias became one of the first expressions of a "new institutionalism" movement in the art world (Kolb and Flückiger 2013) as well as a model for the cultural politics of socially engaged art in Spain in the years to come.

In 2003 La Fiambrera were invited to form part of yet another ambitious curatorial and urban-based project that went by the name of New Cartographies of Madrid (Doctor Roncero 2003). At once a sociological investigation and an artistic exhibition, the project was commissioned to mark the opening of a new cultural and social center in the city, La Casa Encendida. Handsomely funded by a publicly owned and not-for-profit regional savings bank, the building of the new cultural center sat next door to The Laboratory. Unlike any other art institution in the country, La Casa Encendida was generously funded by its financial alma mater, while simultaneously subjected to its social-responsibility agenda. The New Cartographies of Madrid project showcased this ambiguous, almost contradictory set of alliances—the glamor of the financial and institutional art worlds, on the one hand, and the public-value philosophy of its not-for-profit orientation, on the other—and did so from a specific emplacement: a flagship cultural center whose very location at a marginal neighborhood was bound to set in motion gentrifying dynamics in every direction. How to position oneself amid such a convoluted and contradictory set of dynamics?

At the time of La Casa Encendida's opening the debates about "new institutionalism" were still up in the air. In this context, it was perhaps inevitable that given the center's location next door to The Laboratory it would gradually get pulled into the latter's gravitational field. In 2003, for example, members of The Laboratory approached La Casa Encendida to help fund a three-day workshop on "copyleft and intellectual property." The cultural center provided €12,000, which funded the international travel and accommodation of, among others, Franco "Bifo" Berardi, the Wu Ming Foundation (a Bologna-based subset of Luther Blissett), the Agencies project from MACBA, and Glen Otis Brown (executive director of Creative Commons) (Vidal 2003).[2] Toward the organization of the event, activists set up an email list under the name "Copyleft," which quickly outgrew its immediate purpose and over the next decade became the principal site for the discussion of *cultura libre* (free culture) in Spain. The list became a space where educators, librarians, designers, architects, hackers, lawyers, and autonomous activists discussed the legal, philosophical, and technical capabilities underlying the "copyleft" affordances of different types of cultural content and knowledge, from school textbooks to furniture, from urban infrastructures to typographic designs.

Indeed, the very definition of "free culture" as a term of art to describe the challenges of intellectual property law in the digital age soon became hotly contested. For example, on June 2004, the attorney, hacker, and academic Javier de la Cueva—one of the leading experts on Internet law and technology in Spain today, who was at the time embarked in challenging the entitlement of copyright management entities to a fiscal canon over digital copies—wrote to the list with the first draft of the legal argument he was then advancing. De la Cueva was exploring the doctrine of the "social function of property" in Spanish law—in particular, its application in urban law to prove the unconstitutional nature of existing copyright legislation. To everyone's surprise, he noted how the urban condition offered a conceptual background for leveraging the "commons" as a category with legal purchase. As he put it:

> I am making use of the legal argument about the social function of property (*función social de la propiedad*), which is established and recognized by Article 33 of the Spanish Constitution, whereby:
> 1. The Constitution recognizes the right to private property and inheritance.
> 2. The content of the aforementioned rights will be delimited by their social function, in accordance with the law.
>
> In this sense, I am trying to develop a legal argument that illustrates the social function of property in terms analogous to how Urban Law limits the extension of private property. That is, when it comes to intellectual property law we need analogous "common spaces" (*the equivalent in Urban Law would be green areas, urban equipment, natural parks . . .*) because inasmuch as intellectual property law is just one kind of the property genus, then of course it only makes sense that it, too, is limited by the social function of property. (de la Cueva 2004, emphasis added)

Thus, the complexion of free culture as a social function—a social function for which the ecological joviality and multiplicity of the city provided its most suitable metaphor—gradually empowered activists to imagine conceptual and practical alternatives to the delimitative and punitive directives of copy-right legislation. While "copyleft" or "creative commons" offered useful legal and technical solutions to existing copyright management frameworks, Spanish free-culture activists were quick to recognize that they otherwise offered limited purchase as political and conceptual vocabularies. Thus, in the search for alter-natives, some members of The Laboratory already offered, as early as 2004, the notion of *procomún* (commons) as a political and vernacular expansion of "free culture" beyond its strict digital circumscription. Miquel Vidal, a historic figure in the free-culture movement in Spain, summarized the debate with eloquence in an email to the Copyleft list on June 2004. I quote at length:

> "*Procomún*" is a genuinely Castilian term and of very old origin. . . . There are documented appearances in the XV, XVI, XIX and XX centuries. . . . In every case its use is similar to the way we use it today ("that which is com-mon and useful at the same time"). The Dictionary of the Royal Academy of Language has an entry for it in every one of its editions, including the last one where its usage as "public utility" is accepted (from "pro", benefit or advantage, and "común", common). In other words, the term has long been used in a very similar way to how we use it today to denote "that which is of public use." Therefore *procomún* would serve as a good transla-tion of "commons" (although there are even more precise translations such as "ejido") and it has the advantage over other translations—such as com-mon property, common goods or public goods—that it is both short and that it can be used as a generic. . . . *Procomún* does not refer to forests, land, nor irrigation systems. Nor does it refer to culture. It is sufficiently generic to encompass all of the above; it is intuitive, one doesn't need the diction-ary to understand its meaning; and it has the term "común" [common] embedded within (which gestures to "communal", "community", even "communism"). It's not as if we want to impose one term above others, nor to show off our philological expertise. . . . We just want to see how the term fares as a political tool enabling the circulation of a concept that can do just what we aspire for. What matters is the concept rather than the word that embodies it (copyleft, commons, procomún, ejido . . .). (Vidal 2004)

By 2004, then, free-culture activists in Spain had already tested the limits of digital technologies and legal licenses as tools for the liberation of culture and knowledge. Heirs to a tradition of autonomous and social-squatting activism, in particular one with a long history of struggles for the rights for housing and public space, free-culture activists reappropriated the emancipatory impulse and discourse of an emerging global network culture (Juris 2008) to situate it in specific urban contexts. Importantly, they did not do this alone. At the turn of the century, free-culture activists established an unsuspected alliance with a number of progressive art institutions, which funded and promoted their work and agenda. Hand in hand, curators, hackers, and autonomous activists took "free culture" out to the streets and plazas, resignifying the notion of "liberation" as a material, aesthetic, and technological concept.

Autonomia Ethnographica

I arrived in Madrid for my first research sabbatical from the University of Manchester on September 2006. I had set out to do ethnographic fieldwork among a group of humanities scholars (Hebrew and Biblical philologists, on the one hand, and historians of science, on the other) at the Spanish National Research Council for a year. In this context, some six months into my fieldwork I met the historian of science Antonio Lafuente. A couple of years earlier Lafuente had convened a public series of roundtables on "hybrid science" at La Casa Encendida, which included a session on "common goods." News of the workshops circulated on the Copyleft email list (Aitor 2004), which prompted Miquel Vidal, one of the founding hackers of The Laboratory's "telematics zone" (whose definition of procomún we encountered above), to invite Lafuente to give a talk at an event on the alternative uses of an old tobacco factory in Lavapiés, which squatters had long identified as a possible site for occupation.

On April 9, 2005, Lafuente gave an open-air talk at a public square in Lavapiés on the "museum as a house of the commons" (Lafuente 2005), where he first essayed an idea that would become foundational for the free-culture movement in Spain in the years to come: the idea of the commons not as a resource or property form but as a "laboratory," a sociotechnical assemblage striated by the tensions of intellectual property, autonomous self-management, and open-source technical affordances—a *laboratorio del procomún*, "laboratory of the commons" (Estalella Fernández et al. 2013).

Some months after delivering his talk, Lafuente was approached by Marcos García, then head of the educational program at Medialab, a digital arts center funded by Madrid's municipality, with a proposition to help set up a laboratory of the commons at the center. Lafuente accepted, and the first event of the new laboratory, a one-day workshop introducing the concept of procomún held on May 17, 2007, included talks by the hacker Miquel Vidal, the lawyer Javier de la Cueva, the artist and philosopher Jordi Claramonte (a founding member of La Fiambrera Obrera), and the art historian Jesús Carrillo (head of culture programs at the Reina Sofía Museum, Spain's national museum of contemporary art)—a neat crystallization of the concept's situated entanglement in the histories and ecologies of autonomist telematics, intellectual property law, insurrectional aesthetics, and the public institutional art world. I attended a couple of events of the laboratory that spring, and I myself even gave a talk at the invitation of Lafuente on "cooperation and the commons from an anthropological perspective" (Corsín Jiménez 2007). When I next returned to the laboratory a few years later, however, the notion of "an anthropology of" is one that I would learn to contest. Let me briefly set the stage.

The Medialab had opened in 2002 as a digital arts center. By 2006, however, the center had set in motion an original research program that overhauled its previous agenda as a curatorial and exhibition space, partly in response to the "new institutionalism" agenda, partly due to the complicity that some of its curators had with autonomous and free-culture circles. In its place, Medialab positioned itself as a "prototyping" workshop. The notion of "prototype" would become foundational to the center's redesign of its ecology of practices. Borrowing from the philosophy of free software, the practices of prototyping that Medialab staged called for investigating how to open-source the technical, juridical, and pedagogical dynamics of every sociotechnical assemblage (see Corsín Jiménez 2014). To this end, the center developed a two-prong agenda. On the one hand, three times a year it convened international prototyping workshops where people were invited over a two-week period to develop prototypes responding to theme-specific calls. The calls invoked loosely the social dimensions of technology—for example, Magic and Technology, Technologies of Laughter, or Aesthetics and Data. The real emphasis, however, was set not on the topics of the projects but on the rules by which they ought to operate. Two rules were to be followed: (1) a requirement that every step in the making of the prototype had to be profusely documented with a view to facilitating future replications, such that the process of documentation often became a pedagogical prototype itself, and (2) a requirement that all such documents be archived and made publicly and openly available using free licenses. Therefore, in different degrees of accomplishment, most projects ended up turning their own problematics—the technologies of magic, laughter, or aesthetics—into problems of documentation, archiving, and pedagogical redescription.

On the other hand, Medialab invested in designing a culture of "mediation" whose aim was to facilitate the encounter between the center's users (makers, artists, participants at the workshops, and visitors). To this end, a team of so-called mediators was employed to help users navigate the technical, aesthetic, and cultural complexities of the projects and activities therein developed. Many of the mediators had a shared history of militancy in autonomous and squatted social centers, and it was not unusual for them to take participants for walks, drinks, or parties at neighboring squatted social centers. Therefore, over time, the complicity between autonomous and prototyping projects, inside and outside Medialab, became a paragon of a "culture of 'free culture,'" one where the concerns of autonomists and insurrectional artists (housing, public space, common and affective knowledge) met with the preoccupations of hackers and digital artists (archiving, interfaces, infrastructures of collaboration, and licenses). In other words, autonomy became a problem of design and experimentation, a project in the prototyping of autonomy itself.

When I returned to Madrid in 2009 after landing a job at the Spanish National Research Council, I took the opportunity to return also to the laboratory of the commons as an ethnographic field site. My reencounter with the laboratory was a wake-up call in a number of ways. As my fieldwork progressed, I became ever more confused as to who or what I was in the company of: a social movement, an artistic expression, a technical and design vanguard? I felt at a loss on a theoretical level also. Most of my interlocutors were sophisticated analysts who had published more, more eloquently, and more critically than I could ever hope for, in topics as diverse as the philosophy of autonomy, network culture, art theory, or intellectual property law. And they had done so in registers, formats, styles, and venues—under anonymous or multiple-user-name identities, in street performances or open-air seminars, building networked infrastructures and open-source documentary archives—that cast my old academic habits in a somewhat arcane light. Who was my *anthropology for* in this context? And what was my anthropology an *anthropology of* anyway?

Therefore, when my colleague Adolfo Estalella and I began working with free-culture communities in 2009, it soon became obvious to us that it would require on our part developing practices of documentation, archiving, and reportage concurrent to those of the people we were working with. It would have been hardly possible for us to gain the trust of our informants without being part of the open-source culture they were so passionately building. As we have put it elsewhere, "One can hardly study free culture prototypes without becoming a prototype for free culture oneself" (Corsín Jiménez and Estalella 2017, 858). Initially this entailed experimenting with infrastructures of writing, accompaniment, and encounter: keeping a blog, organizing urban walkabouts and itinerant seminars, and developing an open-source platform for urban apprenticeships in collaboration with guerrilla architectural collectives, street artists, and urban social movements (Corsín Jiménez and Estalella 2016). This was part of the moment of awakening to which I referred above: coming to terms with the realization that our research practice had to be "re-functioned," as George Marcus and Douglas Holmes have put it (2012, 129), from an *anthropology of/for* to an *anthropology with*—where the mutuality of the fieldwork encounter between researchers and their interlocutors is turned into one of "epistemic partners[hip]" (Holmes and Marcus 2012, 129).

However, there is a further aspect to this refunctioning and redesigning of anthropology that I believe has not drawn quite as much attention. This regards what I have called the moment of autonomia ethnographica: the labor, scenographies, and modalities of attentiveness through which ethnography is wireframed and designed into a tentative project in complicity and complexity—that is, as a tentative space of autonomous enunciation. Let me explain by way of a conclusion.

In *Fragments of an Anarchist Anthropology*, David Graeber has drawn what at first glance may appear a surprising analogy between the practice of ethnography and the practical aspirations of anarchism. Not unlike what ethnography aims to accomplish, Graeber notes, anarchist revolutionary practice aims "to look to those who are creating viable alternatives, try to figure out what might be the larger implications of what they are (already) doing, and then offer those ideas back, not as prescriptions, but as contributions, possibilities—as gifts" (Graeber 2004, 13). In this light, Graeber calls for refashioning the project for social theory "in the manner of direct democratic process," a project that would then have "two aspects, or moments if you like: one ethnographic, one utopian, *suspended in a constant dialogue*" (Graeber 2004, 13, emphasis added).

While Graeber anchors his call for a new anthropological project in a theoretical vision of how ethnography and anarchism may enrich one another, the figure of "suspension" that he uses as a placeholder for such an exchange echoes the moments of experimentation and prototyping that characterize the practices of free-culture activists that I have described here. The call for suspension, as I read it, is not a call to surrender or abandon the possibilities of critique (hardly, for an anarchist revolutionary project) but a call to measure up to the designs of its contemporary forms of complexity. In the case of ethnography, it is a call to bring to the fore the ecologies and architectures that make the moment of suspension possible in the first place. Ethnography is a field of intellectual, operational, and affective commitments and interventions constantly struggling for a position of autonomous enunciation. As I hope to have shown, the autonomous is not a space of self-sufficiency, detachment, or refuge. Instead, we should think of it as the ecology of tensions that makes inquiry and problematization both feasible and sustainable. As such, the autonomous moment is always reckoning and grappling with a sense of both excessiveness and constraint, of both possibility and impediment. Thus "What is the autonomy of ethnography?" is a question that anthropologists have always grappled with yet rarely made explicit in these terms.

In the specific case of the free-culture movement, such a stance, I wish to argue, offers a position of liberation. In the Anglophone academy, the free-culture movement has too often been associated with the Californian ideology and, as such, fundamentally inscribed by the liberal values of possessive individualism and market exchange. As a rule of thumb, such cultural economy has been taken as the endgame of the biopolitics of late liberalism, where "design thinking," "innovation" or "open-source" developments are (not without reason) seen as the latest fads in a perpetual economy of global and unequal accelerations (Irani 2018).

By focusing on the question of autonomy my aim in this chapter has been to trace a path outside the frameworks of post-Marxist or biopolitical interpretations and instead articulate a space of anthropological thinking that can work analogously to the problem-spaces of experimentation and prototyping of the free-culture collectives I work with. The history of free culture in Madrid, I have attempted to show, is part of a larger history of autonomous movements, insurrectional aesthetics, antagonist telematics, and the role of the institutional art world in reclaiming a right for the city. To study the history of such a movement, however, is not simply to show that the designs of liberalism differ in different contexts of market or state welfarism, nor is it (just) a call for situated and embodied analyses of the liberation agendas of different techno-aspirational cultures. Rather, mine has been an attempt to describe the artful and tactical relocations, as Lucy Suchman has long been calling us to do (Suchman 2011), that hold every critical design culture in tension, not least the culture of anthropology as itself a practice of critical intervention. In particular, I have worked in detail through an ethnography of autonomy in order to throw into relief the problem of the autonomy of ethnography: about its resources and equipment; about the specific material vectors, experimental assemblages, and collective methods through which ethnography navigates the frictions and frissons of liberal designs; and therefore about the complicities and complexities through which ethnography alloys and allies spaces of shared enunciation. This is a story, then, not about how ethnography studies liberal designs, nor even about how designs liberate fields of praxis, aspiration, and reclamation, but about the liberation of design as an anthropological affordance and orientation.

Notes

1. See http://www.sindominio.net/fiambrera/convocatoria.html.
2. I have obtained information on the organization of the Copyleft workshop from the online archive of the Copyleft email list. The archive is available to subscribers only here: https://listas.sindominio.net/mailman/private/copyleft/. I follow a standard referencing convention and cite messages to the list by author and date.

CHAPTER FIVE

The Kinship between Ethnography and Scenography

Design Proposals and Methods Working within Ethnographic Projects

GEORGE E. MARCUS

I address in this chapter the operation of a particular tradition of design practice—scenic design or scenography—within projects defined by methods and
goals of ethnographic research in anthropology. The ethnography itself, as
genre form, and to a lesser or indirect degree the methods of fieldwork that
generate it were collectively and reflexively rethought in anthropology during
the last two decades of the twentieth century. However well this period may
have prepared anthropological ethnography for the dramatic transformations
in media and visual technologies and in global/planetary awareness during the
first two decades of the new century, the classic model of ethnographic research
still prospers in the launching of anthropologists' careers, thus forming the
substance of critical first projects.

The critique of global neoliberalism, as well as the condition of postcolonial-
ism in many of the places that anthropologists have traditionally worked, like
capitalism more generically before it, has performed well enough as the leitmotif
context of anthropological writing and analysis. But somehow there is a widespread sense, which I observe day to day, that the analytics that these frames
provide as a research program do not capture the full intensities and range
that fieldwork produces in its rather humble, but deeply personal recordings.
Controlled speculative thinking about the emergent future, much in fashion as
the knowledge product of ethnography, requires more than the sharp insights
of the reflexive participant observer. To an extent the attraction of design generally for ethnographic practice is in its reliance on and critical reworkings of
speculation as a means of material inquiry and research, leading to a result. In

this sense, design methods provide ethnography with a satisfying working ideology that suggests products, outcomes, techniques, and relations other than those that cluster around "writing up" results from the private archives of field materials in the traditional genres.

During the 2000s especially, and forward, collaborations with design traditions and designers became a matter of increased interest as anthropologists met them on terrains and in the pursuit of topics in which both were present (see, for example, Rabinow et al. 2008; Smith et al. 2016; Estalella and Criado 2018) and shared some obvious kinship. (This relationship has been much more long-standing and more routine in the Scandinavian countries; see Smith et al. 2016.[1])

Particular design practices not only are interesting partners for ethnographic research but actually form a key resource for rethinking, expanding, and experimenting with how the latter might be conducted as the core methodological paradigm within anthropology's own disciplinary culture. That is, this relationship is posing more than the asking of designers as collaborators into the frames and protocols of ethnographic research; rather, it suggests the assimilation of design methods, aesthetics, and norms into anthropology's ethnographic research protocols themselves. The latter is a position that I want to explore in this contribution. And my means of so doing is to think specifically of scenic design, or scenography, inside ethnographic projects since that is where I have had direct experience of collaborations (Cantarella et al. 2015, 2019; Marcus 2008, 2016a, 2016b) and because for their own part, scenic designers have conceived an "expanded" practice for themselves exceeding the world of theater and evoking resemblance to traditions of ethnographic method and writing.[2] I don't so much want to argue emphatically for design within the anthropological tradition of ethnographic research (as I can be understood to have done elsewhere; Rabinow et al. 2008), but rather I want to move through some selected positions on ethnography and problems in defining it today that I have thought important to opening this canonical form to design collaborations (operations? interventions?) within ethnography's established habits and customs of developing research projects.

I proceed in three movements. The first is to consider the major line of resistance—the problem of the ethics of minimalist intervention or nonintervention—that Keith Murphy has so lucidly and powerfully discussed in a recent essay (Murphy 2017). The second is to examine the character of the surplus knowledge (sacralized in private stores of "fieldnotes"; see Sanjek 1990 and

Sanjek and Tratner 2016) of subjects and places that all anthropological projects have each accumulated in their emphasis on open-ended curiosity and attentiveness in fieldwork, as well as the problem of constituting this surplus from open-ended fieldwork curiosity as relevant knowledge today (this turns out to be a question of forms of reception and performing knowledge that anthropology might not yet have articulated or recognized, beyond those that it creates for its own professional discussions). The third is to consider renewed discussions of how ethnographic research intervention perceives or establishes place, locality, mise-en-scène, and especially enclosure. This third movement, stimulated by tenets of scenography, is of special interest to me, who, before the digital era settled in, raised issues of multisited fieldwork (Marcus 1995) and evoked complicity (Marcus 1997) as instilling senses of the local operating sensorially in place at differing levels of scale and politics. Now through an interest in scenic design thinking and practices, how imaginaries of place, space, and enclosure are created in ethnographic research—so concerned with movement, scaling, and following processes, relations, and chains—returns with intensity. To me, in retro mode, this makes the production/elicitation of "local knowledge" all the more significant, through the material production of an imaginary of enclosure in defining locality, place, and dwelling today. This is something at which scenographers are expert, resourceful, and delightfully imaginative in their own version of field research (see, for example, TILT Collective 2013).

In defining these movements, I depend on certain readings and relations that have influenced me, rather than a literature review or summary. The first is Murphy's revealing treatment of ethics and differences between design and anthropology, as well as how definitively and consequentially ethics are regulative in anthropology as defining a limit or inhibition on practice. Then in the juxtaposed quotations by Marilyn Strathern and James Faubion I present the idea that ethnographic method is bountiful, surplus collection, the more or less systematic collection of an archive of data, with unused knowledge potential that requires forms that are lacking or have not been anticipated. Here I use two quotations from early and late in the first decade of the new century, each recognizing deep changes in the positioning of ethnographic research by anthropologists, during a period when an enthusiasm for design anthropology grew. And finally, through more extensive quotation to evoke and mimic the experience of dialogue in shared projects, I present and respond to an expression of the working principles of scenic design articulated by Luke Cantarella with whom I (and our partner Christine Hegel) have worked on a number of projects over the past five years (Cantarella et al. 2015, 2019). Cantarella's articulation of these principles, established centrally on the shaping of spaces into places for dramatic (and social) action, is cumulatively powerful, intriguing, and resonant with ethnography, but how do these principles actually work within the presumptions of the ethnographic projects of lone fieldworkers? They encourage a sense of the mise-en-scène of intensive fieldwork as well as active experiment and presentation long before and long after "results" are reported to the academy. Such scenographic interventions in ethnographic research projects thus have the potential of altering finally in form and content those authoritative receptions that have held the ethnographic research program resolutely in place.

So I undertake this review of what I think about the prospects for (specifically scenic) design modalities merging with ethnographic research method in anthropology... in suspense.[3] What is at stake is the autonomy of ethnography, on which its professional practice insists even in deep, exploratory collaborations—an issue that Alberto Corsín Jiménez also raises as a result of a certain beguiling, productive, and long-term working together with (in his case, architectural) designers, and the issue on which I end this essay.

The following sections are presented in the form of commentary that mimics and evokes dialogic engagement, which is a representation of the course that every ethnography/design collaboration takes and nurtures. The endpoint of each section is an implied invitation to my evoked interlocutors (Murphy, Faubion, Strathern, Hegel, and Cantarella) and to any readers of this essay to respond and continue, off-text.

Ethics . . .

In his essay "Art, Design, and Ethical Forms of Intervention," Keith Murphy (2017) raises the following series of points:

> What would happen if we admit, rather than ignore, that our presence is inherently interventionist—and then play with that form to make the intervention more productive; for our interlocutors, for our research, and for knowledge-building more generally? (102)

The American Anthropological Association adopted its first code of ethics . . . in 1971, and since that time ethics has become big bureaucratic business

for the organization. . . . One consequence of this is a generalized resistance to methodological innovation, especially in the domain of explicit
intervention. . . . But unlike anthropology, there is no substantive code of
ethics for artists. (103–7)

Design is always, even in its smallest details, interventionist in ways that
constitute the very discipline itself. And this is a condition whose implications most design disciplines, and most designers, don't spend much time
worrying about; because intervening is just what they do. (109)

Framing ethnography as an aesthetic process that's centrally concerned
with creating and studying social forms helps shift perceptions of the profession of anthropology in ways that promote thoughtful, considered, ethical intervention as an explicit and significant knowledge-building aspect
of ethnographic research. . . . By viewing ethnography though the practices
and values of adjacent disciplines that both treat intervention differently
than anthropology does, we can heed Lederman's (2007) call for reimagining anthropological research by other means. (111–12)

Murphy captures well the limits, or at least inhibitions, that the history of ethics
and ethical concern in anthropology since the 1960s has placed on innovations
within both the broad postulates and the specific practices that have defined
anthropology's emblematic ethnographic research method. This is particularly
so for one who is interested in aesthetic experiments in inquiry, drawn from
recent histories of art and design disciplines. The key ethical barrier seems to
be suspicions that surround experiments of aesthetic or design intervention,
especially those that rearrange or distort the found conditions of life within
field research, beyond the minimalist, but that are powerfully invested in acts
of intervention that make fieldwork possible at all. At least, there is no room for
more outside this ethically regulated act in apprentice ethnographic research.

What is also effective about Murphy's account is that he shows contrastively
how rigorous this care about ethical intervention is in anthropology compared
to ethical codes in design and art disciplines. Not without ethical concerns,
"design," he says, "is always, even in its smallest details, interventionist in
ways that constitute the very discipline itself." So, anthropological ethics is not
merely an addendum or a caution to fieldwork underway, but it is a shaper of
anthropology's basic method, which focuses on a paradigm of only one kind of

intervention, that of the lone fieldworker or fieldwork project, deeply inculcated in the training of anthropologists and, in turn, prizing above all else the skill of the reflexive and attentive observer.

I had little conscious appreciation of this relation when I heard comments by the artist Neil Cummings at the 2003 Tate Modern Conference on Art and Anthropology concerning a project with his partner Marysia Lewandowska that moved between the Bank of England and an interactive installation they were preparing at the Tate Modern, which involved unsuspecting visitors being presented with the gift of a beautiful poster from the Bank of England (see Cummings and Lewandowska 2001). Motivated by ethnographic example and several classic readings from anthropology (including Strathern), I was not so impressed with the design itself, which was implemented as a performance of relational aesthetics. But to me at the time it seemed an exciting enactment of a multisited ethnography of elite institutions intervening in their services to the populace.

On responding to a question from me asking whether this work might be related to ethnography, Cummings immediately denied it, by remarking that artists were not "ethically rigorous enough" to be anthropologists. This wording struck and puzzled me. It deferred to anthropological ethnography in a way that Hal Foster did not in his 1990s essay distinguishing site-specific, conceptual art from ethnography. "Ethical rigor" made the difference, but what did Cummings mean? I would have thought it would have been something like "objective knowledge vs. aesthetics" a la Foster. I could only presume that what was synonymous with fieldwork intervention was not controversial from an ethical standpoint for the artist. (Did artists not care about ethics in their form of fieldwork? Perhaps their ethical concerns focused on what was made spectacle to a public. The moment of spectacle or performance, not de facto backstage work or fieldwork, might indeed be a focus of ethical concern for artists but, even then and there, not to the degree of ethical concern about intervention in once colonially immersed anthropology.)

Cummings's reference to "rigor" in differentiating ethnography from what he did as an artist had for me the uncomfortable association with piety (to which he seemed politely to defer in differentiating what he did from what anthropologists do). I wanted to embrace or be embraced by shoptalk on this project, but instead I came away a bit discouraged. In subsequent years, for whatever reasons, I have usually found it easier to be an anthropologist amid artists and their projects rather than to have the same sort of rich conversations with artists when invited into my projects. (Although more recently I have enjoyed this anthropology-inflected contact with artists in a modest atelier of projects with Luke Cantarella and Christine Hegel. It could be the character of the particular aesthetic design discipline—scenography; see the "Enclosure" section below. Still, even here, there are implicit rules in effect for not "converting" each other.)

Finally, then, there is an important change in older anthropological ethics that partnerships with design disciplines would pose within the conduct of classically conceived ethnographic projects, and that is exposure or production of work/results, usually reserved for the write-ups, talks, articles, and monographs in the academy, in forms of performing ethnography, in various states of development, to a variety of situations of reception for inner or micro "publics," constituted at varying degrees of closeness and relation to the fieldwork. This challenge may be the hardest but most important innovation that introducing interventions into the monopolistic course of fieldwork might pose—both to reigning ethical concern and to the complexity of knowledge making where professional authoritative response mixes with a variety of test runs and experiments with granular receptions among those who have been subjects and associates of the fieldwork. Anthropologists would have to risk more, and invent more, when they report their research to those in the field as well as to the academy. This is where design collaborations within the circuits of ethnographic reporting, as part of fieldwork, could be most important. Such collaborations need designed forms for articulating knowledge as it is created. There is no lab in the field, but there are theaters, and there are studios.

Murphy's essay is clarifying about a strongly held inhibition in anthropological research. While ethical concern, associated with anthropology's past, can be fully respected, its inhibitions also must inevitably be challenged because of the changing assumptions almost everywhere concerning participation—being part of a community or a project. The access that an ethnographer requires nowadays can almost never be justified by subjects in their agreement to being studied by a "marginal native." In other words, how one gains access inevitably involves revisable agreements more complex than the negotiation of allowing a fieldworker to be present. Indeed, in my own experience the entry of aesthetic or design disciplines into collaborations with anthropologists and others in the spaces or sites of fieldwork occurs almost always as an evolution of a project that begins in the presumption of the classic ethical norms of anthropology. The progress of research demands more. It requires the renegotiation of rigorous ethics within their principles and results in the emergence of collaborations, interventions, and a logical frame for design experiments emerging within the sites of ethnography classically construed. How far it goes should be predicated on how productive it is and how ethical it remains (according to a pragmatic sense of ethics rather than a canonical one). At present such forms of work in anthropological ethnography are likely to emerge out of and following the form of qualifying dissertation research in which the ground for interventions drawing on design disciplines might be prepared. But is there a doctoral program in anthropology moving in this direction in its norms of producing dissertation research or anticipating its more matured results?

Surplus . . .

Two quotations have resonated with me over the years since they appeared, and in opposite ways they have allowed me to think both hopefully and differently about how design interventions could fit (modestly) into emerging, ongoing, or dormant ethnographic projects of research taken up again. The first is from Marilyn Strathern:

> What research strategy could possibly collect information on unpredictable outcomes? Social anthropology has one trick up its sleeve: *the deliberate attempt to generate more data than the investigator is aware of at the time of collection. Anthropologists deploy open-ended, non-linear methods of data collection which they call ethnography;* I refer particularly to the nature of ethnography entailed in anthropology's version of fieldwork. Rather than devising research protocols that will purify the data in advance of analysis, the anthropologist embarks on a participatory exercise which yields materials for which analytical protocols are often devised after the fact. . . . We may speak of anticipation by default, to be found in tools already there or in open-ended modes of study, such as "ethnography," which allow one to recover the antecedents of future crises from material not collected for the purpose. If one were to formalize it, then it would be to anticipate a future need to know something that cannot be defined in the present. (Strathern 2004, 6–7, emphasis added)

The second quote is from James Faubion:

> *A perusal of my mental card file has yielded not a single instance of an*

ethnographic monograph that has succeeded through the deployment of
its own substantive resources alone in establishing a generative program-
matic—not just an analytical category or two, but a technology of disciplined
question-formation. Those that have succeeded in doing so in the glorious
Dreamtime of the anthropological past—from Malinowski's *Argonauts*
(1922) to Leach's *Political Systems of Highland Burma* (1956)—have in every
case had the support of one or another of the vastly abstract dichotomies,
the master tropes or myths, in which we can no longer believe: traditional vs. rational; preconceptual vs. conceptual; the economy of status vs.
the economy of material capital; above all, the primitive vs. the modern.
(Faubion 2011, 269, emphasis added)

These ruminations by Strathern and Faubion have particularly resonated for
me in my own participation, first, in a team ethnographic project at the World
Trade Organization (WTO) from 2008 through 2010, followed by a "second
act" in 2013 of a commissioned scenographic installation, with me and another
researcher from the original project joining scenic designers to make an installation in the WTO spaces in which the earlier ethnographic research occurred
(see Marcus 2016a; Cantarella et al. 2019).

Surplus material, data, and thinking with speculative potential, I believe,
are the key resources or thematics evoked by both Strathern and Faubion,
with different inflections. They also each point to doing more with the collection and writing of the larger corpus or archive of material that any classic
fieldwork project generates, quite separate from the conventional writings of
articles, reports, and monographs. Strathern is "sunnier" here and means to
save anthropology from what seems to be limited expectations for its role in
collaborations (usually those that are entrepreneurial, institutional, technical, or natural-science related, as she was involved in, with some discomfort,
just before and perhaps when the writing of the working papers in which her
"defense" of anthropological ethnography in such collaborations appeared).
The implication for me is that anthropologists themselves might not see the
potential of material that they have collected until they are marginalized or
somewhat misunderstood in broader and more powerful collaborations in
which they frequently participate these days (as in the Cambridge science
park project in which Strathern was involved; interestingly, anthropologists
can no longer be naysayers or obstructionists as they sometimes were when
serving with pride in Third World development projects of the last century).

Seeing this surplus in a corpus of notes and archives already collected, developing it, and sending it back into the world requires more than more fieldwork; it also needs innovations in method, as well as forms that are otherwise outside the frame of disciplinary ethnographic projects as usual. It requires bringing in congenial partners (designers with experience working in the arts as well as business), negotiating the authority of anthropological knowledge, and seeing what kinds of forms can be produced that shape the "surplus" and give it occasions to be presented in the original "field" or beyond it, before, while, or after it takes customary shapes as articles or monographs in reporting to the academy.

So, Strathern's modest and playful evoking of the "surplus" has, I believe, great implication for incorporating situationally and practically design aesthetics and methods (scenic design still being my preferred imaginary—see Cantarella below) into an act of ethnographic research with all of its loose and open ends. However, although I suspect she might have thought it did at the time, making use of the surplus does not necessarily lead to more enriching, recognizably disciplinary discourse among anthropologists. That surplus locked in field archives has many different ways to go in the incorporation of other partners or collaborators (such as designers) before it might emerge as something else. But this is for second or later postdoctorate projects (for one very apt recent example, see the extraordinary industry and design enterprise that transduced the "qualifying" ethnographies of Sherine Hamdy and Coleman Nye into the graphic novel *Lissa* [Hamdy et al. 2018]). The important skill is to see the potential of the surplus and its possibilities that are accumulated in any fieldwork project, and here bringing in design exercises and interventions is most valuable. This is a sort of therapy for the untapped potential of projects while they are being shaped by disciplinary discussion. Design interventions pragmatically experiment with the surplus in various possible forms while more customized thinking and writing from research is being pursued. They also legitimate and explore the realm of "controlled speculation," precisely the attractive dividend that Strathern sees in the development of the excess thinking and data that exist in fieldwork notebooks.

I see a similar potential for design methods within the tradition of generating anthropological ethnographic research in the more austere and critical comment of Faubion, who ends his extraordinary book on the anthropology of ethics (2011) with a rider about standards of first career-making projects of fieldwork. Generally, I think he is writing about the same surplus that

Strathern evokes in any project of observant, attentive fieldwork in its stores and archives of notes and gathered materials. Speaking more to the initiate than the anthropologist who participates in a collaboration on others' terms and as a partial knowledge maker in later career research entanglements, Faubion is most concerned with the lack of even a skein of programmatic investigation in many canonical projects today—the absence of "a technology of disciplined question-formation," as he says, and without even the support of the master tropes and myths of the past. Faubion goes on to outline the strategies of ethnographic writing that produce impressive works despite the lack of programmatic pursuits in fieldwork. What then would make contemporary fieldworkers program their fieldwork by a "technology" of question-asking? This probing question alludes to the same surplus to which Strathern refers that could be structured in collection by design interventions. These would not be for data gathering or testing, but they would lend the procedures of fieldwork the sort of aesthetic character that Murphy (2017) describes in his review of the much discussed and criticized (in art circles) relational aesthetics trend of the early 2000s (Bishop 2012).

In his final chapter, Faubion goes on to define a kind of diagnostics that seems to inject the programmatic back into fieldwork without the older mythologies defining its conceptual boundaries and imaginaries of purpose. I see in his (Foucault-derived) category of diagnostics a mise-en-scène for design experiments and interventions in the terms that early ethnographic research in its nonprogrammatic license has defined and set out upon.

The point is that the surplus, as either Strathern or Faubion evoked it, within projects of ethnographic research, as the potential energy in private reserves of ethnographic writing, does not resolve itself by anthropologists becoming poets or, as called for in the 1980s, by reinstilling poetics in scholarly genres of signature, composed ethnographic writing for the sake of politics. Instead, the surplus opens ethnography to translating and negotiating its projects into more aesthetic forms with experienced partners. Or else, the surplus just remains surplus and as a comforting, controlled sense of the value of ethnographic work in exciting, ever underdeveloped, and undeveloped potential or excess. In effect, the "surplus" of any project unaddressed—for example, by design collaborations—offers a contribution to the self-esteem and mystique of the discipline as it makes important, but limited contributions to partners and collaborators, who increasingly shape the potential questions of originary research within anthropology itself. In this transformation, anthropologists need to make the surplus reserves from each project kinetic through other partnerships negotiated on its own terms. For this, designers of the surplus are needed.

Enclosure . . .

The following quotations are extracted from Luke Cantarella's articulation of the principles of scenography as a capstone piece within the account of our five-year collaboration (Cantarella et al. 2019). I have made them extensive, since they offer an unusual reflective perspective on a design craft after a practitioner's long-term and variable participation in working within and on ethnographic projects. If there is one key theme for the ethnographer in considering these deepening relations with a design practice suited to it, it is his or her impulse and need to return repeatedly, and constantly with new vision and thinking, to fieldnotes—the diverse, often raw archives of research projects that are sacred-like private spheres—to articulate new insights and new sources of commentary than what might be offered by the work of, or toward, disciplinary publications.

> [Mise-en-scène] In the theater, scenography functions to make plausible or necessary the symbolic actions of a performance. It is created collaboratively by designers, directors, writers, and performers. In the world, the scenography utilizes similar powers of mise-en-scène to frame built environments that condition encounters. . . . The scenographic can be found in many places within everyday life but may be especially noticeable in architecture, urban planning, politics, gardening, cartography, and of course a wide variety of art projects from painting to installation. (16)

> Scenography's manifest intentionality, the practice of staging scenes in order to engineer encounters, is more explicit than in ethnography where there remains a strong connection to the discovery of the ethnographic scene rather than its invention. In theatrical terms, this might be thought of as an affinity towards naturalism over artifice. . . . By making the seams in the enclosure of the field visible, the scenographic experiment co-constructs representations of the culture concept while simultaneous[ly] questioning its stability and pointing towards what it is in the process of becoming. (24)

[Design-Based] Scenographers are aligned towards the traditional status and relationships of the design fields in which utility (i.e., the solving of problems and evaluating successes based on that problem-solving) precedes aesthetics. However, because scenographers work in the service of fictions, as opposed to physics, they may redefine the terms of their efficacy based upon the discipline of aesthetic laws, not natural ones. In this sense, while they may choose solutions that are minimal, efficient, and feasible, they are equally attracted to Rube Goldbergian strategies that emphasize the impossible, complex, childlike or failure-prone. (20)

[Supplemental] In contrast to theater-making as a whole or art practices that have traditionally been held to be autonomous forms, a scenographer's work is decidedly supplemental. . . . Scenographers, with their habits of framing, decorating and setting works, occupy this double position of the necessary yet extraneous. They always operate *in relation* to another thing. The scenographer's task is to think through how the large-scale visual, spatial, and aural fields can provide context. Unlike history painting, frescoes, murals, or panoramas, architecture or installations, scenographers request no autonomy. They understand that their work is partial and cannot be evaluated on its own, but rather must be evaluated on the basis of its co-constructed collaboration with authors, directors, performers and spectators. (20–21, emphasis in the original)

[Without Form] While the framing and conditioning of space have always been considered central to the medium, the scenographic gesture implicates all aspects of the visual and aural fields. They exist in a multitude of forms from architecture to lighting to sound to kinetic and haptic events, even to commentaries on institutional framing. (21)

[Without Isms] There are no aesthetics of "good scenography" in the way that there have been an aesthetics of "good design." A scenographer can be wicked or tame, debased or refined. And their attitude is determined primarily through relations to a client or project. . . . In contrast to other designers and artists whose primary concern is with establishing a mark, look, style, or market, scenographers do not need to maintain aesthetic fidelities. (21)

[World-Making] Scenography is a speculative practice that invents worlds. Using its status as a fiction (something illusory, false, and pretend), it makes real materialized representations of the imaginary. (21)

[Scaled to Individuals] Scenography (like anthropology) understands and speaks to humans most effectively at the scale of the individual and small groups. . . . Primary users in scenographic terms are specific performing bodies (characters, participants, or attendants), whose motivations and anticipated behaviors shape the design process. Secondary users are publics or audiences that have traditionally been understood more generally. . . . In the development of scenographic ideas, these two groups are evoked through research, speculations, and the push and pull of people that create the central resistances and affordances in the scenography process. (22)

[Aligned to Spectators] Scenography exists in relation to performers or publics. It is the result of observations made on a certain viewing vector(s) that establish indices between the fields of meaning created by performer and spectator. Codified as the sightline, the scenographer controls the directionality, positionality, and magnitude of these vectors to determine limits and spaces of the scenographic space and to create linkages between viewer and spectacle. A proscenium-like stage, for instance, aligns all the vectors in one direction privileging surface decoration, unity, and hierarchical relationships. The thrust theater or arena collides multiple vectors shifting the emphasis towards materiality and dissensus. (22)

Cantarella defines scenography as the perfect design partner (utility over aesthetics) to work within other disciplines (e.g., the scene of ethnographic research displacing theater), but with a playfully mischievous proviso: "However, because scenographers work in the service of fictions, as opposed to physics, they may redefine the terms of their efficacy based upon the discipline of aesthetic laws, not natural ones. In this sense, while they may choose solutions that are minimal, efficient, and feasible, they are equally attracted to Rube Goldbergian strategies that emphasize the impossible, complex, childlike or failure-prone." Is this a problem, though, at least constitutionally, for scenography working within the agendas of ethnography rather than theater? I say, not if the engagement of scenographic thinking is with the full range of thinking observantly, imaginatively, and speculatively that is evident in the fieldnote archives of ethnographic research.

There is an interesting issue here, however, about who in such collaborations are differentially willing to give up, or diminish, aesthetically interesting and exciting ideas when facts qualify imaginaries, even though grounded. Ethnographers tend to become committed through, after, and alongside their fieldwork to certain interpretations and investments in hardwrought concepts and imaginaries that guide writing and argumentation. Collaborations with scenographers often pose creative challenges to the emergent analytic in one's work and frequently send the ethnographer back to the trove of fieldnotes for "second, closer looks." How does one recover the analytic script serving the ethnographic narrative or "write-up"? Through serving the needs of scenographic design collaborations around the character of place as thought through and designed. Enclosure is a major creative challenge of this form of design collaboration.

But for the purposes of a design discipline working within ethnographic objectives, scenography, according to Cantarella, is formally and sometimes deceptively yielding in its "supplemental" character: "The scenographer's task is to think through how the large-scale visual, spatial, and aural fields can provide context. . . . Scenographers request no autonomy. They understand that their work is partial and cannot be evaluated on its own, but rather must be evaluated on the basis of its co-constructed collaboration with authors, directors, performers and spectators." The professionally skilled deference of design to ethnography may seem like the freedom of an ethnographer to develop her favored interpretations in an enhanced way. Actually, though, this supplemental deference of the scenographer makes trouble (good trouble!) for an ethnographer (or theater director) moving toward a line of interpretation. The response for the ethnographer is in finding new inspirations in fieldnotes — where Strathern's surplus exists. And here also we come to the theme of enclosure, or in the scenographer's practice, place-making (see TILT Collective 2013). This place-making occurs in the ethnographer's multisensory and multimodal rethinking of locale in an age of thinking of research practice as mobile and recursive, while hypostatizing the value of situational attunement to the closely observed: "While the framing and conditioning of space have always been considered central to the medium, the scenographic gesture implicates all aspects of the visual and aural fields. They exist in a multitude of forms from architecture to lighting to sound to kinetic and haptic events, even to commentaries on institutional framing" (Cantarella et al. 2019, 21).

The rethinking of the "the local" site or place as at least operationally enclosing the scene or scenes of ethnographic research, without isolating them, is crucial to a kind of multisited ethnography that performs and produces its insights
in different locales, from those of inception to those of reception.[4] Mise-en-
scène requires a material scenographic practice. Enclosure, I would argue, is a
much-needed powerful tenet of contemporary method, a context that must be
literally and materially constructed as part of fieldwork—especially in collaborations with scenographers. "World-making," "scaled to individuals," and "aligned
to spectators" are precisely the values that parallel those that imbue contemporary ethnographic sensibility.

My own position (Marcus 2014) has been that anthropological research
needs prototypes drawn from its trove of surplus knowledge in intermediate
semi- or micro-public forms of response in addition to, or in relation to, the
production of knowledge in the standard modes (texts, articles) of reporting to
the academy. Scenic design principles enacted within performance allow this.
Anthropologists themselves, as peers, are the secondary, but authoritative audiences for disciplinary research that has always traveled by other routes of receptions and reaction. They have been recognized as part of the data or record of
fieldwork. But they can and should be more—they are participatory, dialogic
commentaries (see Fabian 2008) alongside disciplinary methods. Only scenic
design provides anthropology with a method for bounding, enclosing, and thus
giving standing and expression to these responses buried in the archives ("fieldnotes") of inquiry performed.

In Conclusion . . .

Ethnography is a field of intellectual, operational, and affective commitments constantly struggling for a position of autonomous enunciation.
(Corsín Jiménez this volume)

The struggle to which Corsín Jiménez refers, which in his case derives from long-
term daily engagements with activist architectural designers in Madrid, is more
generally a problematic aspect that accompanies the pleasures and insights of
aligned collaboration with a design craft partner. Scenographic inventions, for
example, in their self-defined "supplementary" positioning plumb and call on

the most intimate, speculative thinking within projects of ethnographic research. The value of ethnographic thinking is tested to its cognitive and creative limits, sometimes in odd and uncertain ways. This is the "surplus"—ethnography's own supplements—that resides emblematically in fieldnotes and is the off-stage source of the creative concept work and analytics that traditionally emerge in the professional arena, are assessed, have influence, and make careers. Often one's collaborative partners in design processes elicit from ethnographers what is held back; or they transform, for the sake of aesthetic invention, what secures authority and reputation in the circles and forums that define what anthropological knowledge is. At its best, though, ethnographic enunciation—what long ago was thought of as "mere" description—is enhanced by the combination of trouble and opportunity that opening to the craft of scenic design makes for the expression within ethnography's richness of reserve abundance and surplus: "more data than the investigator is aware of at the time of collection" (Strathern 2004, 6).

My wager is that design collaborations, such as those described in this chapter, in the scenographic mode will increasingly be a powerful means of doing something significant with the "more data" in the realm of producing controlled speculation from ethnographic research. Giving over to design collaborations at the intimate, preconceptualized, or incompletely conceptualized heart of its investigation is a risk, an unsettling, and a renewal of possibility in the continuing evolution of this very settled form in anthropology of making and claiming knowledge.

The ethnographer's inevitable concern with her own autonomy in collaborations that immerse her in the exercises of scenographic design thus becomes a probe; a useful, but unresolved struggle; and a renewal of anthropological discourse rooted in a core tradition of inquiry. But this concern also signals the morphing of the fieldwork model in ways that design collaborations, as described in this chapter, only begin to facilitate and make known.

Notes

1.　The idea of intervention or active design strategies in pursuing anthropological research would be no problem for Tim Ingold, who with great inspiration and insight has displaced some of the key norms of ethnographic research by disassociating any identification of anthropological research with a tradition of discussing ethnographic method and essentially by valorizing, restating, and

aestheticizing the observation "function" of field method as a rich phenomenology of perception, embedded sensorily in materiality and movement (Ingold
2008, 2011). This indeed has been a powerful renovation of British anthropology
of much broader influence. My personal hesitation is in having been bred in
a moment when the dialogic was emphasized over the observational—see,
for example, Maranhao 1990. The influence of this tendency might have run
its course with the so-called theory moment of the study of culture in the last
quarter of the twentieth century, but I think it is powerfully and regrettably
neglected now (but see Matti Bunzl's 2004 interpretation of method in the work
of Franz Boas for an ever-potential dialogism; Boas, so immersed in material
culture interests of his time, is actually a progenitor of dialogic fieldwork
style). In any case the theory and practice of dialogics in projects of fieldwork
are made even more kinetic by an overlay and intervention of scenographic
design within them. If one were to look for an embryonic movement toward
design interventions in fieldwork materials thought through as dialogics, one
might consult Johannes Fabian's 2008 *Ethnography as Commentary*. Dialogics, renewed by design—scenic design—stimulates, I would argue, a renewed
interest in processes of emplacement or enclosure, rather than embodiment
(much more tied to the perceptual). Mikhail Bakhtin's poetics have their complex spatial enclosures as in his exploration of the dialogical world-making of
Dostoyevsky's plots (Bakhtin 1984). Designing the scenes of speaking is another,
alternative route to the same aesthetic concerns with the observational and
perceptual, but with the problems of ethnographic method seamlessly recognized once again as "anthropology."

2. As Luke Cantarella explains, expanded scenography

> refers to artistic practices that derive from the traditions of stage design but
> exist outside the normal institutional frames of theater or play-making. . . .
> Expanded scenography has design-like habits of problem-solving while also
> making use of aesthetic fictions. It is a zone of thickly rendered representa-
> tions; it relies on detail and correspondence, similar to the way that ethnog-
> raphers in the Geerztian tradition have valued thick description of the "real"
> (non-fictional) social. In the ethnographic model, the ethnographer observes
> things and makes meaning; she articulates the authoritative interpretation.
> In the theater model, the three-dimensional field of signifiers is produced
> and recursively interpreted by not only designers and performers but also
> audiences. The fictionalized and often playful space of expanded scenogra-
> phy creates opportunities for embodied and participatory meaning-making
> about the emergent real. (Cantarella et al. 2019, 4–5)

Cantarella's mention of "thick description" suggests evoking here the actual
scenographic imagery in the writing of Clifford Geertz (and Erving Goffman

before him) as a source that is deeply and accessibly within the shaping of ethnographic thinking and writing in anthropology and that also provides the "stuff" of its analytic acuity.

Here is, for example, Clifford Geertz in "Notes on the Balinese Cockfight" (1973, 424) at his most scenographic—and analytic:

> The crosswise doubleness of an event which, taken as a fact of nature, is rage untrammeled and, taken as a fact of culture, is form perfected, defines the cockfight as a sociological entity. A cockfight is what, searching for a name for something not vertebrate enough to be called a group and not structure-less enough to be called a crowd, Erving Goffman has called a "focused gathering"—a set of persons engrossed in a common flow of activity that focuses them is discrete—a particulate process that reoccurs rather than a continuous one that endures. They take their form from the situation that evokes them, the floor on which they are placed, as Goffman puts it; but it is a form, and an articulate one, nonetheless. For the situation, the floor is itself created, in jury deliberations, surgical operations, block meetings, sit-ins, cockfights, but the cultural preoccupations—here, as we shall see, the celebration of status rivalry—which not only specify the focus but, assembling actors and arranging scenery, bring it actually into being.

Geertz toward the end of this famous essay settles on the notion of "text" as a framing descriptor for the cockfight in order to establish most aesthetically his paradigm of interpretation as the study of culture. But in the above passage, he evokes the scenographic in common cause with the most scenographic (dramaturgical?) of sociological theorists of ethnography. Indeed, one could find such references to the scenographically observed and constructed, not only in other passages throughout the Balinese cockfight essay, but in many others of Geertz's ethnographic treatments. While the notion of "text" might have been a better strategic choice in establishing the vision and practice of ethnography as reading/interpretation, he actually had the sensibility of a scenographer without disrupting the classic participant observation method. The same could be said of many other scenographically minded ethnographers such as Gregory Bateson and Victor Turner. All that was missing from this sensibility of such ethnographers was the idea of intervention of the scenic designer (though Goffman himself was frequently there in his interactional experiments) beyond the ethically coded intervention of the lone ethnographer.

3.   So much of the ideology of success or pleasure that I hear in the "corridor talk" among both anthropology professors and students is wrapped up in the almost physical, certainly existential, pleasure of being surprised in the course of one's fieldwork. Surprise, as such, is a very prized feeling/claim in anthropological discourse—maybe more than it should be. In a topic as stimulating as the

possibilities of design projects within ongoing ethnographic ones, I am more "existentially" moved by the tension of suspense, rather than surprise. Suspense emphasizes the unresolved, "yes, and . . ." improv nature of current enthusiasms for design in ethnographic research. To me, suspense is as attractive and emotional a reward as surprise is in inquiry or working through a question (see especially the classic work on the productivity generated by the related emotion of stage fright; Aaron 1986). The pleasure is not so much in the anticipation of surprise as it is in the sustained feeling of suspense about whether such collaborations, as performances, can be "pulled off." Surprise, if it occurs, is a bonus.

This "suspense" over or above "surprise" value in producing creative work (film, in this case) emerged as a theme in Francois Truffaut's discussions with Alfred Hitchcock about his style of plotting (Truffaut 1985). Also, I am inspired by a remark of the social theorist and philosopher Etienne Balibar to a student who was reading with him a text of Spinoza's on which he was a recognized expert. The student asked for an authoritative interpretation of some aspect of the text, and Balibar replied that he didn't know, but was personally in a state of suspense about how this particular reading would turn out. Likewise in my experience design intervention within ongoing fieldwork inspires in me not so much the hope or expectation of surprise (this is a very hard emotion to satisfy, sustain, and trust) but that of suspense—the anticipation of whether a "plot" of fieldwork (driven by hunches), without being a "hypothesis," will turn out. Such a "plot" needs tests of performance that only the design process—and intervention—can produce. The controversy might be whether anthropologists, in an ethical sense and by their own norms of ethical rigor, might entitle themselves to such a defined expectation of suspense in confronting alterity. With design, they are left in suspense, but with little hope for surprise. Personally, I don't trust "surprise" in the way that I do trust "suspense," which more plainly recognizes what the fieldworker has invested in inquiry and can discover as a result rather than evoking the disconnected emotion of "surprise" as a result of discovery and dispassionate observation.

4. In thinking through a "scenic design within ethnographic project," one imagines scenographers being brought into or entering ongoing, in-progress ethnographic research. (Incidentally, the reverse role for ethnographers in theater productions is in serving as dramaturgs—see Kondo 1996—but in my view the potential influence is far less than in scenographers' assumption of their roles in the sites of ethnography.) In my experience, with Cantarella and Hegel, this is how the WTO project unfolded—actually they arrived after the major period of ethnographic research had ended in the creation of a "second act." However, our most satisfying project of scenography within ethnography emerged in the opposite way. This was the 214 sq. ft. project summarized in Marcus 2016b. Luke and Christine as artists were commissioned to construct an installation for a charity banquet concerning the virtually

homeless in Orange County—entire families living in derelict motels. So they produced ethnographically informed scenographic art for a wealthy public. It was only when I joined them in moving the work, a full-size production of a family motel room (214 sq. ft.) to different sites of installation throughout the county—for example, universities, churches, parks, shopping centers—that the installation became the core of fieldwork: ethnographic investigation. It was ethnographic investigation not on the nearly homeless per se, but on attitudes, awareness, and notions of charity among diverse segments of Orange County's wealthy middle classes. The 214 sq. ft. installation provided a literal, traveling enclosure that intervened within bounded places, where fascinating ethnographic interviews and conversations occurred.

Here ethnography followed scenography, but the latter gradually became the former's agent. So stories of the operation of scenography within ethnography can have different developmental narratives, other than the obvious one of recruiting scenic design skills within a process of ethnographic research. In fact, ethnography that begins in theater provides prototypes for fieldwork. There are, of course, many precedents here, especially in the history of art and activism (Bishop 2012). In my experience, however, in the design within ethnography paradigm, much finally depends upon the patience of the scenic designer with the slowness of the ethnographer. The tempos and crescendos of practice and patience—the issue of duration—are quite different in the two crafts . . . though, I personally have found mutual adjustment and accommodation possible and enlightening.

CHAPTER SIX

Form-Giving as Moral Mediation

KEITH M. MURPHY

There has been considerable attention paid in anthropology to several kinds of general human action that touch upon and combine, in different ways, features such as intentionality, aesthetics, expertise, and embodied practice. Each of these — including, most notably, creativity (Wilf 2014), making (Ingold 2013), planning (Holston 1989), and design (Murphy 2015) — represents a specific angle or analytical inclination for understanding the conditions under which humans *build* and *make sense of* the social and material worlds they inhabit. While these and other kinds of action tend to overlap in both concept and practice, as each one tends somehow to "involve" the others, they have nonetheless emerged as separate frameworks for explaining world-building anthropologically, in part because of the particular ethnographic contexts in which they have been observed and discussed. I wonder, though, if there is more to be said not only about how these ways of world-making relate to one another, but also about how they operate as basic mechanisms of human sociality.

What I provide in this essay is not so much a synthesis of these kinds of human action, in which I describe how they are all really just the same thing with different labels, but rather an elaboration of some underlying commonalities that subsist between them, with the hope of forwarding a set of terms and ideas that align them more closely and productively. First, drawing explicitly from design registers as a way to reimagine old anthropological concepts, I will introduce the notion of form-giving, which I think permeates and supports creativity, making, planning, designing, and many other identifiable social actions, and discuss its significance as a generative component of most, if not all, kinds of world-building. Next, I will argue that form-giving is always fundamentally a *morally charged* phenomenon. What I mean by this — and I will stress this again below — is not that form-giving (or creativity, making, design, etc.) is always fundamentally *good*, but rather that it always centers on, and traffics in, questions about and possibilities for the relative goodness or relative badness of its effects on human lives.

Finally, the second part of the chapter will be devoted to unpacking what I mean by all of this by critically exploring "design"[1]—the source of the term and the concept—through the linked prisms of form-giving and morality. This essay is thus primarily an attempt to formulate a way to think about a range of domains, such as design, making, creativity, planning, and many other kinds of human action, that anthropologists can use for more deeply understanding how humans engage in the general flows and trajectories of world-making.[2]

Giving Form

"Form-giving" is neither a new term nor a new concept, though I am applying it in an uncommon way here. Within the world of design, "form-giving" describes acts of creation. It is often applied to stages or modes of designing specifically directed toward drafting the physical forms of designed things, whether it is the facade of a large building, the shape of chair, or the graphic layout of a poster. In several European languages, such as Swedish, a cognate of "form-giving" is a synonym of the word "design" itself.

In recasting "form-giving" for anthropological analysis of the social world, I'm consciously exploiting the term's blunt simplicity. As a category of social action, form-giving is exactly what it seems to be, an actual "giving" of "forms." But whereas designers "give" what is typically characterized as physical or perceptible forms—such as the shapes, sizes, and colors of material objects, or the contours of private and public spaces—a more broadly conceived form-giver is a social actor who "gives" all kinds of forms, be they physical, political, linguistic, and more. And the giving is important, too, because giving implies— requires—a relationship between someone who gives, and has the power and authority to give, and someone who receives; and such relationships are rarely neutral. From this perspective there are certain kinds of actions that count as form-giving and certain kinds of people who give certain kinds of forms, and all of this has specific social and political consequences. From this perspective, forms of all kinds matter specifically as forms. They do not merely exist, but are contemplated, created, deliberated, and "given" to the world by certain social beings, and as such that is partly what gives these forms power. Both form and giving have particular histories in anthropology, of course, and before I go on I should say more about them.

FORM

Anthropology has historically maintained a cautious and uneven relationship with the notion of form. In some subfields form is relatively central and treated as a basic analytic. In the anthropology of art, for instance, especially in the early days of the discipline, the formal properties of artistic works were examined for their wider cultural significance, historical development, and social transmission. And in linguistic anthropology, a notion of form underlies everything from the phoneme to higher-level grammatical constructions, such as morphemes, words, and sentences. In these and other areas of anthropological research, what shape a form takes and what gets included in the formal container are, of course, always up for debate, but the notion of form itself is rarely called into question.

Elsewhere in anthropology, however, where it is less literally applicable, form has faced waves of both intense popularity and withering criticism. Its most obvious appearance has been in the guise of different "formalisms"—theoretical frameworks built around a notion of form—notably in economic anthropology, functionalism, and structuralism. Following Karl Polanyi's (1944) influential delineation of "formalist" and "substantivist" approaches to understanding how economies work, economic anthropology characterizes formalists as emphasizing abstract rules, goals, and values—and how they are "formalized" in institutions—as universally relevant, regardless of cultural particulars. The substantivists, in contrast, treat economic activity as always embedded in social and political contexts, many of which are, especially in nonindustrial societies, "informal," which is to say, loosely organized and variable. Outside of economic anthropology, both functionalism and structural-functionalism relied on highly formalized models and metaphors for explaining social relations at every scale, from interpersonal taboos to the ordering of entire societies. And of course the concept of structure itself, central to both structural-functionalism and structuralism, has been one of the most influential and highly formalized "forms" in all of social-scientific theory.

The critiques of all of these formalisms vary, to a degree, but they also overlap on several key points. First, these formalisms imply a "universal" portability of form that does not tend to bear out upon close ethnographic comparison, a point forcefully argued by Marilyn Strathern (1988). Second, and following from that point, form also implies a high degree of rigidity that is not always present—for instance, that a market is a market is a market—or that is drawn significantly from forms already apparent to the ethnographers and are then "discovered" in ethnographic materials. Third, researchers who adopt formalist positions are often overstating their claims by trying to accommodate an overwhelming amount of data in too elegant a form, and in so doing they are missing many important ethnographic details that have fallen out of the model.

Such shortcomings of formalist approaches have understandably led to a suspicion of form in contemporary anthropology. Tim Ingold (2012, 432–33), for example, has critiqued the "hylomorphic" model of creativity inherited from Aristotle, which stresses "that the origination of things is reducible to the imposition of preconceived abstract form on inert matter." Instead, he argues, form is a *result* of complicated interactions between humans and the materials they work. Meanwhile Susana Narotzky (2016) sees a "hegemony of form" produced under capitalism, in which practically all attempts to mobilize for social justice are organized within the very market models they seek to destroy, as the principal barrier to successful resistance. It is the unrecognized reliance on form itself, in her view, that impedes actual social progress.

While both the critiques of formalist approaches and the suspicions of form warrant serious consideration, that does not imply that the notion of form itself is useless for anthropological theorizing. Literary scholar Caroline Levine (2015) maintains that researchers in the humanities and social sciences have tended to treat form either too literally or too metaphorically, all the while treating different kinds of forms, be they "aesthetic" or "political," quite differently (even if they share similar features). To counteract these antipodal positions and to make the notion of form more useful, she suggests focusing specifically on the formed-ness of phenomena, but with an agnostic attitude toward their specific compositions. This would methodologically place all sorts of forms—in Levine's (2015, 3) words, "all shapes and configurations, all ordering principles, all patterns of repetition and difference"—on relatively equal footing, a move similar to the "generalizing" of agency in actor-network theory (see Latour 2007).

GIVING

Since Bronislaw Malinowski's (1922) work on reciprocity, and especially Marcel Mauss's (2000) reappraisal of that work, anthropologists have treated giving as an iconic kind of social action, one mostly predicated on building and maintaining equitable relations between individuals and groups. Gift exchange, as one prominent example, in contrast with other kinds of exchange, typically involves something that is given without an expectation of an immediate return; thus it represents something approaching, but not quite reaching, a "pure" mode of giving. Marshall Sahlins (1972) called this "generalized reciprocity," a time-delayed system of exchange in which the act of giving takes precedence over the specifics of the gift. To prioritize the act of giving, of course, is not to say that the value of the gift itself is unimportant, but rather that short-term accounting for equivalent gifts between givers and receivers is prioritized lower than the direct experience (and expectation) of giving and receiving. Over time, according to the logic of the gift, social relations between individuals and groups are managed and controlled through multiple acts of gift giving.

One central supposition in theories of the gift is that kinship, as well as the relative strength of kinship ties, heavily influences how giving and receiving are performed (see, e.g., Lévi-Strauss 1969; cf. Rubin 1975). In societies in which kin relations delineate the contours of political organization, generalized reciprocity figures most prominently among closely related kin, while exchange with more distant kin, or nonkin, looks something more like a market economy. In industrial societies, where kinship ties are complexly dispersed, commodity exchange, in which individuals directly exchange specific goods for specific values, is the dominant framework, and gifts assume a different social role. According to Jonathan Parry (1986, 467), gift-giving in such societies, typically treated as "disinterested" and, indeed, "pure," stands as an ideological counterpoint to self-interested commodity exchange and "assume[s] a much more voluntaristic character as their political functions are progressively taken over by state institutions." With the work of social and political management largely conducted by nonkin entities in industrial societies, individuals are free to perform acts of seeming altruism in their gift-giving without any real expectation of a return.

Of course a neat distinction between gifts and commodities, once used to separate small-scale societies from industrial societies, is largely overstated (Bowie 1998; cf. Appadurai 1986; Strathern 1988). In certain contexts single items can flip back and forth between gift and commodity without adopting a stable status (Herrmann 1997). Moreover, as Asif Agha (2011) has articulated, the concept of the commodity—and to which we might also add the gift—is not simply a physical thing, but rather an intricate bundle of materials, discourses, and values that all mutually reinforce one another in their social existence. And even if gifts and commodities are exchanged according to different valuation regimes in industrial societies, both systems nonetheless ensnare givers and receivers into complicated, morally inflected relationships and, in so doing, contribute to social and political world-making. In other words, while there are certainly many real differences between gifts and commodities as social objects, their commonalities nonetheless show that the transfer of culturally valued and complexly organized phenomena is a fundamental aspect of building and maintaining human relationality.

FORM-GIVING

In developing a general anthropological notion of form-giving, then, we might heed Levine's (2015) exhortation and adopt a light and flexible concept of form, one that regularizes a tendency already evident in anthropological writing. A cursory examination of the anthropological lexicon reveals plenty of form-related language, including formation, order, organization, construct, shape, and many others, though mostly these terms are used as metaphors, and not used to discuss or analyze form in any literal sense. What I am suggesting here is that rather than use a phrase like "social form" as metaphorical shorthand, we instead take it seriously as actually manifest, as relatively organized, relatively bounded, and relatively coherent both to ethnographers and to people in their own social worlds. One task for the ethnographer, then, is to identify forms, to trace out their rough outlines, and to understand how humans go about manipulating them. By adopting this perspective, and examining how forms of all kinds—material, digital, social, political, cultural—are created, maintained, brought together, and made meaningful, Lévi-Strauss's (1966) character of the bricoleur, the formalist improvisor, is revived and refashioned in a more workable guise, as one who brings together and shapes the bricolage that constitutes the social world.

The case is similar for approaching giving too. In reflecting upon how gifts and giving have figured in anthropological thinking, at least two premises follow. First, what is given in an act of giving, and the act of giving itself, can take many different forms, both within a society and cross-culturally. While the specifics of actual gifts matter in particular contexts, what seems more broadly relevant is that acts of giving forge certain kinds of links between people, including between people who occupy very different social positions. These links do not always mean or do the same thing in all contexts, of course; they simply act as binding agents that help give shape to the ways in which a social group coheres. Second, because giving relies on and can create asymmetries between people—at the very least, sorting them into "givers" and "receivers," even if only temporarily—then it always at least partly traffics in questions of morality, of good and bad, and of right and wrong ways of interacting with others. At least since Mauss's analysis of the gift, we have recognized that expectations around gift-giving, while often not explicitly articulated, are deeply implicated in consequential moral evaluations. On a small scale, if one does it wrong, or does not do it at all, it reflects badly on them as a person. On a large scale, if a group fails to fulfill its prestation-related obligations, it could lead to upset, or even violence.

Taking these elaborations of both form and giving, and combining them into something new, we can finally say that form-giving is a category of action, or perhaps an imbued generator of action found in different kinds of human activities, that is focused on shaping, in multiple real senses, the lived conditions of the social world. Certain people (or institutions or groups) undertake form-giving in certain contexts. It always involves a social actor who does some sort of work to shape some aspect of the world beyond themself—which is to say, to *intervene* in the world by means of forming some part of it—and social actors who "receive" the forms they shape by means of using them, observing them, living with them and in them, and so on. As such, this (typically asymmetrical) intervention of some social actors in the lives of others necessarily raises questions about whether the intervention is "good," "beneficial," or "right," on the one hand, or "bad," "detrimental," or "wrong" on the other, two poles demarcating the boundaries of a morality space within which the relative goodness or badness of things can be debated, determined, manipulated, and reformed.

I should say more about what I mean by morality here. When one enters into this sort of discussion, it is usually common to spend some time throat-clearing about the differences between morality and ethics, which often means drawing distinctions between specific values (morality) and general principles (ethics), or virtuous ways of living and normative obligations (see the introduction to Keane 2016 for a useful discussion).[3] For my own purposes, "morality" and "ethics" are interchangeable, and their meaning is very blunt: philosophical ruminating on this topic pertains to *questions*—not necessarily *determinations*—of goodness, on the one hand, and "right action," on the other, which together reduce to questions of relative goodness or badness, relative rightness or wrongness, or in other circumstances relative helping or harming, relative improving or worsening, and so on. Thus in my discussion of the morality of form-giving, I'm simply (and broadly) referring to the ways in which these and related categories are implicated in the manifestation of form-giving, whether in the actions (and beliefs and decisions) of form-givers, or in the effects of given forms on individuals and society. This doesn't require a universal definition of "good" or "right" that is applicable in all circumstances, as anthropologists have pointed out; rather, it assumes that while goodness and rightness are always entailed in form-giving, *how* they are entailed, and how they are assessed, is always contingent on locally determined parameters.

Contemporary anthropological studies of many different domains—large-scale phenomena such as welfare (Fennell 2015; Muehlebach 2012) and philanthropy (Bornstein 2009); interpersonal phenomena, such as organ donation (Hamdy 2012) and filial sacrifice (Shohet 2013); or those that are a mixture of both, such as religious charity (Erie 2016) and open-source software (Kelty 2008)—demonstrate that in most situations, the act of giving, as well as its relative moral valence, is always inextricably linked to the specific forms being given. Take, for example, welfare, in which governments act as form-givers. In the United States, the form of what is given—which is not to say the "gift," because the "gift" status of welfare benefits is a perpetual political debate—is critical to understanding how welfare operates in people's lives and, in a recursive move, "gives form" to the broader social world. Cash assistance is not the same as electronic debit cards, nor is either the same as actual physical items of food, and which form recipients get directly impacts their patterns of living, including movements in space as they work to find sustenance. The same goes for housing vouchers, which can only be used in certain buildings in certain neighborhoods, which, functioning as an instrument of exclusion, itself has the effect of shaping city blocks, neighborhoods, and entire urban areas. Moreover, only certain "kinds" of people qualify to receive these welfare forms, which has the effect of interpellating entire population segments that also take very specific forms.

We can see similar patterns in other governance strategies too. For example, as Annette Weiner (1992, 7–8) notes, in many societies ruling parties often attempt to fashion continuity between present and past by giving specific forms for subjects to consume in order to obscure change: "Consider how the leaders of the T'ang dynasty used regalia from earlier times to fabricate their genealogical connections to former rulers. In much the same way, Joseph Stalin used V. I. Lenin's body to create an inalienable monument that helped legitimate his legal right to rule." In these cases, a constructed form of past glory and the form of the present governance are intentionally made equivalent though the giving of specific material forms (sartorial and corporeal, respectively) that, their givers hope, can credibly bring past and present together.

All of these examples demonstrate that, when viewed from a wider angle than we are typically accustomed to using, and with a more ecumenical sensibility toward both form and giving, many kinds of human action begin to appear as critically linked and morally charged practices of world-building. By considering form *as such* and not just as a shorthand, and giving as involving more forms than gifts and commodities, we can begin to see how the world is actively and consistently shaped and reshaped through the accumulation and alignment of different social forms through specific acts of form-giving, including struggles over who gives, who receives, and what forms things of all kinds should take.

What I want to do now, in order to explain this in more detail, is return to design, the domain that produced the concept of form-giving, to explore the morality of form-giving in a specific context.

Design: The Prototype of Form-Giving

One of the most well-known definitions of "design" was proposed decades ago by Herbert Simon, a polymath scholar who, among other things, pioneered the development of artificial intelligence as well as theories of decision-making in economics. In his 1969 book, *The Sciences of the Artificial*, he offered a useful description of design, famously stating, "Engineers are not the only professional designers. Everyone designs who devises courses of action aimed at changing existing situations into preferred ones" (Simon 1996, 111). This simple claim, which in one stroke renders design a *technical* discipline by aligning it with engineering, but in the next stroke *democratizes* it by granting it to almost "everyone," was perhaps the most influential conceptualization of design of the twentieth century, not only providing a broad and potentially inclusive definition of design, but also setting the tone for how the field of design research would unfold.

I should say that I'm purposefully overstating Simon's ecumenical stance by interpreting his claim that "everyone designs" as a *democratic* statement. Simon himself was actually quite positivist in his attitude toward design, but his definition, probably due to its bare simplicity, has nonetheless been interpreted quite widely in design and design studies, even against its author's intentions. Indeed, there is an interesting tension in Simon's definition between a drive to *expand* the application of the concept of design and a desire to maintain its unique status, and that tension has trailed design research from the start. Is designing something that is professional, special, and unique to a particular training regime; or is it something more general, pervasive, and basically human?

In recent years that latter framing has become more pronounced, though not quite ascendant, in professional design and design research. Made evident in book titles like *Design, When Everybody Designs* (Manzini 2015), or the first lines of a recent article in *Design Issues* (Campbell 2017, 30) — "We are all designers. Everyone actively plans and intentionally changes their circumstances with the goal of bettering themselves" — this quasi-populist stance appeals to a certain kind of liberal sensibility, one that privileges making the category of "designer" more inclusive over subjecting it to critical scrutiny. I'll return to this genre of "good" design below, but what I want to point out here is that an anthropological take on design faces the same sort of fuzziness of scope: Do we find design everywhere, or only in certain kinds of domains; and if it is indeed restricted to only some domains, does that mean only offices and studios, or only industrial contexts, or only involving certain kinds of "objects"?

Since the early 2010s, following the lead of Tim Ingold (e.g., 2010, 2013; Hallam and Ingold 2016), anthropologists drawn to artifacts and materiality have grown increasingly interested in "making" as a social form. Encompassing actions as simple as purposefully putting hands to materials, making is a concept that is intended to cover a lot of ground. For Ingold, design counts as a specialized genre of making (see Anusas and Ingold 2013), but making, wherein the maker is "a participant . . . amongst a world of active materials" (Ingold 2013, 21), is the superior, which is to say more fundamental category. If we follow Ingold's humanist logic, everybody makes in the material world, but not everybody necessarily designs.

This, I think, is mostly right. If making springs forth from the interaction of humans, tools, and materials, then certainly everybody assumes the role of maker at some point. But design, while of a piece with making, is itself something more complex. It typically involves intention, structure, and foresight, which aren't required aspects of making. And design often involves significant nonmaterial elements. Perhaps most significantly, design is almost always undertaken *explicitly in behalf of someone other than the designer* (though, of course, the designer may take part as well). This is especially clear in the most obvious and prevailing kinds of design, *the design professions*—architecture, graphic design, furniture design, typography, software engineering, and so on—all of which are based on a patronage model. In practically every design situation, professional or not, to design is inherently to design for another.

In a previous piece (Murphy 2016b, 435), I described design as "the most common channel through which humans intervene, directly and indirectly, in the lives of other humans." As a corollary to that framing, I also claimed that design represents "humans provisioning for one another the conditions of life in innumerable forms and at almost every scale" (Murphy 2016b, 435). In other words, design is a very common mode through which humans in one way or another impact the lives of other humans. In all of its versions, design is fundamentally concerned with crafting the details of objects, spaces, buildings, infrastructures, technologies, services, texts, and more, the things that constitute what has fashionably come to be known as the "nonhuman" aspects of everyday life. This perspective, summed up by graphic designer Paul Rand's famous aphorism "Everything is design," is a complement to the perspective that "Everybody designs," though this one is arguably more believable and better supported by evidence. It's typically the case, however, that only a few classes of "everything" are attended to as specifically designed and whose designedness matters to the way people live their lives. For example, it's common in both scholarly and nonscholarly communities to treat "technologies"—such as cell phones, Facebook, infrastructures, or maybe doorstops—as the kind of things that affect humans, social interactions, and the everyday world (more on this below). Everything else, though, is treated as "just there," maybe displaying some form of agency, should some theorist devise a just-so story arguing it, or maybe being merely an inert, uninteresting hunk of matter. (I have yet to read a critical analysis of the vital agency of an Ikea table leg or a discarded square of partially popped bubble wrap.) I think the emphasis on the power of *technology* to impact the world, without full acknowledgment of the role played by everything else, not only misses the forest for the trees, in some respects, but also vigorously focuses on far too few arboreal specimens.

So Paul Rand was right: most things of the world—certainly the "artificial" ones, but also many that are "natural"—are designed, in the basic sense that some human or humans have applied intentional action to give form and other qualities to those things in a way that should (which is not to say *will*) serve some imagined purpose or function. Collectively these things of the world comprise *ecologies of designed artifice* that every human inhabits, ecologies that are composed of not mere things, but things expressly created by humans for other humans. Each of these things in its own small way sets some condition for the lives of the people who experience it: the shape, size, and color of a desk chair; the dimensions of a kitchen cabinet; the user interface of a television; the placement, height, and species of the street tree the town has planted in the sidewalk outside. All of these aren't just things in the world, but things whose form, qualities, placement, and very existence are largely determined by humans—often, many different humans—whose intentional actions have led to one's experiencing them. What's more, people don't usually experience phenomena individually, but in combinations, as integrated segments of an ecology of designed artifice. Viewed from this perspective, one's movements, actions, moods, and emotions are all *conditioned* by—though not *determined* by—one's relation to this ecology.

The form-givers whose actions end up producing these things, which are then placed in commodity chains to be manufactured, shipped, warehoused, sold, and used, all play a part—and, I'm arguing, a significant part—in crafting the worlds that other humans inhabit precisely though the mode of design, even if one designer (or one object, or one space) represents only one tiny detail within the overall artificial ecology. This is how design works as an intervention in human life and why, as such, it is always moral.

"GOOD DESIGN"

There are many ways in which morality explicitly manifests in design. Perhaps the most obvious is the notion of "good design." This phrase, which is typically more rhetorically potent than actually descriptive (Hayward 1998), has thrived for a long time in Europe and the United States. Historically linked to figures like Ellen Key in Sweden, William Morris and Nicolaus Pevsner in the United Kingdom, Frank Lloyd Wright in the United States, Le Corbusier in France and Switzerland, and the Bauhaus in Germany, all of whom advocated for some design reform program linked to social improvement, good design has always had a rather tenuous relationship to the concept of good. As design historian Stephen Hayward (1998) has argued, the idea of good design, which first matured in the 1930s during a period in which elites pushed an agenda of social hygiene, later developed into a method for reshaping and supposedly elevating the aesthetic taste of lower- and middle-class consumers. From the 1930s into the 1960s, especially in countries with capitalist economies, the "good" of good design described several different and shifting referents, including the quality of materials, the functionality of objects, their aesthetics, the power of design to reform society, and the value of design to improve business and economic efficiency. Only in a very limited sense was good design treated as directly beneficial to, or enriching for, the lives of individuals.

By the late 1960s, however, good design was undergoing a new evolution. Dissatisfied with the overly consumerist and overly materialist postwar design culture, a new generation of designers, mostly in Europe, seized the spirit of the political moment to advocate forcefully for a new kind of design proudly driven by a socially conscious ethos. The loudest voice in the pack belonged to Victor Papanek, an Austrian emigré to the United States who, during the 1960s, spent time in the Nordic countries both learning from and lecturing to students and professionals working in some of the longest-lived socially minded design traditions in the world. In 1970 he published a book in Sweden called *Miljön och Miljonerna: Design som Tjänst eller Förtjänst?* (The Environment and the Millions: Design as Service or Profit?), which was described by one reviewer when it was first published in English (as *Design for the Real World: Human Ecology and Social Change)* in 1971 as "a harsh and Biblical blast at the design profession" (Mellow 1972, 21). With chapter titles like "Phylogenocide," "The Myth of the Noble Slob," and "Do-It-Yourself Murder," Papanek (1984) adopted a no-holds-barred tone in excoriating the design profession for its lack of social conscience, and he encouraged young designers to reorient the work they do to improving the conditions of society (see also Clarke 2013, 2017a). By the end of the 1970s, in many design professions *doing good* had become an entrenched aspect of good design (which is not to say an aspect of *all* design), a position most visible today in specific design paradigms such as "social" design, design for disability, sustainable design, and design for development, all of which situate some version of "doing good" as the centerpiece of their missions.

But the category of "good design" is not without evil twins. As Hayward (1998, 223) has put it, over time "'good design' has maintained a dialectical relationship with 'bad design,'" and indeed in some respects there is a kind of "bad design" that operates according to specific counterpoints to good design—cheap materials, poor functionality, ugly aesthetics, wasteful and inefficient objects, and so on. And of course using design for "doing evil"—or at least not necessarily for "doing good"—is always a possibility. So to ward off this haunting dark side of design, many designers today explicitly proclaim themselves to be working in the moral light, engaged in an active and intentional project of beneficence, or of "making good" in one way another. Yet even if designers aren't actively turning their intentions toward causing harm, their work can still produce negative effects, sometimes by inattention, or sometimes simply by accident.

"BAD DESIGN"

Take, for example, the case of the Pruitt-Igoe housing project in St. Louis, where for decades the misguided expertise of the buildings' architects was widely viewed as a causal force behind an insurmountable wave of violence and social disintegration that plagued the community and led to its eventual demolition (see Bristol 1991). Critics of the housing project pointed to specific design choices—for example, skip-stop elevators and open public galleries, both of which were imagined as beneficial design features that could help foster a sense of belonging among residents, but that also offered spaces for violent crime to thrive—declaring them directly responsible for the unraveling of social order that almost immediately beset Pruitt-Igoe.[4] To be sure, Pruitt-Igoe's architects didn't account for the actual lived reality of the building's future occupants, choosing instead to focus more on *who they could be become* through the power of design rather than *who they already were*. But from another perspective, the architects' main failing was a lack of attention not so much to how the residents lived their everyday lives, but to the innumerable felt but unnoticed constraints that public-housing residents continuously face, such as inattentive government bureaucracies, the stigma of poverty, and outright racism, all of which are implicated in design, if not directly designed themselves. Even the very word we use to describe these kinds of buildings—"projects"—implies a kind of temporary status, an assignment to be worked on only for the time being. The buildings and their architects surely didn't cause the collapse of Pruitt-Igoe. But a kind of design that privileged technical expertise and prevailing policy over the ideological currents and social flows that relentlessly buffet human artifice certainly played a contributive part.

Pruitt-Igoe is emblematic of a common problem in design: things don't always work out as intended. In 1936 sociologist Robert Merton famously dubbed this "the problem of the unanticipated consequences of purposive action" (Merton 1936, 894), and over the following decades a whole strain of sociological research emerged that analyzed all the stuff that happens that we don't really plan on happening. This problem of unintended consequences is, of course, a generally familiar one: as, for example, when you buy an arbitrary birthday gift for a friend, and that gift turns out to be exactly the thing she had wanted; or when the simple compliment "You look nice today" unintentionally invokes the insinuation that looking nice is an observably rare occurrence. This genus of phenomena contains a number of different species—accident, fluke, coincidence, happenstance, serendipity, and more—all of which describe versions of events in which the consequences of action turn out otherwise than expected. Given that humans are generally and fundamentally quite poor at controlling the effects and interpretations of their actions, at least in some absolute sense, it's no wonder that the problem of unanticipated consequences would have a particular impact on design, a field largely preoccupied with producing effects at almost every scale.

Several other notable unanticipated design results come to mind. Highway overpasses designed by Robert Moses for the Long Island Expressway were built too low for buses to pass underneath, which consequently kept urban minority families away from Long Island beaches and helped entrench the area as predominantly white and upper-middle class—a situation whose accidentalness has famously been questioned by Langdon Winner (1980; but cf. Joerges 1999). And as Lochlann Jain has argued, while the tail fins ornamenting so many cars of the 1950s were designed to invoke a sense of speed and streamlined freedom, they also contributed to what Jain describes as a "public slaughter" (2004, 65), causing significant undue harm when, for instance, children playing in the street accidentally slammed their heads into the trunks of sleekly pointed parked cars.

Then, of course, there is PowerPoint. On February 1, 2003, after sixteen days in orbit, the space shuttle *Columbia* catastrophically disintegrated as it reentered Earth's atmosphere, killing all seven crew members onboard. The proximate cause of the disaster was relatively simple: during the launch a lightweight piece of foam had broken off of one of the shuttle's fuel tanks and struck a section of the left wing. This created a hole in the wing's thermal protection—which was innocuous while in orbit, but proved fatal once the shuttle began its descent. Because it was caught on film, NASA controllers were immediately aware of the strike—though not the hole—and they quickly set out to determine whether the shuttle and crew could, in some way, be adversely affected. Models were consulted and numbers were run, and after a presentation of results to high-level NASA officials, it was decided that the shuttle would be able to withstand the damage caused by the foam, and Columbia was given the OK to return home—with, of course, disastrous results.

The unintended consequence of design in this case was not what would be typically expected, according to statistician and data scientist Edward Tufte (2006), who served as a consultant to NASA in the aftermath of the disaster. The problem, Tufte argues, was PowerPoint. More specifically, the problem was the particular ways in which PowerPoint structures information by default and how those defaults were habitually put to use in real-world presentations at NASA. According to Tufte, on PowerPoint slides, higher levels of hierarchically ordered information—titles and what he calls Very Big Bullets—are typically used for top-level findings and summaries, while more subtle information (such as inconsistencies, doubts, and caveats on the slides used at NASA) is placed at the lowest levels, usually with smaller bullets and smaller fonts. Moreover, this "bureaucracy of bullets" (E. Tufte 2006, 10), as Tufte calls it, is repeated on each new slide, forcing very complicated information into a highly constraining framework determined not by the particular needs of the NASA scientists or their data, but by the default settings programmed by Microsoft engineers. Because people habitually tend to pay more attention to an outline's highest levels of organization, and they tend to ignore or discount their lowest levels, and because those highest levels on the NASA slides were relatively anodyne and insufficiently alarmist, NASA officials were left with the impression that Columbia would survive reentry intact. As Tufte argues, had the information squirreled away in the slides' lowest levels been given suitable formatting—and thereby proper attention—different decisions could have been made and lives could have been saved.

In discussing both good design and bad design it's difficult to avoid extremist language and extremist examples such as these, largely because the operative categories are themselves so stark. What counts as good design is usually obviously good, such that some specific kind of person or social group, someone who is obviously in need, is helped in some way by the intervention of design. Likewise, bad design often traffics in the morbid, in violence, in poverty, and in death, not simply ugly objects. Ironically, when viewed from a certain perspective, it's bad design contributes to the very conditions that good design purportedly ameliorates, creating an endless ouroboros-like cycle of making bad and making good.

Locating "The Good"

I should say that I've overstated my point again. While "doing good" has become a significant aspect of many kinds of contemporary design practice, or at least the rhetoric surrounding that practice, the way it manifests in particular versions of "good design" is mostly blunt and without much nuance, as I alluded to above. The bluntest of these "doing good" formations is "social design," a general label that can be applied to work that somehow accounts for circumstances beyond the form or aesthetics of the specific things under design (see Koskinen 2016). Almost any practice that pays attention to contexts of use can claim to be doing social design, which is why the Papanek-inspired label is all but useless within a political economic environment like today's, in which the *acknowledgment of an existing social world* is valued more highly than actually addressing the kinds of inequalities and structural violence that Papanek originally identified.

One of the most active areas of social design today is "ecological design" or "sustainable design," which tends to target objects and processes that, if improved, will contribute less to vexing issues like climate change, landfill overflow, drought, deforestation, and so on. Following the lead of other professionals and scholars concerned about the degrading conditions of the anthropocene (J. Chan 2017; cf. Fry 2009, 2011), designers working in an expressly "sustainable" mode tend to treat design as a means for disciplining consumers in how to reduce the damage they do to the world (Thorpe 2010), though few see capitalism and consumption itself as problems. Alongside ecological design there is a thriving push for "design for development" or "humanitarian design" by governments and NGOs (Redfield 2016; Schwittay 2014; cf. Escobar 2017, 2018b). This approach, like sustainable design, is nominally concerned with large-scale social problems, but is significantly preoccupied with redesigning human populations by means of designing the objects they use. Also like sustainable design, practitioners in this design space rarely see capitalism or consumption as problems.

There is also an older tradition of social design aimed at specific groups of people with nonnormative needs and abilities. This often means designing objects especially for people with disabilities (Hamraie 2017; Ott 2014; Pullin 2009), or accessible spaces (Hartblay 2017; Rattray 2007), or even furniture for wounded soldiers (Weems 2012). One variant of this is "empathic design" (Postma et al. 2012), which encourages designers to adopt the user and his or her world as basic constituents in the design process, rather than add-ons, and another variant is "universal design" (see Catanese 2012), which encourages designers to design everything in ways that allow everybody equitable access.

In recent years universal design and humanitarian design have grown closer together in some corners, while also taking on a more specifically moral valence in the form of what's called "the capability approach" to design (Dong 2008; Oosterlaken 2009; Oosterlaken and Van der Hoven 2012). Heavily influenced by the philosophies of Martha Nussbaum and Amartya Sen, advocates of the capability approach foreground social justice as a motivator for design decisions, arguing that design should be used to enhance people's capabilities and their opportunities to pursue well-being. As one proponent has framed it (Oosterlaken 2009, 95): "Many different design options are generally available during the development process of a new technology or product. This means that the details of design are morally significant. If technologies are value-laden and design features are relevant, we should—so it has been suggested—design these technologies in such a way that they incorporate our [*sic*] moral values." There are several other schools of thought in design that attend to the work of "doing good" in designing, but the overall point I'm making here is that in the basic organization of the design professions, the most prominent way to include an explicitly moral perspective is to shoehorn that perspective into a labeled and packaged style of designing (if not design style). Every other kind of design that doesn't use the label is, in the implicit contrast, not social, not concerned with a moral position, or not doing much to improve the world.

In addition to particular institutionalized "good" styles of designing, morality plays a part in the discourses and practices surrounding design ethics. These ethics can take the form of official professional codes or unofficial exhortations for designers to behave responsibly in their role as the "Prometheus of the everyday" (Manzini 1992). While there are differences in the details of how design ethics have been promoted (e.g., d'Anjou 2010; J. Chan 2017; B. Friedman and Kahn 2003; Stairs 2005), they all more or less boil down to the same basic principle: *Hey, designer, don't be a jerk.* While this focus on the responsibility and behavior of individual designers in design ethics is important and necessary—and definitely a significant part of the issue—it also helps avoid accounting for the structural, social, cultural ways in which design impacts life. That is to say, placing social responsibility in the hands of individual designers and the choices they make reproduces the solutionist logic of much contemporary design—the notion that social problems can be satisfactorily addressed through single design solutions—by arguing that the problems of design can be solved by quick-fixing designers themselves. Bad designers can become good designers by simply following these easy ethical principles, and thus everything in the world can be made right again.

Conceptualizing Design and Morality

I've been spending time tracing out some of the forms in which morality is explicitly figured in professional design as a way toward making my broader point about exploring form-giving from an anthropological perspective. The takes I've presented thus far all tend to tuck morality away in particular nooks and crannies of design, treating morality as either bluntly good or bluntly bad, and relegating it to only certain kinds of designing. But in contrast to these views, my point is this: these takes on good and bad design are only partially revealing about how morality operates in form-giving. All form-giving and thus all design, not just the explicitly social and responsible kind, is about morality at its core, and the cases I've been discussing represent only the most obvious manifestations of a more general state or moral presence that can be uncovered ethnographically in formed things.

Probably the most robust theoretical analysis of morality and design comes from scholars in science and technology studies (STS) who examine the mediating role of technology in society (cf. Findeli 1994). Building on Bruno Latour's work (e.g., 1992, 1994) on the social agency of artifacts and on Heidegger's post-phenomenological analysis of tools and tool use, Peter-Paul Verbeek frames the issue of designing "behavior steering technologies" (Verbeek 2006, 363) most succinctly: "Technology design is inherently a moral activity. Designers, by designing artifacts that will inevitably play a mediating role in people's actions and experience, are thus helping to shape (moral) decisions and practices" (Verbeek 2008, 99). Verbeek is certainly right to treat design as "a moral activity" and mediation as key to thinking about ethics and morality in new ways ("doing ethics by other means," as he says in Verbeek 2006). The problem with his formulation, however—a problem shared by many STS scholars—is that it is too narrow a focus on "technology" as the designed object that matters (not to mention too narrow an understanding of what counts as technology, despite, or perhaps because of, the Heideggerian influence), to the exclusion or significant demotion of other sorts of phenomena and the relentless emphasis on materiality and thingly artifacts over everything else—including leaving out real, live humans, for all intents and purposes. From a more broadly anthropological perspective, everything and everyone is behavior-steering, not just cell phones and doorstoppers, and the gaze-narrowing effect of attending only to technology helps steer us away from noticing. Moreover, it's easy to understand mediation through functionality when it's intentionally designed into a technology, such as a thermometer displaying the temperature. But what about something as mundane as a rug? Or a trivet? Or the placement of a lamp on a desk, or the height of a traffic sign? All of this, too, can steer behavior and thus play a mediating role in people's experience, but is often considered too trivial to matter. All of which is to say, Verbeek has posed a good way of thinking about design; he just didn't push those ideas far enough.

While morality has always been an inculcated aspect of ethnographic theorizing in one way or another—for instance, incest taboos and norms of gift exchange are deeply moral cultural forms—it's only quite recently that anthropologists have begun centering morality as a specific object of analysis.[5] At its core, this anthropology of morality[6] concerns "how societies ideologically and emotionally found their cultural distinction between good and evil, and how social agents concretely work out this separation in their everyday life" (Fassin 2008, 334), focusing more on "the everyday moral lives of actual living people" (Zigon 2008, 1) than on the philosophical abstractions that have dominated most scholarly thinking about morality. That is to say, from an anthropological point of view, morality is not just a set of principles, norms, and values; it is also—and probably more so—about how those principles, norms, and values are made manifest, negotiated, violated, reconciled, and transformed in the context of humans living in the worlds they construct for themselves and for each other.

In treating design as socially and materially mediated morality, I'm building on Michael Lambek's (2010) concept of "ordinary ethics" (cf. Das 2015). Rather than situating morality primarily in either society or an individual's mind, this perspective treats "the ethical as a modality of social action or of being in the world" (Lambek 2010, 10)—in particular, being in a world populated by others. And further, if designing is always designing for others, it also entails some more or less empathetic stance. Here I'm following work in the anthropology of empathy (e.g., Throop 2008, 2010, 2012a, 2012b), which attempts to uncover the culturally inflected ways in which humans understand the minds, emotions, and lives or other humans. At a basic level, this involves "(1) a decentering of the self from its own historically and culturally situated self-experience; (2) imagining the perspective of another from a quasi-first-person perspective; and (3) approximating the feelings, emotions, motives, concerns, and thoughts of another mind" (Throop 2008, 405).

This, then, is the sort of conceptual material that an anthropological conceptualization of design and designing would be built with. It begins with the idea that design is an inherently mediating form of social action and that all designed things are, even if only in microscopic ways, behavior-steering; as such, designers who design things for others are morally implicated in the worlds those others and their things inhabit. This conceptualization also adopts the perspective that morality is primarily found in and concerned with the lived world and social action—that is, action directed toward other humans. And entangled in this morality is some substance of empathy—or perhaps a notable a lack of empathy—as a method for adopting an understanding of the people for whom designers design.

Almost all of the anthropological research on morality thus far, even though it leans toward emphasizing the social, has within that context focused most attention on individual conduct, individual reason and emotion, and interpersonal interactions. This usually involves exploring culturally situated normative claims about how one ought to act toward others. What I'm proposing here is treating design (and not just "good design") as a kind of "ethics at a distance" in which actual living people (designers, of all different stripes), through the objects, spaces, and interfaces that they create, provision the textures, colors, forms, and structures of the everyday world and, by extension, everyday life. This in turn operates as an extension of the human capacity to reach into, and give shape to, the experiences of others.

To reiterate, design is an ever-present aspect of the worlds humans inhabit. It's not just relegated to special objects and domains (technology, skyscrapers, disability, the anthropocene, etc.), and it's not just influencing us in obviously good or obviously bad ways. Design is a part of practically everything, particularly in the urban and suburban parts of the world, but also to some extent everywhere else too. (There are probably very few places on earth that have not been touched by design.) What follows from this is that issues of morality—a morality mediated through design—are also ever-present.

Among the relatively small number of anthropologists who've spent some time examining design and its implications, the hovering presence of morality, while rarely the topic of explicit attention, has not gone entirely unnoticed. Natasha Dow Schüll's (2014) comprehensive study of machine gambling in Las Vegas demonstrates clearly the complex moral questions implicated in what may otherwise seem to be a neutral design process. For casino owners (and the architects and interior designers who work for them), constructing a successful casino floor involves several related objectives, including leading gamblers into the space, directing them to the games they want to play, making them feel comfortable while playing those games, and keeping them playing for as long as possible. In order to do this, practically every detail of the space is considered and designed, from lighting angles and the arrangement of machines to acoustic levels, ceiling heights, and even ambient aromas. Likewise, slot-machine engineers and software designers have developed increasingly sophisticated ways to help gamblers play faster, stay on the machines longer, and feel as if their on-machine experience is richer, even if they themselves are not. When viewed from a certain angle, this arrangement fits a typical design model touted in market-driven contexts: that casinos and allied industries design products and experiences that increase profits by directly responding to consumer demand—a winning situation for all parties involved. The consequences on the lives of individual consumers are not always innocuous, however, as the drive for more and more play that this design model serves can create and exacerbate compulsive behaviors that, if left unchecked, can spell disaster—financial, emotional, and even physical—for gamblers seduced by the casino's design techniques.

Lochlann Jain (2004, 2006) has explored the intersection of injury law and product design in the United States. In American culture interactions between bodies and consumer products are typically assumed to be either neutral or beneficial to the user, and when something does go wrong, even to innocent bystanders (Jain 2004), the problem is usually at first attributed to some cause outside the object's design (for instance, "user error" or "accident"). But designed objects are, of course, not always benevolent in their operations, and when product-related bodily harm affects large numbers of people in similar ways across space and time, and companies do nothing to address consumer concerns, injury law functions as a primary mechanism for possible remediation. Jain's (2006) analysis is centered on how poorly conceived forms and functions of particular objects—including the the short-handled hoe, a staple of agricultural work before the 1970s, and the typewriter and computer keyboard—lead to specific kinds of bodily harm and how injury law works in the fight to receive that remediation. Jain argues that while injury law cultivates conditions within which links between citizens, the state, and corporations are forged—conditions whose fairness and justice are unevenly distributed—it also, crucially, helps give form and affective inflection to broader cultural understandings of bodies, things, and the relations between them.

In my own work on Swedish design (Murphy 2015), I trace how certain forms, materials, discourses, and everyday objects have historically been, and continue to be, transformed into vectors of moralizing social-democratic ideologies concerning care, equality, and democracy in Swedish society. Krisztina Fehérváry (2013) details the complex parallel relationship between design style, state politics, and everyday affect in Hungary during the second half of the twentieth century. Fehérváry identifies and elaborates five different but related aesthetic regimes, including familiar ones such as socialist realism and more distinct ones such as organicist modern, which have more or less successively given form to the material world in Hungary since World War II. In the transition to socialism, and the subsequent transition away from socialism, particular qualities of architecture, city planning, and everyday objects, such as furniture and other household items, not only indexed dominant design preferences of the ruling political class but also acted as critical affective morality mediators between that ruling class and Hungarian citizens in their everyday lives. As Fehérváry demonstrates, far from plugging along under a tyranny of oppressive architectural forms and washed-out monochromatic decor, as is popularly imagined in the West, during socialism and its immediate aftermath Hungarians relied upon the materiality of their everyday world to both understand and take some control of their own shifting sociopolitical cosmologies.

In all of these cases design manifests in complicated ways, morally implicated in the various lifeworlds in which designers intervene through their creations. None of them portray design or designers as unambiguously good or unambiguously bad. Instead, what we see is that design is both *swept up in* and *generative of* social, cultural, and political—not to mention material, economic, and psychological—conditions that collectively and fundamentally constitute the very worlds that humans inhabit, the scenes in which they enact their own lives. If humans are shaped at least in part by their social environments, and those environments are largely made up of things and structures, and those things and structures are largely designed by other humans, then designers are always playing a part—a mediated part, to be sure—in giving shape and social form to other humans.

Conclusion

This chapter was motivated by at least two factors. The first was to articulate and develop the concept of form-giving, a category of action that underlies and supports many different kinds of world-making. Part of doing so required attending to both "form" and "giving" as concepts, as well as to the moral encoding of form-giving—and thus world-making, more generally. The second motivating factor was to explore design in particular through the lens of social form-giving. The term "form-giving" itself comes from design, of course, but my intention was to expand and extend its application beyond the workaday details of designing objects of various kinds to show how form-giving, in design and elsewhere, reaches outward beyond the things themselves into the social world—and how this is implicated in the creation and reproduction of the moral textures that bind people together. The hope was that this approach, both inspired by and exemplified by design, can help generate new ways for understanding how humans build their worlds with and for one another—for better and worse.

As a final note, to the degree that this analysis stems from the perspective of an "anthropology of design," it raises a problem that faces how such a subfield might continue to take form. It's similar to the problem that Alfred Gell (1992) discusses at the start of his essay "The Technology of Enchantment and the Enchantment of Technology," while ruminating on the anthropology of art: To what degree are anthropologists who study design "captured" by their own object of inquiry? Designers, many design researchers, and many others love to tout the salutary power of design without fully acknowledging design's many downsides (what this means, of course, depends on what particular kind of design one is looking at). One worry I have is that anthropologists of design get seduced by the very seductive discourses of design that espouse the kind of "goodness" we've come to desire in ourselves as a discipline. I often feel myself falling into this trap. But on the other side, there is also the possibility that anthropology's sharp critical edge will dismiss design as merely a tool of capitalism and modernity and, therefore, as an oppressive force that should be pushed back against and heavily critiqued. This is something that I also often feel. It seems to me, though, that a dynamic anthropology of design should tack back and forth between these two perspectives, so as not to settle on one particular hill, but rather to turn a skeptical but curious gaze toward the vast valley in between, figuring out what design is as a form of human action and what it's doing for particular groups of people in their particular social worlds.

Notes

1. For a number of reasons, deputizing design to exemplify a more general analysis is not such an easy task. The phenomenon of design takes many guises, encompassing objects, styles, practices, ways of working and thinking, aesthetics, materialities, and much more. Moreover, people often work with very different

ideas about what design even is depending on their points of entry, or areas of familiarity—for example, while the fields of architecture, software engineering, furniture making, and urban planning all purport to truck in design, they do not position design, or even talk about it, in the same ways. But this inherent variability in how design is discussed, understood, and operationalized in the world is precisely why I think devising a way to analyze it as a broad kind of form-giving, without immediately pigeonholing it as one thing or another, is so worthwhile.

2. I want to thank the SAR participants and Justin Richland for the tremendously valuable feedback they gave on earlier iterations of this chapter.

3. Recently anthropologists have grown interested in questions of ethics and morality from a sociocultural point of view (e.g., Das 2015; Keane 2016; Laidlaw 2013; Lambek 2010; Zigon 2008), but with notable disparities among them, it seems even they haven't been able to resolve the ambiguity in terms.

4. Note that Pruitt and Igoe were originally planned as separate communities for Black folks and whites before the Supreme Court banned such segregation.

5. Folks like Emile Durkheim and E. E. Evans-Pritchard are often cited as having laid the groundwork for conceptualizing morality, but Signe Howell's (1997) edited volume tends to initiate the start of the contemporary trend, though it seems to have only picked up steam since about 2008.

6. There is also a related stream of thought, most notably advocated by Joel Robbins (2013), pushing for an "anthropology of the good." Note that Robbins's call for initiating "an anthropology of the good" pivots on the same stark division cleaving bad design and good design—or in this case, suffering and a better life:

> The point of developing this new kind of anthropology would not be to displace the anthropology of suffering, which will continue for the foreseeable future to address problems we need to face. It would be to help realize in a distinctively anthropological way the promise suffering slot anthropology always at least implicitly makes: that there must be better ways to live than the ones it documents. (2013, 458)

CHAPTER SEVEN

Money Troubles

Designing a Bridge to the Ephemera of Expectations

DOUGLAS R. HOLMES

Monetary regimes are among the most complex and pervasive symbolic systems we know of and yet they are poorly understood—acknowledged even—by anthropologists. In their current form these systems have been designed by tiny cadres of current and former government officials working primarily within central banks (and academic departments) in order to regulate the availability of money and credit to the financial system and the economy at large. As I will argue below, built into the design of the contemporary monetary regime managed by central banks is a series of radical imperatives by which the architecture of markets unfolds as a function of language, an architecture whereby the value of money is anchored by means of expectations.

Why should anthropologists care? To begin with the monetary regime influences virtually every economic transaction, every appraisal of commodity value, and every calculation of wealth and impoverishment. The regime is foundational to any formulation of contemporary political economy. Further, the design features of the regime were repurposed to address the staggering contingencies of the financial crisis of 2008 and the devastating economic consequences of the pandemic that commenced in early 2020. To investigate these remarkable and in many respects unprecedented interventions—whether you agree with them or not—requires an understanding of the basic design elements of the regime and the roles of the people who operate them. It is a regime endowed with extraordinary powers and stunning liabilities to which our economic fates are tethered (Holmes 2014a, 2014b, 2016, 2018; Riles 2018; Rudnyckyj 2019).

This chapter is divided in two parts. The first deals with the basic design brief and the range of solutions that have been worked out over the last three decades to address various exigencies of money and credit. The solutions, particularly since the onset of the financial crisis in late 2008, have undergone continuous revision, refinement, and repurposing. Drawing on my ethnographic work in five central banks—the European Central Bank, the Bundesbank, the Reserve Bank of New Zealand, the Riksbank, and the Bank of England—I provide background material on the intellectual regime underwriting monetary affairs, its communicative technology, and its forward-looking capabilities.

The second part examines how the communicative technology works (or not) from the perspective of the Bank of England, where I am currently conducting research (Gabor and Jessop 2015). For the purposes of consistency and to stabilize as much as possible a series of key analytical concepts, I have repeated (often verbatim) sections from my earlier publications. I have also sought to demonstrate how my own practices as an ethnographer are implicated in the design story, as a necessary adjunctive to the regime and decisive for its performative efficacy (Austin 1961; Callon 2007; MacKenzie 2006; MacKenzie et al. 2007; Searle 1969). The questions addressed herein have an intricate history, and the design challenges have been addressed by a number of luminaries of European intellectual history: Nicolaus Copernicus, Isaac Newton, David Hume, and John Maynard Keynes.

Part 1: Currency of Ideas

DESIGN BRIEFS

Here are the broad challenges and contingencies posed for designing a contemporary monetary regime:

1. Design a regime to anchor the value of money over time.
2. Design the regime employing the institutional apparatus of central banks for the purpose of achieving price stability.
3. Design the regime around the expectational nature of prices.
4. Delineate communicative practices that can shape expectations of individuals, households, and firms on the development of prices across various time horizons.
5. Develop a design solution that can be refunctioned—particularly in financial crises—to address a variety of pricing issues and, above all, to address the failure of financial markets to self-correct.

I explore these challenges via a series of texts and diagrams that illustrate both the design elements of the regime and the actual means and methods by which these features are employed to achieve particular ends. This is a sketch, a schematic, employing a tiny selection of documents drafted in a natural language that opens at least potentially a broad interdisciplinary participation in assessing and revising the fundamental dynamics of monetary affairs.

In contrast to the innovations that are key to the design solutions I am delineating, macroeconomists have arrived, unsurprisingly, at different solutions that they express in quantitative models, notably the Dynamic Stochastic General Equilibrium Models (DSGE). The two approaches manifest in distinctive technologies—quantitative and discursive—are by no means incompatible; rather, they provide different (at times radically different) perspectives on monetary affairs, the role of central bankers, and the means by which policy is formulated and enacted (Morgan 2012).

DESIGN WITHIN THE DESIGN

Major central banks produce on any given day hundreds, if not thousands, of pages of documents, speeches, and analytical texts, as well as graphs and charts, and behind these formal representations are incessant discussions that encompass the rhetorical and analytical practices employed by the personnel of these institutions. Further, many of the most important texts are serialized, articulating ongoing analyses and deliberations within these institutions. These accounts demand continual revision and updating in response to new data, information, and intelligence capturing how the economy unfolds prospectively.

My work as an ethnographer has since the early 2000s been aligned with particular means by which the economy and the financial system are modeled linguistically, communicatively, and relationally by the personnel of central banks. In this regard I have focused on what I term the "economy of words," encompassing the informational dynamics of narratives and other discursive practices (Holmes 2014a; Smart 1999). As we will see, much of my work can be traced back to an unlikely experiment pursued by a group of young economists working in the Reserve Bank of New Zealand beginning in the 1980s, known as "inflation targeting" (Bernanke et al. 1999; Singleton et al. 2006). This experiment is now foundational to the practices of virtually all central banks globally, and it serves as a basis for dealing with some of the most vexing issues posed by the financial crisis that began in 2008 and the economic collapse attendant on the COVID-19 pandemic that commenced in 2020.

As suggested above, I have my own design agenda, which is to open up issues of monetary affairs to broad interdisciplinary investigation as well as to robust scrutiny by the public at large (Holmes and Marcus 2021). I am not alone in this endeavor. Central bankers are themselves asking similar questions and, relatedly, acknowledging that macroeconomics and monetary theory are insufficient for addressing fully the exigencies of money and credit. Further, they concede that for the legitimacy and creditability of their institutions to be sustained they must strive for coherence and precision in their communications, enlisting various segments and strata of the public to participate in the monetary drama (Kelty 2019). I have thus foregrounded the means and methods by which the personnel of central banks employ their technical acumen and rhetorical expertise to recruit the public to achieve the ends of policy. Hence, there is a secondary design brief implicit in this project that speaks to my work as an ethnographer:

1. Design a collaborative relationship aligned with central bankers' institutional preoccupations and their evolving communicative practices.
2. Redesign the language of and for monetary policy such that it is intelligible from either the perspectives of the personnel working in central banks or the perspectives of anthropologists and countless other observers.

Here is the tricky part: these secondary issues are not merely about communicative or analytical conventions; they are essential features of a monetary regime in which reflexive perspectives are integral to the efficacy of policy interventions. Central bankers are experimenting with the deep cultural assumption animating money and credit. This experimentation with very distinctive types of economic performativity poses an acute and uncanny question: Can policy makers influence expectations not merely about the future but *in* the future and thereby shape and format economic behavior prospectively (Holmes 2014a)?

MONETARY REGIMES

Since the creation of the first systems of coinage in the Late Bronze Age, a series of vexing issues have recurred. One question in particular is at the heart of the experiments that have yielded the global monetary regime that emerged in the last quarter of the twentieth century: How can the value of money be preserved over time? This question goes to one of the key functions of money: its role as "a store of value." Luminaries such as Nicolaus Copernicus and Isaac Newton have addressed these design issues with intellectual rigor and, in the case of Newton, with religious zeal.

In 1526 Copernicus published a work entitled "Monetae cudendae ratio," which set out the earliest formulation of the "quantity theory of money." He postulated a fundamental relationship "between a stock of money, its velocity, its price level, and the output of an economy. . . . The supply of money," he pointed out, "is the major determinant of prices."[1] Copernicus's basic insights continue to inform the management of monetary affairs and are the basis of an agenda known as monetarism, which Milton Friedman (1970, 24) summarized as follows: "Inflation is always and everywhere a monetary phenomenon in the sense that it is and can be produced only by a more rapid increase in the quantity of money than in output."

For the last thirty years of Newton's life he served as the warden and then master of the Royal Mint, playing a key role in the Great Recoinage of 1698 and the Scottish Recoinage of 1707–1710, which created a common currency for the new United Kingdom. Further, on Newton's recommendations in 1717, a Royal Proclamation established an official exchange rate between gold and silver that had the effect of driving silver coins out of circulation and creating a de facto gold standard for Britain.[2] Newton was also known for his ardent prosecutions of "counterfeiters" and "clippers," whose actions debased the currency, stripping both its physical and symbolic value. He personally pursued these prosecutions with religious fervor—he viewed debasement as a crime against God and king—and he relentlessly sought the execution of notorious perpetrators.

If Isaac Newton in 1717 established the gold standard for the United Kingdom, then David Hume in 1752 provided the design for anchoring the monetary affairs by virtue of gold within a system of international trade. Here are the basic features of Hume's "price-species flow model":

Hume considered a world in which only gold coin circulated and the role of banks was negligible. Each time merchandise was exported, the exporter received payment in gold, which he took to the mint to have coined. Each time an importer purchased merchandise abroad, he made payment by exporting gold.

For a country with a trade deficit, the second set of transactions exceeded the first. It experienced a gold outflow, which set in motion a self-correcting chain of events. With less money (gold coin) circulating internally, prices fell in the deficit country. With more money (gold coin) circulating abroad, prices rose in the surplus country. The specie flow thereby produced a change in relative prices (hence the name "price-specie flow model").

Imported goods having become more expensive, domestic residents would reduce their purchases of them. Foreigners, for whom imported goods had become less expensive, would be inclined to purchase more. The deficit country's exports would rise, and its imports fall, until the trade imbalance was eliminated. (Eichengreen 2008, 24–25)

Gold did not become a fully global monetary standard until the late nineteenth century, and then primarily within Europe, yet its flaws were already apparent (Desan 2014). Indeed, much of the agenda of contemporary monetary affairs is predicated on overcoming the failures of the gold standard, specifically its constraints on growth, its limitations on the availability of money and credit, and its role in provoking and exacerbating recurrent financial instabilities and crises (Eichengreen 2008).

In the early twentieth century a group emerged known as monetary reformers, notably J. M. Keynes, who contended that human intervention—government policy formulated by a technocratic elite—provided a more workable alternative to the inert metal, what he termed "a barbarous relic." The resulting agendas of "discretionary monetary policy"—underwritten by theory—inserted *ideas* at the center of monetary affairs, ideas that became the basis of what has come to be known as macroeconomics, the epistemic framework guiding the work of central bankers.

WHAT DO CENTRAL BANKERS DO?

Central bankers set periodically what is known as the policy rate—the federal funds rate in the United States, the repo rate in Sweden, the interest rate on the ECB's main refinancing operations (MRO), and the Official Bank Rate in the United Kingdom, to name just a few. These interest rates, determined by the respective banks' Monetary Policy Committee (MPC), can have profound

effects on virtually every transaction in the economy by influencing expectations about the pacing of economic activity prospectively. The policy rate establishes the "risk-free" cost of money against which virtually all other interest
rates are calibrated; therefore, the policy rate is foundational to the pricing of
financial risk in the economy and the financial system. Primarily by means of
central banks' "open-market operations," the buying and selling of government
securities, market interest rates are stabilized by the central bank at or near the
policy rate set by these monetary policy committees.

Central bankers, who number in the dozens globally, are thus required
under normal circumstances and as a matter of law to make one policy decision on the course of interest rates—up, down, or unchanged—every six
weeks or so. That's it, or so it would seem. The rest of the work of monetary
affairs is conventionally understood to be performed elsewhere, by the financial markets and banking systems. In other words, the policy rate by means
of various forms of arbitrage works its way over time through the financial
and banking systems, influencing virtually every interest rate in the economy from the pricing of government bonds and commercial paper to the
interest rates for mortgages, car loans, credit cards, and so on. The change in
the calibration of a single interest rate—again, the central bank policy rate—
can and does have powerful and, in times of crisis, profound effects on the
pacing of economic activity as a whole, reflected most notably in changes in
Gross Domestc Product (GDP), employment, savings, investment, exchange
rates, and prices (inflation or deflation). These variables constitute the key
indices of the macroeconomy. What macroeconomics provides are research
tools—models—for evaluating economic conditions and forecasting their
development across various time horizons. Monetary interventions operate
with what Milton Friedman (1948) termed "long and variable lags," creating a
decisive predicament for central bankers. Monetary policy decisions can take
as long as two years to have a full and measurable effect on the economy at
large. Compounding the predicament, the data the central bankers employ to
inform their decisions in "real time" are typically belated, rendering the current state of the economy difficult, if not impossible, to fully appraise. In other
words, central bankers must make decisions in the present about the future
course of the economy with data that are essentially historical. Resolving this
"intertemporal problem" became fundamental for the design solution that has
come to be known as inflation targeting.

THE DESIGN SOLUTION

In the wake of the collapse in the early 1970s of the system of fixed-exchange rates that prevailed under the Bretton Woods Agreements, a series of experiments emerged that have come to be known, again, as inflation targeting (Bernanke et al. 1999). The inflation-targeting framework, the prototype of which was designed by personnel at the Reserve Bank of New Zealand, imparted to discretionary monetary policy a series of technical innovations to address the practical issues of retaining the value of money prospectively. Over the last three decades virtually all the major central banks of the world have adopted fundamental elements of the New Zealand model to influence the development of the general level of prices. The framework, as we will see, was also critically important insofar as it became decisive for managing some of the most vexing issues posed by financial crises.

A severe financial crisis in New Zealand in 1984, a crisis with overt Orwellian overtones, prefigured the efforts of a group of young economists working within the Reserve Bank of New Zealand to design and build a central bank and monetary regime from scratch (Arthur Grimes personal communication; Singleton et al. 2006). The experimental framework the Kiwis designed provided a practical means to stabilize prices over time. Their solution yielded a sweeping series of innovations, a design solution that revolutionized monetary policy globally (Bernanke et al. 1999; Blinder 2004).

It began with the creation of an "independent central bank," a monetary institution that was insulated from political interventions and manipulations while bound by clearly defined legal mandates with measurable parameters by which the performance of the central bank could be evaluated. These mandates typically specified a target for inflation, usually on or around 2 percent, and in most cases a broad directive for monetary policy to support economic growth and employment. Institutional credibility was an overriding concern. Here are its core features:

1. The logic or theory impelling this experimental design can be summarized as follows: if the behavior of prices is "expectational"—as Irving Fisher, J. M. Keynes, Knut Wicksell, and others proposed as early as the 1890s—then an anticipatory policy that projects central bank action into the future becomes a means to influence these sentiments.

2. The instruments developed to manage expectation are expressed most concisely in official statements—typically running between five hundred and a few thousand words—which the major central banks of the world publish periodically in support of their interest rate decisions. Rounds of speeches and press conferences by senior personnel of central banks elaborate and explain policy statements in relationship to research and analysis on the trajectory of economic and financial conditions.

3. These "macroeconomic allegories," as Alan Blinder and Ricardo Reis (2005) term them—in clear evocation of the persuasive labor these narratives are called upon to perform—draw on the full intellectual resources of these institutions, the research acumen, the judgment, the experience, and the rhetorical skill of their personnel (McCloskey 1985; Morgan 2012; Yellen 2013). They project a forecast of economic and financial conditions over a time horizon of approximately one to two years, along with an explanation of how the respective banks' interest rate policy will achieve particular outcomes.

4. As economic agents—that is, you and I—assimilate policy intentions as our own *personal* expectations, we do the work of the central bank. Our expectations themselves can thus influence the course of inflationary and deflationary processes independent of (or in anticipation of) conventional interventions on interest rates (Merton 1948). The bridge to the ephemera of expectations—expectations that shape economic behavior prospectively—is constructed with words, demonstrating inter alia how markets themselves are fundamentally discursive phenomena.

This initial design breakthrough was almost immediately repurposed to address another fundamental challenge. Ben Bernanke and a group of his colleagues, notably Paul Krugman, recognized that the protocols of inflation targeting could be modified in such a way as to explain and resolve the *deflationary* dynamic that had plagued the Japanese economy since the late 1980s (Tett 2003). Indeed, their design solutions—notably to the problems of a "liquidity trap," a situation in which conventional monetary policy, based on the calibration of interest rates, no longer has any stimulative effect on the economy—were remarkably prescient. They too were subsequently repurposed, becoming the intellectual foundation for managing some of the most troublesome aspects of the global financial crisis of the early 2000s and the economic collapse initiated by the 2020 pandemic. Inflation targeting provided a solution by which to stabilize the economy and restore economic growth in the face of a looming recession or outright depression.

ESCAPING THE LIQUIDITY TRAP

Why had the vibrant and robust expansion of the Japanese economy that marked most of the postwar era suddenly succumbed to the lurching slump that had plagued the Japanese economy into the new century? These "lost decades," as they are termed, posed questions for monetary economics and, indeed, they reopened classic issues about the etiology of the Great Depression.

Paul Krugman in December 1999 began his analysis with a rhetorical statement: "So far only Japan has actually found itself in liquidity-trap conditions, but if it has happened once it can happen again, and if it can happen here it presumably can happen elsewhere. So even if Japan does eventually emerge from its slump, the question of how it became trapped and what to do about it remains a pressing one" (Krugman 1999). This predication, of course, came to fruition within a decade and then reasserted itself with even greater force early in 2020.

Krugman worked out the "essential logic of liquidity-trap economics," and he then laid out a series of alternative monetary strategies to deal with the Japanese situation. He began his analysis candidly with his own initial skepticism about the plausibility of the liquidity trap—viewing it initially as an artifact of "intellectual corner-cutting" of the standard Keynesian/Hicksian IS-LM framework.[3] He then went on to delineate his approach, showing how a liquidity trap *can* happen and, more importantly, how monetary policy—specifically inflation targeting—could be modified to escape the conundrum of stagnation by "promising to be irresponsible":

> So the intertemporal approach led me to a different destination than I expected. I thought it would show that the liquidity trap was not a real issue, that without the inconsistencies of the IS-LM model it would become clear that it could not really happen. Instead it turns out that a liquidity trap can indeed happen; but that it is in a fundamental sense an expectational issue. Monetary expansion is irrelevant because the private sector does not expect it to be sustained, because they believe that given a chance the central bank will revert to type and stabilize prices. And in

order to make monetary policy effective, at least in a simple model, the central bank must overcome a credibility problem that is the inverse of our usual one. In a liquidity trap monetary policy does not work because the markets expect the bank to revert as soon as possible to the normal practice of stabilizing prices; to make it effective, the central bank must credibly promise to be irresponsible, to maintain its expansion after the recession is past.

He concludes:

> Let me say this perhaps more forcefully than I have in the past. Inflation targeting is not just a clever idea—a particular proposal that might work in fighting a liquidity trap. *It is the theoretically "correct" response*—that is, inflation targeting is the way to achieve in a sticky-price world the same result that would obtain if prices were perfectly flexible. Of course in policy the perfect is the enemy of the good, and I would not oppose trying a variety of tactics to fight Japan's stagnation. But it is inflation targeting that most nearly approaches the usual goal of modern stabilization policy, which is to provide adequate demand in a clean, unobtrusive way that does not distort the allocation of resources. (Krugman 1999, emphasis in the original)

Again, within a decade, these circumstances, as Krugman had foreseen, were manifest globally and the design solution he outlined became a basis of emergency measures orchestrated by major central banks. One of the decisive design features of the framework is its dependence on forecasts—its ability to project the behavior of prices, the direction and magnitude of economic growth and employment, and the performance of other macroeconomic variables into the future. To examine the operation of this forward-looking design element I have gone back approximately two years before the onset of the crisis of 2020. Again, twenty-four months is an important temporal horizon because it is roughly the time it takes for the full impact of monetary policy to have measurable effects and, thus, it is the time frame that preoccupies policy makers.

I then turn in the second part of the chapter to the efforts of the Bank of England to deal with a situation in which data have failed, when information on the economy in the present and near future are unavailable. For the Bank to shape expectations it had to find other discursive means to tether expectations. I conclude with a very brief aside about how a democratic public is emerging in crisis (Dewey [1927] 1991; Lippmann [1927] 2002).

Part 2: "Monetary Policy à Outrance"

QUANTITATIVE EASING

In 2009 the Bank of England described the dilemmas posed by the financial crisis and its plan to address them via a strategy, quantitative easing (QE), broadly in line with Krugman's analysis:

> Significant reductions in Bank Rate to date have provided a large stimulus to the economy but as Bank Rate approaches zero, further reductions are likely to be less effective in terms of the transmission to market interest rates and the impact on demand and inflation. And interest rates cannot be less than zero.
>
> The [Bank] . . . therefore needs to provide further stimulus to support demand in the wider economy. It boosts the supply of money by purchasing assets like Government and corporate bonds—a policy sometimes known as "Quantitative Easing". Instead of lowering Bank Rate to increase the amount of money in the economy, the Bank supplies extra money directly. This does not involve printing more banknotes but rather the Bank pays for these assets by creating money electronically and crediting the accounts of the companies it bought the assets from. This extra money supports more spending in the economy to bring future inflation back to the target.
>
> In essence, when spending on goods and services is too low, inflation will fall below its target. With Bank Rate already at a very low level, a further measured stimulus is needed through an increase in the quantity of money. (Bank of England 2009)

As the crisis unfolded, monetary policy interventions shifted from the price of money—regulated by interest rates—to the quantity of money. As the risks of inflation were superseded by the perils of deflation, the major central banks of the world employed their balance sheets to create massive quantities of money— liquidity—to avert what was widely perceived to be a looming economic catastrophe (Bernanke 2020). By early 2020 the scale of these interventions was staggering: the Bank of England held 26 percent of all UK government debt (Vlieghe 2020). It was monetary policy of saturation, "à outrance."

To achieve the full impact of these remarkable monetary interventions, central banks had to inform the public not merely about the behavior of prices but about the operation of the monetary system more generally. Relatedly, the Bank had to communicate its intentions to act prospectively, a practice known as "forward guidance" (Woodford 2012; Fischer 2016).

TWO FAN CHARTS

Two "fan charts," published in August 2018 by the Bank, are "projections" of the development of prices (inflation/deflation) and output (GDP) over the medium term, and as such they are critical to the operation of forward guidance.

The darker bands represent, in the judgment of the Bank's officials, more likely outcomes and lighter bands less likely ones. The black line labeled "ONS data" on the green chart is the more conventional tracking of output as calculated by the United Kingdom's Office of National Statistics. As the green chart also demonstrates, the Bank prefers to view the past probabilistically, suggesting that the past and not just the future remains uncertain from the perspective of August 2018. This uncertainty, graphically represented, is itself important as it reveals the Bank's acknowledgment of the limitations—indeed severe limitations—of macroeconomic forecasting. To say that inflation three years hence will range between negative 0.5 percent and positive 4.5 percent and output will be somewhere between negative 1.5 percent and positive 4.5 percent is hardly an expression of analytical precision. Rather it reflects pervasive uncertainty about the future and the limitations of the instruments used to forecast it (Tuckett et al. 2020). Crucially, the Bank was grappling with a particular problem, the uncertainties surrounding Brexit—the withdrawal of the United Kingdom from the EU. There is obviously no hint of pandemic in the graphic projections.

There is another curious element to both charts that is fundamental to the rhetorical design of the monetary system. The fan charts are representing phenomena, the behavior of prices and output, that the Bank can and will seek to influence by means of its policy actions. They are not representations of natural phenomena governed by forces independent of human agency; they are fully within the Bank's statutory authority to act upon and otherwise influence by means of powerful macroeconomic incentives. Hence, the predisposition of the

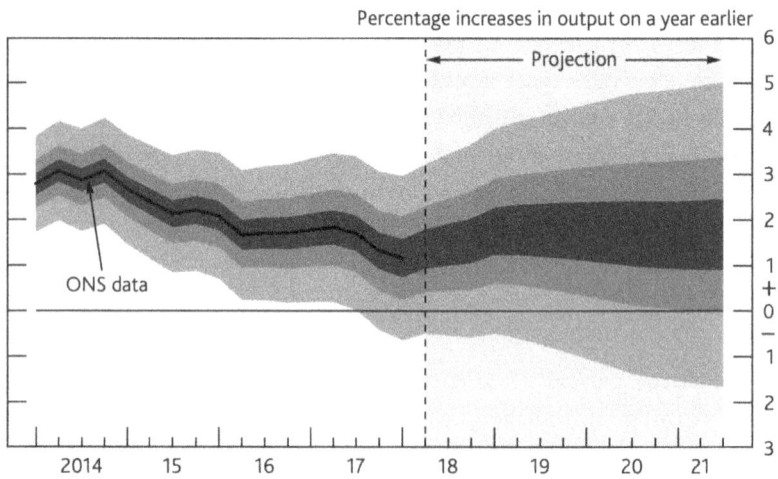

Percentage increases in output on a year earlier

Figure 7.1. GDP projection (wide bands).

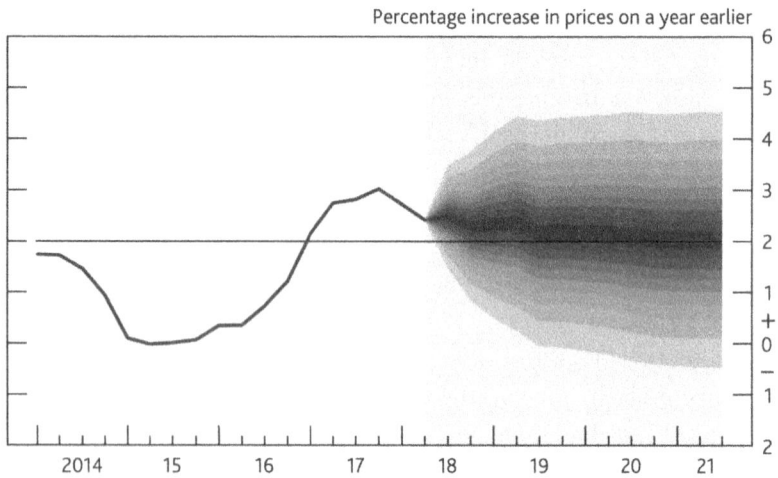

Percentage increase in prices on a year earlier

Figure 7.2. CPI inflation projection (narrow bands).

Bank's officialdom to act in the future is registered graphically in the dark and light hues of the charts.

There is one final point, perhaps the most important point, about these curious representations. The public is a party to them. By means of the monetary policy narrative imparted by these charts and other graphic and rhetorical devices, the Bank seeks to shape expectation in and about the future. Hence the two fan charts are part of a technology of persuasion.

Forward guidance is predicated on communicating the Bank's "reaction function": its commitment to act in relationship to new data and information. Here is how former Bank governor Mark Carney described these commitments in May 2018:

> That is why the Committee provided forward guidance that explicitly linked any potential change in interest rates to the unemployment rate—a clear and widely understood indicator of the degree of slack. The Committee's objective was to secure the nascent recovery while learning more about the supply capacity of the economy.
>
> The message the Committee gave UK households and businesses was simple: the MPC would not even think about tightening policy at least until the unemployment rate had fallen below 7%, consistent with the creation of around three quarter of a million jobs. We reassured households and businesses that, after five years of decline and stagnation, the recovery would not be choked off prematurely. (Carney 2018)

And this commitment to future action is, as we will see below, central to how officials of the Bank of England were addressing the challenges that surfaced in mid-2018 and then again in early 2020.

PRESS RELEASE

Here is the press release announcing the MPC's decision on August 1, 2018, regarding interest rates and the committee's rationale for the decision:

> Monetary Policy Summary and minutes of the Monetary Policy Committee meeting
>
> Published on 02 August 2018

The Bank of England's Monetary Policy Committee (MPC) sets monetary policy to meet the 2% inflation target, and in a way that helps to sustain growth and employment. At its meeting ending on 1 August 2018, the MPC voted unanimously to increase Bank Rate by 0.25 percentage points, to 0.75%.

The Committee voted unanimously to maintain the stock of sterling non-financial investment-grade corporate bond purchases, financed by the issuance of central bank reserves, at £10 billion. The Committee also voted unanimously to maintain the stock of UK government bond purchases, financed by the issuance of central bank reserves, at £435 billion.

Since the May Inflation Report, the near-term outlook has evolved broadly in line with the MPC's expectations. Recent data appear to confirm that the dip in output in the first quarter was temporary, with momentum recovering in the second quarter. The labour market has continued to tighten and unit labour cost growth has firmed.

The MPC's updated projections for inflation and activity are set out in the August Inflation Report and are broadly similar to its projections in May.

In the MPC's central forecast, conditioned on the gently rising path of Bank Rate implied by current market yields, GDP is expected to grow by around 1¾% per year on average over the forecast period. Global demand grows above its estimated potential rate and financial conditions remain accommodative, although both are somewhat less supportive of UK activity over the forecast period. Net trade and business investment continue to support UK activity, while consumption grows in line with the subdued pace of real incomes.

Although modest by historical standards, the projected pace of GDP growth over the forecast is slightly faster than the diminished rate of supply growth, which averages around 1½% per year. The MPC continues to judge that the UK economy currently has a very limited degree of slack. Unemployment is low and is projected to fall a little further. In the MPC's central projection, therefore, a small margin of excess demand emerges by late 2019 and builds thereafter, feeding through into higher growth in domestic costs than has been seen over recent years.

CPI inflation was 2.4% in June, pushed above the 2% target by external cost pressures resulting from the effects of sterling's past depreciation and higher energy prices. The contribution of external pressures is projected to ease over the forecast period while the contribution of domestic cost pressures is expected to rise. Taking these influences together, and conditioned on the gently rising path of Bank Rate implied by current market yields, CPI inflation remains slightly above 2% through most of the forecast period, reaching the target in the third year.

The MPC continues to recognise that the economic outlook could be influenced significantly by the response of households, businesses and financial markets to developments related to the process of EU withdrawal.

The Committee judges that an increase in Bank Rate of 0.25 percentage points is warranted at this meeting.

The Committee also judges that, were the economy to continue to develop broadly in line with its Inflation Report projections, an ongoing tightening of monetary policy over the forecast period would be appropriate to return inflation sustainably to the 2% target at a conventional horizon. Any future increases in Bank Rate are likely to be at a gradual pace and to a limited extent. (Bank of England 2018)

The Bank was anticipating in this decision a gradual and limited tightening of interest rates as the economy improved in late 2018 and 2019 as the uncertainty surrounding Brexit receded. As of this writing in 2020, it turns out that the decisions in August 2018 to raise interest rates .25% as well as the prior interest rate increase of .50% at the end of 2017 were infelicitous, the analysis and the messaging were erroneous. By early 2020 there were signs that the United Kingdom's economy was, in fact, weakening even before the onset of the pandemic.

The two fan charts drafted in mid-2018 with forecasts reaching into 2021 did, however, project the possibility of a decline of output and prices as a nontrivial consequence of Brexit and related economic issues, notably the weakening of the Chinese and German economies. The forecasts also anticipated the possibility, albeit unlikely, of an economic recession, the projection of negative output over two quarters. But, of course, the economic effects of COVID-19 were absolutely unforeseen by means of the Bank's technologies of forecasting and projection.

By March 2020 all the resources of the Bank were being brought to bear on the astonishing medical, economic, and financial consequences of the pandemic—the most severe economic downturn in the United Kingdom since the "Great Frost of 1709." The monetary actions of the Bank were coordinated with the fiscal interventions of the British Treasury to stabilize the economy in the midst of the pandemic. Here are the minutes of the MPC's unscheduled meetings in March 2020:

Monetary Policy Summary and minutes of the Monetary Policy Committee meeting

Published on 19 March 2020

The spread of Covid-19 and the measures being taken to contain the virus will result in an economic shock that could be sharp and large, but should be temporary. The role of the Bank of England is to help to meet the needs of UK businesses and households in dealing with the associated economic disruption.

On 11 March, the Bank of England's three policy committees announced a package of measures to support UK businesses and households through this period. In his Budget on the same day, the Chancellor of the Exchequer announced a number of fiscal measures with the same aim. On 17 March, this combined package of measures was complemented by the announcement by HM Treasury of the Covid 19 Corporate Financing Facility (CCFF), for which the Bank will act as HM Treasury's agent. By purchasing commercial paper, the CCFF will provide funding to non-financial businesses making a material contribution to the UK economy to support them in paying salaries, rents and suppliers while experiencing the likely disruption to cashflows associated with Covid-19.

In light of actions to tackle the spread of the virus, and evidence relating to the global and domestic economy and financial markets, the Monetary Policy Committee (MPC) held an additional special meeting on 19 March. Over recent days, and in common with a number of other advanced economy bond markets, conditions in the UK gilt market have deteriorated as investors have sought shorter-dated instruments that are closer substitutes for highly liquid central bank reserves. As a consequence, UK and global financial conditions have tightened.

At its special meeting on 19 March, the MPC judged that a further package of measures was warranted to meet its statutory objectives. It therefore voted unanimously to increase the Bank of England's holdings of UK

government bonds and sterling non-financial investment-grade corporate
bonds by £200 billion to a total of £645 billion, financed by the issuance of
central bank reserves, and to reduce Bank Rate by 15 basis points to 0.1%.
The Committee also voted unanimously that the Bank of England should
enlarge the TFSME scheme, financed by the issuance of central bank
reserves.

The majority of additional asset purchases will comprise UK government bonds. The purchases announced today will be completed as soon
as is operationally possible, consistent with improved market functioning.
The Bank will issue further guidance to the market in due course. (Bank of
England 2020)

The Bank of England and other central banks of the world were engaged in
emergency interventions that drew on the full repertoire of techniques developed since 2008 to stabilize the financial system and the real economy (Bernanke 2020). These include pushing interest rates to zero, and in some cases below
zero; purchasing government and corporate debt to underwrite asset prices;
employing repo agreements with the US Federal Reserve System to secure
access to US dollars; and developing various ad hoc interventions as needed to
restore the functioning of credit and equity markets.

These actions were accomplished by a tiny cadre of experts who continually
scrutinize the behavior and misbehavior of markets as they appear on computer
screens. They orchestrate technical interventions as outlined in the minutes to
address the profound financial discord ignited by the spread of the COVID-
19 virus. They also observe, at times instantaneously, the effects of their own
interventions on multiple screens that track movements across various markets
(Knorr-Cetina 1999; Abolafia 2020).

The other domains of concerns were and are acutely communicative: model-
ing linguistically the relational dynamics underwriting stability and confidence
for market participants and the public at large. And this is accomplished, as I
have argued above, in a natural language designed to engage the public in particular forms of thought and action.

On the morning of March 11, 2020, Mark Carney, at the time the outgo-
ing governor of the Bank of England, and incoming governor Andrew Baily
held a joint press conference. It was the first effort by senior officials of any
major central bank to address systematically the gravity of the situation
posed by the pandemic as well as to delineate a meaningful course of action.

The performance was in many respects masterful, if only because it fully acknowledged the profound human and economic cost of the pandemic. In a candid conversation with the press corps that morning on Threadneedle Street, the two officials shared the Bank's view on the emerging crises—what was known and what was unknown—and explained the first series of interventions that were developed to address them. The crises were unpredictable, and available information was uncertain, but there was one overriding design imperative that the officials of the Bank were committing (or recommitting) themselves to.

If the crises were to be made tractable within the design framework outlined above, that could only be achieved by means of fidelity to the relationship that the Bank had sought to cultivate over three or four decades, a relationship that imparted a decisive analytical challenge for the Bank. Can the Bank articulate the predicaments—the dilemmas in the present and foreseeable future—facing various strata and segments of the public? Can these challenges be articulated not solely or necessarily by means of high-level mathematical reasoning and quantitative analysis, but in a language that captures the pragmatic contingencies of economic life entangled within a public-health emergency and a financial calamity? Stability and recovery were, thus, predicated on building a bridge to the ephemera of expectations of individuals, households, and firms—expectation that could inform their pragmatic problem-solving and planning and, thus, lay the foundations for recovery.

SCENARIO

The Monetary Policy Report for May 2020 runs approximately four thousand words. Rather than containing the usual analyses and forecasts, the report sought to explain discursively the channels through which the pandemic was likely to affect the economy. It is crafted as a narrative, a plausible "scenario," as the report notes, "conditioned on a set of stylized assumptions about the pandemic and the actions of governments, households and businesses and, as usual, on the prevailing levels of asset prices and the market path for interest rates. While the scenario is highly conditional, it helps illustrate the nature and potential scale of the impact of the pandemic on the economy." I have excerpted key elements of the scenario and the conditionalities shaping how the personnel of the Bank understood the challenges they faced in mid-2020. Here is a narrative template, the heuristic device by which bank personnel sought to explain to themselves and to the public at large the challenges they faced at the outset of the crisis:

Global GDP recovers from the sharp fall in activity in 2020 H1

Global GDP is estimated to have fallen sharply over the first half of 2020. While the exact paths of the falls in activity vary across regions, reflecting differences in the timing of public health measures being put in place, the impact of those measures is assumed to be broadly similar across the UK's main trading partners. The falls in GDP also partly reflect the tightening in financial conditions which has resulted from falls in risky asset prices around the world. Moreover, global spillovers—through supply chain disruption, for example—amplify the domestic shocks arising from the virus, including in the UK. As a result of some of these spillovers, the fall in world GDP is accompanied by a large reduction in world trade.

In the scenario, conditioned on the assumptions above, global activity recovers over the second half of the year, as social distancing measures are rolled back. The recovery is aided by the macroeconomic policies that have been put in place in many countries, which act to prevent significant longer-term damage to the global economy. There are some variations in the extent of support across countries, however.

In the scenario, PPP [purchasing power parity]-weighted world growth falls sharply from 3% in 2019 to -12% in 2020. It increases strongly in 2021—to 15%—reflecting the recovery in activity, before growing by 5% in 2022. Weighted by UK export shares, world GDP growth falls from 2% in 2019 to -13% in 2020. It recovers to 14% in 2021 and is around 4% in 2022.

The outlook for the UK in the scenario

UK GDP falls sharply in 2020 H1: it is expected to be close to 30% lower in Q2 than it was in 2019 Q4. Under the assumptions outlined above, it recovers relatively rapidly in Q3, as social distancing measures are gradually lifted, and rises further in Q4....

UK GDP in the scenario falls by 14% in 2020 as a whole. Activity picks up materially in the latter part of 2020 and into 2021 after social distancing measures are relaxed, although it does not reach its pre-Covid level until the second half of 2021. . . . In 2022, GDP growth is around 3%. Annual household consumption growth follows a similar pattern. . . . Household income growth is volatile. It falls in 2020, partly reflecting the fact that furloughed workers are paid 80% of their pay (up to £2,500 per month). It then picks up as those employees return to work. On average over the scenario period, consumption growth is weaker than household income growth, such that the saving ratio rises somewhat. Business investment declines very sharply in 2020, by 26% on average relative to 2019. Annual growth rises to 19% in 2021 and is then around 12% in 2022.

Conditioning assumptions underlying the illustrative scenario (abbreviated)

1. The illustrative scenario is conditioned on social distancing measures and government support schemes remaining as they are until early June, before being gradually unwound by the end of Q3.
2. The Coronavirus Job Retention Scheme lowers the number of jobs that are lost.
3. It is assumed that most furloughed workers do not seek work elsewhere.
4. Some companies are assumed to cease or scale back their operations for a time.
5. Some of the spending foregone while social distancing measures are in place is assumed to be made up . . .
6. . . . but lower confidence and higher uncertainty are assumed to persist for some time and dampen spending.
7. Falls in risky asset prices also weigh on GDP.
8. But monetary and fiscal policy actions support spending.
9. The illustrative scenario is conditioned on the assumption that the UK moves to a comprehensive free trade agreement with the EU on 1 January 2021.
10. . . . although heightened uncertainty weighs on spending by consumers and businesses for some time.
11. Lower investment and less innovation weigh on productivity further out.
12. GDP falls sharply in 2020 H1 before recovering following the relaxation of social distancing measures.
13. Lower demand in 2020 is assumed to lead to some downward pressure on inflation.

14. CPI inflation is very low in 2020, largely reflecting the marked decline in the oil price.

15. CPI inflation is around 2% in 2022.

Key sensitivity 1: the global economic outlook (abbreviated).

1. Policy actions around the world will affect the outlook for the UK . . . the evolution of the pandemic and the measures taken to contain it are assumed to be similar in other countries to those in the UK.

2. . . . including via spillover channels. For example, if firms in other countries supplying intermediate inputs to UK companies remain closed, the resulting supply chain disruption could lower UK activity, even if UK restrictions are lifted.

Key sensitivity 2: the persistence of the fall in UK activity (abbreviated).

1. The timing of the recovery will depend in large part on how long social distancing and support measures are in place.

2. The speed of the recovery will also be affected by how households and businesses respond once measures are lifted.

Key sensitivity 3: the degree of long-lasting scarring in the economy (abbreviated).

1. The eventual recovery in GDP will be affected by developments in the economy's supply capacity.

Key sensitivity 4: the impact of changes in economic activity on prices (abbreviated).

1. CPI inflation will be affected by how companies respond to changes in demand.

There are countless moving parts to the illustrative scenario and the conditioning assumptions and sensitivities underlying the account. In May 2020 the Bank had little in the way of reliable data on the state of the United Kingdom economy to draw on to perform their conventional policy analyses and interventions. As the Bank sought to look out over a profoundly uncertain time horizon of two years, they relied on narratives and other discursive devices to model the economy and financial system (Beckert 2016, 263).

LOAD-BEARING NARRATIVES

The repair of the United Kingdom economy was and is contingent on how individuals, households, and firms act in relationship to immediate and diverse challenges they face. The Bank can help by aligning macroeconomic incentives—most notably interest rates—but the restoration of consistent and reliable growth is in the hands of the British people, in how they conduct their lives, in how they appraise their livelihoods, and in how they understand their economic futures. The Bank acknowledges the damage to confidence and the potential of long-lasting, economic "scarring." It is reasonable to ask: Is the system capable of self-repair and of the restoration of confidence?

I have argued that there is within the inflation-targeting regime an alternative way of understanding *relationally* the role of the central bankers that can help us understand the challenges of repair and renovation prospectively.

> Central bankers seek to endow the future with discernible features that we—the public—can reflect and act upon, animating or curtailing our propensities to produce, consume, borrow, and lend. . . . Central bankers, rather than predicting the future, seek to create elements of a tractable future. They do this with words. They use language to explore, promulgate, and sustain the ideas that animate our economic future, as well as the structures of feeling, the sentiments, expectations, and desires that make them real. (Holmes 2018, 85)

I further argue how this can be understood as an "ethnographic challenge," or as a representational task:

> Central bankers create and enter, as it were, a communicative field in which countless protagonists model economic phenomenon for their own purposes, employing their own pragmatic insights and grounded truths. They (and we) are confronted with actors whose futures are enlivened by just about every emotional sensibility, every constellation of thought and belief, reason and unreason, rationality and irrationality, as well as every human proclivity to create truth, untruth, virtue, beauty, and depravity (Bronk 2009; Rudnyckyj 2014). The stories told by these unruly figurers can impel or impede the leaps of faith that ratify or foreclose a tractable future (Beckert 2016, 263). The efficacy of monetary policy thus rests on the

representational enterprise of these protagonists with whom central bankers must orchestrate prospectively the contingencies of economic stability and growth. (Holmes 2018, 85)

To complete the design of the regime thus requires fully acknowledging how economic and monetary affairs are enacted and by whom. The load-bearing capacity of monetary narratives relies on a certain form of alchemy—persuasion—by which expectations are translated into a regime of planning, animating (or curtailing) incrementally the propensities of a vast array of individuals, households, and firms to produce, consume, borrow, and lend. The monetary system depends on stories that can impel the leaps of faith that can ratify or foreclose a tractable future. This design solution also creates a place, a role even, for the anthropologist, a role in redrawing the boundaries of the monetary system and the parameters of thought and action that unfold across its dynamic mise-en-scène.

MONEY TROUBLES

My effort to recast the role of the central banker relationally began in 2008–2009 as I observed how the protocols of inflation target were modified by QE and forward guidance and around the problems of zero or negative interest rates. What I observed was that monetary policy was no longer a matter solely or necessarily for financial institutions, the banking system, and the interests of market participants; it fully implicated the public, a diversely constituted "democratic public." Further, I wondered if and how members of this emerging public would attain a voice. The Occupy Wall Street movement provided an inkling of a popular rejoinder to the discontents, the money troubles, posed by the financial crisis in 2008. It was, however, the measures orchestrated by central banks themselves to thwart the crisis that may well have fully legitimated the role of a democratic public in the management of money and credit.

In practice central bankers are aware of "distributional effects"—that is, who stands to benefit and who stands to lose as a result of a particular policy stance. In fact, every policy move has distributional consequences that need to be balanced against the aims and outcomes of particular interventions. When QE was initiated it was understood to be an emergency measure of limited duration, and its distributional effects were understood as temporary. That is certainly implied by the statement, given above, by the Bank of England in 2009 when it first announced its "unconventional" policies.

The effects of QE were not meant to be subtle or indirect—far from it. The massive purchase of assets had immediate consequences, stabilizing the value of financial assets and thus protecting or boosting the wealth of those individuals and institutions who held them. Central bankers fully understood this and only embarked on this and similar programs as a means to protect the broader economy—Main Street and Wall Street—from calamitous outcomes. Hence, there was little outcry at the outset when QE was understood to be a temporary measure to stimulate job creation, to lower interest rates, to encourage borrowing and investment, to increase GDP, and to rekindle inflationary expectations.

But QE lingered and central bankers found it tricky to fully exit. Programs for reducing the size of central bank balance sheets and tapering asset purchases have been initiated and repeatedly curtailed in the face of recurring signals of economic weakness. What was initially understood as a temporary expedient is now widely regarded as a permanent feature of monetary policy (Bernanke 2020). And, of course, the pandemic has initiated in early 2020 what are by far the largest programs of QE to date, programs that have been rightly credited with thwarting the immediate collapse of the economy and monetary system.

But as QE has taken on an enduring, if not permanent status, its potential to alter fundamental dynamics of political economy and to disrupt assumptions underwriting the social contract are worth noting. The enormous deficits accrued by governments to address the crisis have been largely placed on the balance sheets of central banks. QE allows governments to issue debt at extremely favorable interest rates (at or close to 0%), and this debt in the form of government securities is purchased immediately by the central bank. This kind of relationship has the potential, at least in theory, to incentivize elected officials to "monetize the debt," eroding its value by stimulating inflation. More immediately, as QE and other emergency measures become entrenched, their distributional effects become enduring, and significant shifts in wealth are thereby accomplished.

If, as I have argued, members of the public are not merely served by monetary policy, but they enact it, then words matter. And if words fail—if members of the public suspect that they are being recruited by central banks to achieve unworthy or unjust ends—then the architecture of the monetary regime is compromised. The bridge to the ephemera of expectations is rendered unsound. If monetary policy is seen to be consistently serving particular

distributional ends—instilling what Edward Shaw (1973) and Ronald McKinnon (1973) termed "financial repression"—then it is likely, inevitable even, that
a democratic public will assume an ardent voice in the monetary drama. It is
this new, critical design element that I have turned my attention to.

Notes

1. See Wikipedia, s.v. "Monetae cudendae ratio," accessed April 22, 2019, https://
   en.wikipedia.org/wiki/Monetae_cudendae_ratio.

2. See Wikipedia, s.v. "Later Life of Isaac Newton," accessed April 22, 2019, https://
   en.wikipedia.org/wiki/Later_life_of_Isaac_Newton.

3. IS/LM stands for Investment Saving / Liquidity preference Money supply. See
   Paul Krugman's short overview of the significance of John Hick's 1937 representation of Keynes's 1936 theoretical model, "There Is Something about Macro,"
   accessed March 4, 2021, http://web.mit.edu/krugman/www/islm.html.

Anthropology, Designing, and World-Making

ARTURO ESCOBAR

This constructive and farsighted statement on the potentialities, tensions, and difficulties characterizing the encounter between anthropology and design is a most welcome intervention into what has been an uneven, but steadily growing affair for close to two decades now. The engagement between the two fields has elicited all kinds of positions, from attraction and even fascination to suspicion and repulsion, with diverse critiques all along the spectrum. The conviction that there is something mutually enriching in the encounter is growing, even if the particular forms that such collaboration should take, if it wants to go beyond a purely utilitarian and instrumental relation, are still hugely contested. *Designs and Anthropologies* helps us move this agenda in useful ways, suggesting an initial mapping of this relationship in terms of the tripartite distribution of anthropology for and of design, on the one hand, and design for anthropology, on the other. From here, it arrives at the open-ended conclusion that the relation between design and anthropology will always have the character of a multiplicity, never to be singularized through any overarching formulation, nor rendered into a single idea of what "design anthropology" might be. In this brief text, I will offer some thoughts that I believe complement the volume's main contributions, partly coming from different sources or going in different directions, and sometimes in a contrapuntal relation to the arguments, in the musical sense of the term. I am tempted to suggest—in the spirit of what was a well-known rendition by Marilyn Strathern, from a seemingly bygone era (1987), of the relation between anthropology and feminism encompassed under the rubric of "feminist anthropology"—that in their attempt at coming together anthropology and design "mock each other"; in the dissonance of their encounter, they question each other's epistemologies, location, practices, their respective relations to the academy and "the real world," and their contrasting understandings of theory and the political. Many aspects of this awkward encounter surface in the volume's diverse chapters.[1] Despite the tensions, however, just as in the case of feminist anthropology, the encounter between anthropology and design is proving productive. Just to mention one of the most discussed tensions: while design's embeddedness in capitalism and commercialism constitutes an impassable red flag for many anthropologists from the perspective of practice-oriented design, anthropology's entrenchment in the academy, conversely, appears as an unwillingness to dare any sort of meaningful intervention, if not a cop-out of responsibility altogether. This is an old tension, of course, one long found at the heart of anthropology—for instance, in the debates between academic or applied and engaged forms of anthropology. In design contexts, however, the tension takes on new meaning, perhaps moving academic-oriented anthropology to be more self-reflexive about its own status as a practice beyond the academic walls. I will return to this issue since it continues to be a persistent trope at the anthropology/design interface.

There is another area of anthropological transdisciplinary engagement that comes to mind. In the heyday of anthropological science and technology studies, there was still a sense in which those working in the subjects at hand—nuclear physicists, molecular biologists, imaging technicians, biodiversity experts, computer modelers, development professionals, or what have you—were still our "tribe." No matter how much the anthropologist tried to get proficiency in the field in question, one could still practice a sort of distancing epistemology and nonengagement vis-à-vis his or her subjects. While this approach is still possible and legitimate in the anthropology of design, today's varieties of engagement are clearly more diverse. Design theorists and practitioners can be objects of study, interlocutors, collaborators, inspirations, and even sources of theory production, or several of these at the same time. This makes the relationship very complex, even if the dissonances persist. One could also mention cultural studies as another area of anthropological engagement that has seen these oscillations.

I believe there are a number of sources of unease that have permeated these encounters and that are still at play at the anthropology/design interface. One of these stems from academic anthropology's traditional hesitancy, especially in the Euro-American context, about "intervention" and what could be called the fear of the normative, sometimes failing to take into account that nonintervention is already intervention and that any discipline, anthropology included, is profoundly normative, even in its styles of critiques. As the introduction to the volume puts it, this amounts to a sort of "parochialism." It's high time, then, for the boundary between "academic" and "applied" (in whatever configuration, including better known appellatives now, such as "public" and "engaged") to fall, which does not mean the absence of critique, but perhaps even a heightened sense of critique and self-critique, although on somewhat different registers. The same applies to the fear of intervention and the normative.

I would say that, taken as a whole, what is considered "anthropology" in the canonical journals and teaching programs continues to operate largely as a set of interdisciplinary and normative conversations within the academy. As Lucy Suchman suggests (this volume), anthropology needs to embrace in earnest the task of decolonizing the taken-for-granted practices of knowledge and world-making in which it participates — indeed to decolonize knowledge practices as a prerequisite to decolonize practices of world-making. This is well known, but it merits bringing it back into the conversation as a reminder of what is still an open question. As I will suggest, certain trends in critical design studies, a subfield that is predicated on the very awareness that designing is about world-making, can help us rearticulate this question in novel ways. Above all, it seems to me that the volume's call for critical, but actively engaged participation in world-making, whether through design or otherwise, needs to be brought to the fore again and widely discussed.

Anthropology and Design as Form-Giving Practices

I find very productive the volume's main framing, that given that design is an important domain of human action, it is eminently deserving of anthropological attention. Design is about creation, about form-giving and world-building, in the language of the volume.[2] My current take is that design/ing — as both a practice and a field of studies or, in fact, as acting-knowing — is emerging as a fundamental domain for thinking about life itself and the making of worlds. I have arrived at a definition of design *as a praxis for the healing of the web of life*, an important praxis against what some Indigenous women activists in South America call *terricide*.[3] Allow me to belabor this definition a bit from the perspective of form.

I've long been attracted to the concept of form, from the biological to the social, from built structures to knowledge structures (epistemes), within a very loose conception of morphogenesis, meaning the creation and differentiation of forms and behaviors, including patterns (for instance, in the sense of architect Christopher Alexander's well-known attempt at building a pattern language in Alexander et al. 1977). Form is the expression of the creativity of the natural world, including the so-called nonliving world, which possibly explains the persistence of the emergence of form from chaos as a recurrent trope in many narratives of creation. There is thus an intimate relation between life and form, and this relation is reenacted every day in myriad ways (think about the spring season, for instance, in the plant world). Between "the life of form" and "the form of life," a formulation I borrow from the late complexity theorist Brian Goodwin (2007), there opens up a vast terrain for investigation into form-giving and meaning-making; understanding this process, as Goodwin insists, requires cultivating our capacity for feeling our way through form-making and acknowledging the sentience in the universe, from matter to organisms. This nondualist approach is needed as a corrective against the taming and normalization of form by expert-driven modernity, functionalist design, state-driven "law and order," and patriarchal/colonial capitalism. From plantations to contemporary agroindustrial agriculture, and from suburban neighborhoods to monetary regimes, and in every field of human endeavor, we have witnessed a progressive impoverishment and colonization of form.[4]

One of the volume's central ideas, that "form-giving is *a category of action*, or perhaps an imbued generator of action found in different kinds of human activities, that is focused on *shaping, in multiple real senses, the lived conditions of the social world*" (Murphy this volume, my emphasis), points to the dynamic nature of form. Form-giving, like designing (and perhaps everything in life), entails a knowing-acting, and so it is always ethical and political—a relational praxis. As form-giving, design/ing is always an intervention into the world, into the lives of others, humans and not. In making the world-within-the-world in which we live (Fry 2012), humans become the product of their own designing. Murphy's notion that we exist in the midst of "ecologies of design artifice" summons anthropologists to become active form-givers in those realms of practice and materiality in which we want to see new worlds emerge. It's also a call to contest explicitly the form-giving power of the merchants of life and their capitalistic and liberal ontology.

As a type of situated action, design has valuable implications for anthropological theorizing and ethnographic practices, as the volume's discussion of "design for anthropology" expounds. Not that this is an easy relationship, which Alberto Corsín Jiménez (this volume) describes in terms of "complicities and complexities." But the potential connections are readily visible—for instance, and perhaps most politically, when such relation is played out in activist worlds where design languages and practices circulate, sometimes in conjunction with the search for alternative and transformative ways of living that are intended to strengthen futuring and autonomy. Such engagements, as Corsín Jiménez and the volume as a whole suggest, can lead to a reconfiguration of anthropological interests and practices, through an "anthropology with," in epistemic partnership around concrete political projects or set of interventions — in other words, the idea is that activist-generated designs for liberation "can inspire the liberation of anthropological designs" (Corsín Jiménez this volume), the never-finished project of other anthropologies and anthropology otherwise.[5]

This also means considering those types of designing that are not done by professional designers, or not even done under the banner of design, but which are de facto designing practices by other names, sometimes veritable practices of ontological designing from the perspective of, and aiming at, other kinds of form-giving and world-making (Gutiérrez 2017; Alvarez and Gutiérrez 2017). The question posed by the volume, of which designers to engage, needs to take this issue into consideration. In activist contexts in particular it also implies deepening the deconstruction of the premise that "we have theory, they [activists, designers] have practice." The problematization of this divide is taken seriously in some of the chapters in this volume, although not infrequently the theory/practice divide resurfaces in the hypertheoretical anthropologies of the present informed by poststructuralism and postdualism.[6]

I was attracted to the field of design because there I found an epistemic community engaged in discussions and debates that I did not find in the academic disciplines, or at least not with the same poignancy and sense of urgency. What I found in design worlds was a sophisticated production of social, cultural, and political theory, even if rarely explicitly presented as such. For reasons of space, instead of talking about particular theorists to demonstrate my point, I will refer to salient areas of theory production in recent design literature. I should hasten to say that "theory production" in these cases signals entanglements of theory and practice, indeed areas of "acting-thought," designing as process rather than design writ large. To take one of the best-known areas — that of "design for social innovation," spearheaded over the years by Ezio Manzini and Virginia Tassinari at the design PhD program at the Politecnico di Milano but involving a network of sites in a number of other countries,[7] and, more recently, by Mariana Amatullo and Andrew Shea at Parsons School of Design as a practice-based transnational project — here one finds significant theoretico-practical rearticulations of notions of community, collaboration, innovation, agency, social transformation, sustainability, democracy, alternative economies, activism, life projects, commons, and many more. Wresting away the concept of innovation from its individualizing, neoliberal, and capitalistic framings and toward collective and collaborative understandings has been a main achievement.

A second example is the rich inquiring domain of ontological design, with a strong foothold in Australia and increasingly in several Latin American countries; I will not belabor it here, since I discuss it at length elsewhere (Escobar 2018b). This was my entry point into the idea that design is about world-making; coupled with anthropological and activist concerns, it led me eventually to posit the idea that what we are witnessing today with many forms of protest against extractive capitalism is the political activation of relational worlds, as well as to posit the need for a pluriversal politics capable of transforming our understanding of the real and the possible (Escobar 2020). And there are many other important areas in current design research and practice from which one could glean important theoretical contributions to areas of anthropological concern, such as decolonial design, designs from the South, and transition design (to list those most salient in my own work), but also concerning technology and the artificial, urban design and planning, nature and sustainability, networks and distributed agency, food and health. Taken together, and considering contributions from both the Global North and the Global South, I believe we are witnessing the emergence, over the past decade and a half, of a dynamic transnational critical design studies field (Escobar 2018a).

Let me mention one final example, closer to home: the Design Studio for Social Intervention, DS4SI. The Studio's recent book (2020), based on ten years of work with ethnic and working-class communities in the Boston area, develops the apparently simple formula that "ideas are embedded within arrangements, which in turn produce effects," or the I-A-E triplet. The originality of the book stems from the amazing degree of complexity that this formula enables its authors—and all of us, in reading it—to unfold. Complexity about what? About the highest stakes of all—namely, social reality itself. Rather than this complexity leading to paralysis or defeatism about the seemingly unsurmountable problems that leak from all aspects of social life, the analysis delivers with incomparable lucidity a palpable sense of the kinds of actions needed to address many of these problems and, in so doing, to rearrange the social. The I-A-E triplet is an intricate theory of how we have gotten stuck with profoundly oppressive social orders. The framework is indebted to critical academic currents, from poststructuralism and intersectionality to assemblage theories, yet whatever it has borrowed from these often highly abstract theories has been thoroughly rewoven into an original conceptualization. For the Studio, common people and activists are knowledge producers are designers in their own right, resulting in a framework for transformative social change.[8]

A Few Additional Areas of Anthropology/Design Engagement

The following are some loosely related reflections bringing together anthropology and design as form-giving and world-making practices.

A VIGNETTE, NOT ETHNOGRAPHIC,

BUT FROM THE ARCHIVES OF PHENOMENOLOGY

Gaston Bachelard is the phenomenologist of form par excellence. His well-known *La poética del espacio* (The Poetics of Space) speaks lovingly of the relation between form, experience, place, and space in countless elements, from the house to small drawers, and from furniture to nests and shells. In other phenomenological works he muses over water and air as materialities of daydreaming. In his writings on artists (painters, sculptors, poets), particularly in *The Right to Dream*, we find wonderful lessons on artistry and form, on forms as the product of the creative imagination. Commenting on the work of the Basque artist Eduardo Chillida, the sculptor of iron, he talks of Chillida's becoming a blacksmith so he could experience "the diverse dramas of iron and fire," the "metallic cosmos" of iron (Bachelard 1985, 58). He follows the sculptor-blacksmith's invitation "into his prolonged daydreaming about the material image of iron. He knows the complex soul of iron; he knows that this metal experiences strange sensibilities" (58). Chillida's art helps us realize that from long ago, "in a past that is no longer ours, there still live within us the dreams of the forge." As he ventures, "it is a healthy act to awaken them again" (60). In Albert Flocon, the engraver, he finds "a poet of the hand . . . his tracings and drawings carry with it masses, instigate gestures, work up the materials, confer on each form its force, its direction, its dynamical being. . . . His landscapes embody a rapture of the will, an impatient drive to act upon the world. The engraver sets a world in motion, summons the forces that fuel the forms, provokes into being the forces that slumber on a flat universe" (71–72).[9]

For Bachelard, Flocon's prints dream cosmically; the engraver of sinuous landscapes decidedly walks toward the encounter with the great dream that is the work of the earth. Artists entreat us to genuine cosmodramas, to "anthropocosmic agonisms" (Bachelard 1985, 72). Bachelard considers the world to be always an open notebook, an unfinished task, a space in which to make forms and worlds, to sculpt them lovingly and laboriously, taking our cue from the infinite forces of life themselves. Form is memory, life feeling its way into being in particular ways; hence his lament: "In this age of combine harvesters, we have lost the sense of the chaff" (24). Witness also his steadfast determination to understand phenomenologically the will of the earth, as in this passage about the vegetal world, which anticipates contemporary anthropology's and biophilic design's concern with the life of plants, mushrooms, forests, trees: "An entire life of roots and shoots inhabits the heart of our being. In actuality, we are very old plants. . . . A philosophy of the vegetal remains to be created" (83). These interpretations explain his assertion that "the eye is an entire world looking out" (91), as we are discovering perhaps with our anthropological and more-than-human relational reveries. Artists can be our guides, too, as what they set into motion is often a Bachelardian "illustrated philosophy" (103), simultaneously thought and daydreaming. In the printmaker's imagination, "everything with form has a force" and participates in a geometric oneirism (116). At its best, art displays "an ontological vibration" (156) that requires an oneiric, not just an empiric, will. The anthropologist, the designer—could she or he become, like the artist, "a cosmic dreamer"? Could she or he thus participate, in this capacity, in the cosmic project-dream of re-earthing human practice and the liberation of Mother Earth? (below).

THE REEMERGENCE OF RELATIONALITY AS A FUNDAMENTALLY DIFFERENT WAY OF UNDERSTANDING REALITY

Cosmic dreaming, like Thomas Berry's "dream of the earth" (1988), summons a deeply relational view of life. The concept of relationality is remerging as a foundation for the onto-epistemic reorientation of design, based on the increasing awareness that the presuppositions that structure the ways in which we live, think, act, and design are at the root of the contemporary crisis of climate, energy, poverty, inequality, and meaning (Escobar et al. forthcoming). It is well known that these presuppositions, often encompassed under the rubric of "ontological dualism," have propitiated a profound disconnection between humans and the nonhuman world, bestowing all rights on humans. The result, to stay with Berry, has been "the first radically anthropocentric society," thus breaking "the law that every component member of the universe should be integral with every other member of the universe" (1988, 202). The realization that the key to constructing livable worlds lies in the cultivation of ways of knowing and acting based on the fundamental interdependence of everything that exists is growing. The philosophical premise of relationality works to show that complex interdependencies and relationships are at the heart of reality. The fact that radical interdependence has been a fundamental feature of life from the get-go 3.5 billion years ago has been passionately and brilliantly argued by Lynn Margulis (1998) and collaborators through their notion of a symbiotic planet and vividly shown through their multiple form-displaying drawings and diagrams, in another potent instantiation of form-giving.

The shift in cosmovision toward relationality—stemming from multiple sources at present, from a renewed appreciation of ancient cosmovisions and contemporary social struggles to philosophy, anthropology, and some science trends—has the potential to deeply affect the ways in which we live, think, and act, as well as design and do social change. One could go as far as to claim that the failure to recognize relationality is at the basis of many of the crises and destructive forces we currently face, including climate collapse. Many of the dominant practices, institutions, and designs actively work to make this constitutive relationality invisible. Shifting to a relational worldview may be key to creating a more livable future. Radical interdependence is thus a crucial onto-epistemic premise for new visions of social change and of design/ing, even if its premises run counter to the values we customarily hold. Living life under the principle of interexistence would demand from us a significant reorientation of our actions toward the healing, caring, repairing, and sustaining of the web of interrelations that make up the places, communities, regions, and worlds we inhabit. There is something potentially wondrous about relational living so envisioned as well as of designing from this perspective (Escobar et al. forthcoming).

There are momentous implications for design/ing.[10] Relational ontological designing will require a renewed awareness of how the creation of conditions for life-sustaining coexistence will necessarily have to engage with the dominant logic of defuturing and unsustainability. Working against the grain of such logic, design could become a key agency in the transitions from toxic to healing existence. This reorientation in our modes of existing and designing will take a lot of work. Only slowly will we discover the considerable potential of acting and designing from interdependence, care, and repair. A language will eventually emerge that articulates a robust notion of designing as a mindful and effective praxis for the healing of the web of life. This would imply liberation from the straightjacket of narrow conception of reality and the expansion of what we view as desirable and possible, well beyond the impoverished notions of what's real and what's possible with which we have gotten stuck at present (Escobar 2020). This ethics and politics will give us a different sense of being at home in a world of aliveness and to designing otherwise with this realization in mind. This movement might find support in attempts at relearning to walk with the peoples whose major cosmovisions are still nourished by the sources of interexistence, as they rise up in defense of their life territories—again, an area of considerable potential for an anthropology designed and for acting-knowing at the anthropology/design interface.

REPAIR AS EMERGENT LANGUAGE AND PRACTICE OF DESIGN/ING

The current appeal of terms such as "repairing," "care," "regenerating," "mending," "refashioning," "reusing," "repurposing," "makers' cultures," and so forth is a hopeful sign of the times. A recent exhibit at the Rhode Island School of Design (RISD) put it thus: "A humble act first born of necessity, repair is an expression of resistance to the unmaking of our world and the environment. . . . Repair invites renewed forms of social exchange and offers alternative, holistic ways of facing environmental and social breakdown. [It considers] the ways in which mending can serve as a visual and emotional aid to socially engaged design thinking."[11] Historically, repairing was a primary aspect of the quotidian task of weaving the web of life—that is, of sustaining the meshwork of interactions and interrelations that made up each place, locality, and community. Philosopher Elizabeth Spelman (2002) posits a veritable subjectivity of repair (*Homo reparans*), effected on all kinds of materials, from objects and machines to bodies, nations, and even our souls. This reparative ethics is more clearly at play in women's worlds and in those of poor people, peasants, and ethnic minorities in the Global South than in the densely populated liberal worlds of the urban middle classes worldwide, where the cultures of individualism, consumption, and waste have percolated more thoroughly, but even in these latter worlds there seems to be a nascent concern with conserving, mending, and repairing as meaningful and valued activities in themselves.

The fall into desuetude of the practice of repair was an unintended effect of the consolidation of advanced capitalist consumer societies with their "planned obsolescence," technological rationality, and the consecration of ever-increasing productivity as a central element of capital accumulation, features that were much discussed by critics such as Herbert Marcuse, Eric Fromm, Jacques Ellul, and Ivan Illich during the second half of the twentieth century. Tony Fry ([1999] 2020, 2012) has unveiled the profound implications of these critiques in design terms. For Fry, these traits of advanced industrial society are an aspect of defuturing, itself the name he gives to the complex onto-epistemic and material assemblages that create systemic unsustainability, taking all other possible futures away. Indelibly associated with war and technology since the dawn of modernity, if not before, defuturing became a worldwide impetus with the rise of industrialism, productivism, and Fordism in the nineteenth and early twentieth-century United States, a veritable world-designing machine. To summon again the world-(re)building potential of an ontology of repair is thus at once to deconstruct the manifold ways in which it has been derailed and to provide elements for a reconstructive effort, an ontological rearranging of the existing defutured and defuturing social orders beyond design as usual. This calls into being the need for a new foundation for design, one that recognizes "design's powers of world-making" and that "radically transforms what design is and does" (Fry [1999] 2020, 241, 237); such foundation would enable the actualization of design's ability to sustain the web of life and to mindfully and effectively heal and repair such web. By identifying the logic of defuturing, one is able to clear a path for futuring as the space for a redirective practice intended for making otherwise:

> The full story of the defutured can never be told, for it requires a rewriting of everything. However, demonstrating that one understands the method of telling is essential. Defuturing is a necessary learning that travels before any design or constructional action if any effort is to be made to acquire the ability to sustain. The fact that so far the defutured and defuturing (the method by which the defutured is understood) have not been learnt means that even the well intentioned go on sustaining the unsustainable. (Fry [1999] 2020, 237)

Looking at the history of the modern period, one realizes how much other futures have been progressively closed down. The defuturing effects have been particularly striking in the case of colonized and Indigenous peoples in many world regions, whose resistance to ontological erasure continues to this day in many cases. But it is equally true of the modern West, which has been robbed of many other potential futures by the suppression or annihilation of endogenous alternative history-making trajectories and world-making skills, including some that emerged in the very encounter with diverse peoples through colonization.

Defuturing takes on new dimensions with the full arrival of the artificial as onto-epistemic force and a new horizon for being human, posing new challenges and perhaps opportunities for designing understood in terms of relational healing and repair. In this context, the retrieval of the world-making potential of healing, caring, and repair has to face this novel problematic of relationality and dependence established by the artificial while avoiding its powerfully seductive traps. It's very difficult to navigate this theoretical-political landscape. On the one hand, it requires grasping the ontologically and politically structuring role of the emergence of the artificial as a horizon for being; on the other, it has to resist yielding to the naturalized and luring attempts at convincing us that this is all there is, as glamorous media accounts of nanotechnology, synthetic biology, genomics, cognitive enhancement, robotics, interstellar traveling, and artificial intelligence (AI) suggest. These techno-patriarchal imaginaries require the de facto continued devastation of the planet. The salience of the artificial should not lead to Modern Man on steroids, so to say, but to novel cultivations of the future, born out from the acknowledgment of our dependence on the artificial but opening up to different logics of becoming, in complete awareness of the fact that this futuring is "negotiation with the possible through the artificial, just as it is also negotiation through the conditions of natural existence" (Dilnot 2015, 169); this latter aspect is completely overlooked by those seduced by the narrative of the artificial-as-world.

In other words, designing might be a domain for a redirective practice of technology as a space for mutually enriching articulations between the biophysical and the techno-cultural infrastructures inhabiting any and all world-making practice. In this context, the praxis of repairing, healing, and caring for the web of interdependencies that makes up life might be constituted as a means to overcome the most destructive aspects of the technological construction of worlds, perhaps in tandem with those social groups not yet fully instrumentalized and with ongoing efforts worldwide at resisting such instrumentalization in the name of making and living otherwise. The existential and political onto-epistemic conditions for moving toward this goal demand from us a reappraisal of the constitutive relationality of all existence, as well as a reclaiming of a broad understanding of care as an ethics and politics pervading life's entire living web (Puig de la Bellacasa 2017).[12]

Design, Anthropology, and Transitions

In what remains of this text, I would like to share my own sense of strategies for transition from the perspective of the interface of anthropology and design. Transitions and transition design have been an active focus of my research and practice since *Designs for the Pluriverse* (2018b, but published in Spanish in 2016), particularly through transition-related projects in Colombia and, more recently, in the context of the intense debates on the postpandemic, as they have been taking place in Latin America. I mention the latter aspect because while many narratives of transition have focused on the relation between the pandemic and capitalism, in my view the most interesting tackle this relation through the broad lens of civilizational ruptures and transitions, which have been prominent in Latin America. What follows is a schematic rendition of the tentative argument to which I have arrived (see Escobar 2020c for an extended explanation). It takes the form of suggesting five axes or principles for thinking about strategies for transitions, whether through design or through many other forms of collective action. Each of these five axes is easily connected to pressing issues and open questions in anthropology and design, including ontologically oriented inquiries.

THE RECOMMUNALIZATION OF SOCIAL LIFE

This first axis of acting-thinking begins with a resounding *no* regarding individual solutions to the current pandemic or coming crises; they obscure roots of the crisis and promote the stigmatization of particular groups. Generally speaking, it is decisively important to actively and explicitly resist the ever more efficient individualization of subjectivities imposed by modern capitalism in its global phase. Intent on creating subjects who see themselves primarily as individuals making decisions in market terms, globalization has entailed an uncompromising war against everything that is communal and collective. History teaches us that human experience has largely been place-based and communal, carved out at the local level. This condition of existence is an important dimension of relationality and responds to the symbiotic coemergence of living beings and their worlds, resulting in "communalitarian entanglements" that make us kin to everything that is alive (Gutiérrez Aguilar 2018). Oaxacan activists refer to this dynamic as the *condicion nosótrica de ser*, the "we-condition of being." If we see ourselves *nosótricamente* (in terms of a "we"), we cannot but adopt the principles of love, care, and compassion as ethics of living, starting with home, place, and community—this not in order to isolate ourselves but to prepare for greater sharing rooted in autonomy, for communication and *compartencia* (sharingness). These emphases might be translated into design guidelines, even to deepen the insights of existing notions, such as those of "resilient communities."

THE RELOCALIZATION OF SOCIAL, PRODUCTIVE, AND CULTURAL ACTIVITIES

Human history has always seen movement, flows, and regroupings. Delocalizing pressures, however (oftentimes imposed by force, as with the various experiences of enslavement throughout history, and with today's dramatic dispossession of peoples and communities by large-scale extractivist projects), increased exponentially with the development of capitalism and even more in the age of development and globalization. Given their high social and ecological cost, we need to oppose these pressures; the pandemic is fostering a new awareness that capitalist globalization is not inevitable when life is at stake. As Gustavo Esteva (in press) states, the crisis reestablishes fully the importance of the local and of real people, many of whom are abandoning the role assigned to them by society in order to recommunalize. It is imperative to relocalize multiple activities in order to regain the rootedness in the local. Food is one of the most crucial areas; it is also one of the domains where there is greater communalitarian and relocalizing innovations—that is, innovations that break with the patriarchal, racist, and capitalist way of living. The emphases on food sovereignty, agroecology, seed saving, commons, and urban gardens are instances of this renewed will. These relocalizing activities, even more if they take place on an agroecological register and from below, might foster transformations of national and transnational production systems, revaluing the commons and reweaving ties between country and city. Emphasis is placed on relocalization on the basis of a series of active-verb strategies: to eat, to learn, to heal, to dwell, to build, to know. This involves a significant reorientation of the worlds we inhabit. There is a plethora of relocalizing activities worldwide, which can be tapped into through active anthropology/design interfaces (for instance, in transition movements and in debates on degrowth, commons, energy transitions, and so forth).

THE STRENGTHENING OF AUTONOMIES

Autonomy is the political correlate of recommunalization and relocalization. Without the former, the latter would only go halfway or might be reabsorbed by newer forms of delocalized reglobalization. There has been a vibrant debate on *autonomía* in Latin America since the Zapatista uprising of 1994. Autonomy is thought of at times as the radicalization of direct democracy, but also as a new manner of conceiving and enacting politics, understanding politics as the inescapable task that emerges from the entanglement of humans among themselves and with the earth, oriented to reconfigurations of power in less hierarchical ways, on the basis of principles such as sufficiency, mutual aid, and the self-determination of the norms of living. All of this requires thinking about strategies of "overturning and flight" in relation with the established orders of capitalist modernity and the state (Gutierrez Aguilar 2008, 41). In many parts of the world, autonomy is at the crux of a great deal of political mobilization but also of less openly political practices. At its best, autonomy is a theory and practice of interexistence and of designing for and with the pluriverse.[13]

These first three areas aim at the creation of dignified lives in the territories, rethinking the economy in terms of everyday practices of solidarity, reciprocity, and conviviality. There are many clues for this project among those groups who, even during the COVID-19 pandemic, have continued to be dedicated to the production of their own lives, constructing instead of destroying, reuniting instead of separating. These are tangible and actionable principles of "dream-designing" (*disoñación*) and redesign required for a selective but substantial deglobalization. We can intuit the end of globalization as we know it, or at least the beginning of a globalization in different terms, such as the paradigm of *cuidado*, or "care" (Svampa 2020)—in which case it might not be called globalization—and an impetus toward the pluriverse, or a world where many worlds fit. They could be seen as an antidote against destructive globalization, against a normative middle-class way of life marked by agonizing consumption, against the ever deeper grafting of bodies onto ubiquitous digital technologies, whether cell phones, laptops, earphones, "apps," or "Alexas," that subvert our personal and collective autonomies with our complicity and seemingly to our liking.[14]

One final comment: to relocalize, recomunalize, and strengthen autonomies necessarily involves the reconstitution of the naturalized concept of the economy: on the one hand, to decenter it—that is, to see it as one of the most influential civilizational onto-epistemic operations of capitalist modernity, which separated the economy from the rest of life, assigning it the central role in society (Quijano 2012); on the other hand, to undertake in earnest the task of constructing other economies on the basis of relationality, centered on livelihoods, the commons, and the reproduction of, and care for, life (Bollier and Helfrich 2019). There is much to be done along this crucial path, which involves the decolonization and de-economization of social life, labor, and markets. We find clues for this endeavor in popular economic practices that, operating in multiple worlds at the same time, interweave processes of communalization with capitalist processes, thus deglobalizing economies through their "persistent disobedience to capitalist markets" (Rivera Cusicanqui 2018, 66), albeit in a tense and contradictory way (Gago 2015). Contemporary movements in defense of the commons, social and solidarity economies, and degrowth point in one way or another in this same direction.[15]

THE DEPATRIARCHALIZATION, DERACIALIZATION, AND DECOLONIZATION OF SOCIAL RELATIONS

The worlds, ontologies, and civilizational projects associated with patriarchal capitalism are seemingly immune to attempts at dismantling them. Its power assemblages are strongly naturalized in our desires and subjectivities and in the concrete designs of the worlds that we inhabit and that entrap us. It is necessary to go through them, day in and day out, in order to etch out other ways of inhabiting the world. We are reminded of the stakes at hand by the Latin American feminist dictum that there is no decolonization without depatriarchalization and deracialization of social relations. To depatriarchalize and deracialize requires repairing the damage caused by the heteropatriachal white capitalist ontology, practicing a "politics in the feminine" centered on the reappropriation of collectively produced goods and the reproduction of life (Segato 2016, 2018; Gutiérrez Aguilar 2017). In places inhabited by racialized and ethnicized women, such politics involves following the peaceful routes they travel as they reconstitute their territories and maintain dignified lives, as the Afro-Colombian philosopher Elba Palacios suggests in her work with poor Afro-descendant Black women in Cali, Colombia. "In their territories, women give birth to life and to modes of re-existence," says this activist-researcher (Palacios 2019, 143); the women teach us that "to re-exist means much more than resist; it involves the creation and transformation of autonomy in defense of life, through a sort of contemporary urban maroonage that enables them to reconstitute their negated humanity, reweaving communities in the historical diaspora" (150). This feminist and antiracist optic is essential for understanding and strengthening the processes of recommunalization and relocalization in many places (see also Lozano 2019; Hartman 2019 for the historical experience of young Black women in the United States).

The depatriarchalization and deracialization of social existence imply repairing and healing the tapestry of interrelations that make up the bodies, places, and communities that we all are and inhabit. This emphasis is particularly well articulated by the diverse movement of communitarian feminisms led by Mayan and Aymara activist-intellectuals, such as Gladys Tzul Tzul (2018), Julieta Paredes (2012), and Lorena Cabnal. Tzul Tzul (2018) highlights the potential of the communal as horizon for the struggle and as a space for the continuous reconstitution of life. Her perspective is absolutely historical and anti-essentialist; it designates the complexity of thinking from and living within *entramados comunitarios* (communitarian entanglements), with all the forms of power that traverse them.[16] From this perspective, the reconstitution of life's web of relations in a communitarian manner is one of the most fundamental challenges faced by any transition strategy. As Argentinean anthropologist Rita Segato has stated: "We need to advance this politics day by day, outside the State: to re-weave the communal fabric as to restore the political character of domesticity proper of the communal." She continues: "*To choose the relational path is to opt for the historical project of being community*. . . . It means to endow relationality and the communal forms of happiness with a grammar of value and resistance capable of counteracting the powerful developmentalist, exploitative, and productivist rhetoric of things with its alleged meritocracy. *La estrategia a partir de ahora es femenina* [the strategy, from now on, is a feminine one]" (2016, 106, my emphasis). This feminist and radical relational politics needs to be incorporated into many, or all, designing practices and into anthropology designed.

THE RE-EARTHING OF LIFE

We arrive, finally and necessarily, to the Earth (Gaia, Pachamama, coemergence, self-organization, symbiosis). By "Earth" I mean—based on Indigenous cosmovisions as much as on insights from contemporary biological and social theory—the profound interdependence of everything that exists, the indubitable fact that everything exists because everything else does, that nothing preexists the relations that constitute it. Earth signals the capacity of life for self-organization, life's ceaselessly unfolding flux of changing forms, forces, behaviors, and relations, and signals the fact that entities, processes, and forms are always in the process of dependent coarising. As the great biologist Lynn Margulis put it, "Gaia, as the interweaving network of all life, is alive, aware, and conscious to various degrees in all its cells, bodies, and societies" (1998, 126). I take this notion of Earth as the horizon for a renewed living praxis and as the basis for the essential act of human dwelling. There are many expressions of the intensely felt need of reintegrating with Earth at present, from liberal and economistic notions of sustainability to amazingly lucid frameworks in terms of a "Commonsverse"—the commons as pluriverse—to mention one of the most recent (Bollier and Helfrich 2019).

One of the most politically and onto-epistemically radical proposals in this regard has been offered by the Nasa Indigenous people of Northern Cauca in the Colombian southwest. For nearly two decades, their Social and Communitarian Minga has been articulating a powerful project around the concept-movement of the liberation of Mother Earth, as part of their strategy of "weaving life in liberty." As they say, Earth has been enslaved, and as long as she is enslaved, all living beings on the planet are also enslaved. Their struggle involves both the active recovery of lands and a different mode of existence. "This struggle," they say, "comes out of Northern Cauca, but it is not Northern Cauca's struggle. It comes from the Nasa people, but it is not the Nasa people's. Because life itself is at risk when the earth is exploited in the capitalist way, which throws the climate, the ecosystems, everything out of balance." As they hasten to clarify, it's a project for everybody, since we are all Earth and pluriverse. "Every liberated farm, here or in any corner of the world, is a territory that adds to reestablishing the balance of Uma Kiwe ["Mother Earth"]. This is our common house, our only one. Yes, indeed: come on in, *the door is open*." What does it mean to accept this invitation, whether in the countryside or in the city, in the Global South or the Global North? The liberation of Mother Earth, conceived from the cosmocentrism and cosmoaction of a peoples-territory such as the Nasa, invites us to disoñar (dreamagine) different worldings and designings, ones propitious to the reconstitution of the entire web of life, the sustainment of the territories, and communalized forms of economy, wherever we are.[17]

The liberation of Mother Earth, as an imaginary for peoples and collectives, wherever they happen to be, is not as utopian a project as it might seem. For historical reasons, Latin America has been preparing for this fundamental project at many levels, generating little by little an entire onto-epistemic and political space where the Earth-centered struggles, knowledges, and critical thought all converge. This convergence has become more noticeable in the wake of the multiplicity of struggles triggered by resistance to the brutal extractivism of the past few decades, in the conviction that the devastation of the planet is not an inevitable destiny. The Earth question has attained an incredible urgency, powerfully expressed by environmental philosopher-activists such as Mexican Enrique Leff (e.g., 2014) and Colombian Ana Patricia Noguera. For Noguera, Latin American and Abya-Yalan environmental thought responds to the "geometries of atrocity produced by a calculating world" with a "geo-poetics of weaving-dwelling" geared toward original modes of inhabiting the planet (2020, 271). There is, in these expressions of environmental discourse—as in Indigenous, Black, peasant, feminist, and ecological struggles—an entire archive of categories and practices for thinking of paths to concrete transitions.

Concluding Thoughts

The anthropology/design interface may be considered a space in which to visualize the huge challenges faced by all human action in the current planetary/political conjuncture: how to resituate such action, design and anthropology included, within communality and the Earth, without overlooking the multiple power relations that circumscribe such an open-ended onto-epistemic and political horizon. "Can there be a design culture and practice that stops being anthropocentric . . . and embraces the idea of radical interdependence . . . and [is] capable of operating in the reality of the contemporary world?" ask Manzini and Tassinari.[18] What does it mean to live, act, and design within a living Earth, one deeply traversed by fierce destructive forces, ontologies, and political economies, according to the insights of interdependence? What tools, collective inquiries, and concrete actions can we imagine from the perspective of communality, relationality, pluriversality? Which communalitarian and relocalizing innovations can we imagine that break with the state- and market-dependent patriarchal, racist, and capitalist way of living and recenter human praxis on the defense and care of life and Earth, thus opening up novel paths for existence?

"When we think with the audacity of world builders," the practitioner-theorists from the Design Studio for Social Intervention tell us in their "Letter to Our Readers" in their recent book (DS4SI 2020, 166), "we begin to see not just new ways of fighting for a more just and vibrant society, but whole new ideas about what that world might be like." What profound rearrangements are we yearning for, they ask. In their view, thinking in this way requires seeing ourselves as designers of everyday life, interested in what is possible at the level of social life. Let's heed this call with all our hearts and minds, so as to give collective form and impetus to our deepest yearnings for other worlds and worlds otherwise.

Notes

1. There was an active debate on the subject, partly motivated by the question "Can there be a feminist ethnography?" with thoughtful contributions by Judith Stacey, Lila Abu-Lughod, and Kamala Visweswaran.

2. For instance, the design graduate program with which I am affiliated in Colombia (Universidad de Caldas, in Manizales) is called PhD Program in Design and Creation. (It's almost impossible to imagine a PhD program in anthropology and creation, isn't it?)

3. The notion of terricide is being articulated by the Movimiento de Mujeres Indígenas por el Buen Vivir (Indigenous Women's Movement for Good Living), initiated by Mapuche women in Argentina, particularly Moira Millan; see https://www.facebook.com/movimientodemujeresindigenasporelbuenvivir/. It seems to me a more capacious term, in terms of intellectual-political action, than "anthropocene" or even "climate collapse."

4. Alexander and colleagues have no qualms in their characterization of the taming of form: "The languages that people have today are so brutal, and so fragmented, that most people no longer have any language to speak at all—and what they do have is not based on human, or natural, considerations" (1977, xvi). Alexander's work could be said to involve an autonomous framework for people's form-giving and world-making—that is, one not driven by experts.

5. I have suggested elsewhere (Escobar 2020) that the liberation of Mother Earth proposed by the Nasa Indigenous people of southwest Colombia can be taken as an axis for codesign strategies and for knowledge practices otherwise.

6. This point has been made poignantly by African American anthropologist Irma McClaurin in a recent piece in the *Anthropology News*. "We need a new anthropology. It must practice what it theorizes," she says; decrying the lack of diversity in the field, she concludes: "Perhaps COVID-19 has provided a call to action for a public anthropology with a relevant curriculum that contributes more directly to conducting research for public good" (McClaurin 2020). Lack of social and epistemic diversity and theory-dependence are not unrelated.

7. The Design for Social Innovation and Sustainability Network, DESIS (https://www.desisnetwork.org/about/), with "labs" in many countries, is well known in the design world. In terms of theoretical contributions, Manzini's two most recent books (2015, 2019) are, to my mind, a clear example of sophisticated theorization of social change that involves a complex and unique understanding of modernity, globalization, collaborative praxes, and civilizational transitions. See also the DESIS Philosophy Talks curated by Manzini and Virginia Tassinari, which build bridges between design practices in the field of social innovation and theory and philosophy, at http://www.desis-philosophytalks.org/. On the newer Design for Global Social Innovation project at Parsons, see https://globalleapbook.com/. I am not suggesting that these trends should not be subjected to critique, but that such critique needs to be based on a thorough engagement with them as complex instances of practice theory; in doing so, anthropologists might discover important insights for their own work, theoretical or otherwise.

8. For instance, the notion of "arrangements" points at a certain kinship between the I-A-E framing and theories of assemblages; the latter have no doubt shed new understanding on how the social is the result of complex interrelations among disparate human and nonhuman elements that may acquire, over time and often at great cost, a greater or lesser degree of stability and sturdiness. However, I often find in the diverse approaches going on under the rubric of assemblages a lingering standard geometry of entities, nodes, and interconnections, as well as a vague notion of politics. The I-A-E proposal eludes these problems since, in staying closer to the pragmatics of social life, it arrives at a more grounded, practicable, and political relational vision.

9. The translations from the Spanish version of this work are mine.

10. For a recent design-oriented discussion of the implications of postdualist social theory for design, see the sessions on "The Politics of Nature: Designing and the Ontological Turn" organized by the DESIS Philosophy Talks at the Politecnico di Milano design PhD program (February 21, 2020, http://www.desis-philosophytalks.org/desis-philosophy-talk-7-2-the-politics-of-nature-designing-for-an-ontological-turn/) and at the International Participatory Design Conference, PDC2020, organized by Universidad de Caldas (June 18, 2020, https://www.pdc2020.org/programme/conversations-2/). This latter session, organized by Manzini, Tassinari, and Escobar, included commentaries by Mario Blaser, Marisol de la Cadena, and Alfredo Gutierrez.

11. Exhibit entrance poster, *Repair and Design Futures*, RISD Museum, October 5, 2018–June 30, 2019.

12. I develop the argument on repair from the perspective of the artificial in a recent text (Escobar 2020b). My thanks to Clive Dilnot and Tony Fry for enlightening exchanges on this particular issue.

13. For a European view based on a related notion of autonomy at the place/communal level, see Manzini 2019.

14. The challenge of dedigitalization and the slowing down of the intensification of the virtual is huge; as a recent Spanish text put it, "Digital life cannot be a permanent substitute for real life, and the surrogate debates that take place today on the internet will never be able to replace the presence in flesh and blood and the live dialogue" (Riechmann 2020).

15. We may quote Raoul Vaneigem, the Situationist, to bring home the civilizational stakes in rethinking the economy: "The economy is everywhere that life is not. . . . Economics is the most durable lie of the approximately ten millennia mistakenly accepted as history. . . . There is only one terror: For most people it is the fear of losing the last illusion separating them from themselves, the panic of having to create their own lives. . . . Civilization was identified with obedience to a universal and eternal market relationship... *Nature cannot be liberated from the economy until the economy has been driven out of human life. . . . As the economy's hold weakens, life is more able to clear a path for itself*" (1998, 17, 33, 36, my emphasis).

16. Contrary to common thinking, Indigenous communitarian formations are not homogeneous but plural; neither do they suppress personal expression: "The communal does not place limits on the personal, it rather potentiates it. The communitarian entanglements provide the grounds on which personal and intimate lives are sustained" (Tzul Tzul 2018, 57), even if the organization of life, of politics and of the economy is realized collectively and every family has to engage in these practices.

17. Statement taken from: "Lo que vamos aprendiendo con la liberación de Uma Kiwe," January 19, 2016, accessed March 19, 2021, https://www.onic.org.co/noticias/934-lo-que-vamos-aprendiendo-con-la-liberacion-de-uma-kiwe. There is an extensive Nasa archive on the liberation of Mother Earth. See NASA ACIN, "Libertad para la Madre Tierra," May 28, 2010, http://www.nasaacin.org/libertar-para-la-madre-tierra/50-libertad-para-la-madre-tierra; "El desafío que nos convoca," May 28, 2010, http://www.nasaacin.org/el-desafio-no-da-espera; Vilma Almendra, "La paz de la Mama Kiwe en libertad, de la mujer sin amarras ni silencios," August 2, 2012, http://pueblosencamino.org/?p=150. See also "Libertad y alegría con Uma Kiwe: Palabra del proceso de Liberación de la Madre Tierra," accessed March 19, 2021, https://www.rebelion.org/docs/220925.pdf. I must emphasize that the movement for the liberation of Mother Earth is currently divided and, at the same time, heavily repressed by landowners and government forces. For a full account of the movement and the situation, see Escobar 2020, chap. 3.

18. Prompt for the session on "The Politics of Nature: Designing and the Ontological Turn," organized by the DESIS Philosophy Talks, International Participatory Design Conference, PDC2020, June 18, 2020; see https://www.pdc2020.org/programme/conversations-2.

Aaron, Stephen. 1986. *Stage Fright: Its Role in Acting*. Chicago: University of Chicago Press.

———. 2020. *Stewards of the Market: How the Federal Reserve Made Sense of the Financial Crisis*. Cambridge, MA: Harvard University Press.

Adamson, Glenn. 2015. "Victor Margolin, *World History of Design (2 vols.)*." *West 86th: A Journal of Decorative Arts, Design History, and Material Culture* 22, no. 2 (Fall–Winter): 223–26. https://doi-org.ezproxy.lancs.ac.uk/10.1086/685873.

Agha, Asif. 2011. "Commodity Registers." *Journal of Linguistic Anthropology* 21 (1): 22–53.

Aitor. 2004. "Fwd: Marzo." Copyleft. February 2004. https://listas.sindominio.net/mailman/private/copyleft/2004-February/000953.html.

Akama, Y., S. Pink, and S. Sumartojo, eds. 2018. *Uncertainty and Possibility: New Approaches to Future Making in Design Anthropology*. New York: Bloomsbury.

Alexander, Christopher, Sarah Ishikawa, and Murray Silverstein. 1977. *A Pattern Language: Towns, Buildings, Construction*. New York: Oxford University Press.

Álvarez, Fernando, and Alfredo Gutiérrez. 2017. "Diseño del Sur: La interculturalidad en la vida cotidiana." In *Quinto encuentro de investigaciones emergentes*, edited by Actividad Creativa, 11–27. Bogotá: Idartes.

Anusas, Mike, and Tim Ingold. 2013. "Designing Environmental Relations: From Opacity to Textility." *Design Issues* 29 (4): 58–69.

Appadurai, Arjun. 1986. *The Social Life of Things: Commodities in Cultural Perspective*. New York: Cambridge University Press.

———. 2013. *The Future as Cultural Fact: Essays on the Global Condition*. New York: Verso.

Aureli, Pier Vittorio. 2008. *The Project of Autonomy: Politics and Architecture within and against Capitalism*. New York: Princeton Architectural Press.

Austin, John L. 1961. *Philosophical Papers*. Edited by J. O. Urmson and G. J. Warnock. Oxford: Oxford University Press.

Bachelard, Gaston. 1985. *El derecho de sonar*. México: Fondo de Cultura Económica.

Baena, Fernando José. 2013. "Arte de acción en España. Análisis y tipologías (1991–2011)." PhD diss., Universidad de Granada.

Bakhtin, Mikhail. 1984. *Problems of Dostoevsky's Poetics*. Minneapolis: University of Minnesota Press.

Bank of England. 2009. "Bank of England Monetary Policy and Asset Purchases 2009." Accessed April 24, 2009.

http://www.bankofengland.co.uk/monetarypolicy/assetpurchases.htm.

http://www.bankofengland.co.uk/publications/Documents/inflationreport/2013/ir13augforwardguidance.pdf.

————. 2018. "Monetary Policy Committee Voted Unanimously to Raise Bank
        Rate to 0.75%." August 2, 2018. https://www.bankofengland.co.uk/
        monetary-policy-summary-and-minutes/2018/august-2018.

————. 2020. "Monetary Policy Summary for the Special Monetary Policy Committee
        Meeting on 19 March 2020." March 19, 2020. https://www.bankofengland.
        co.uk/monetary-policy-summary-and-minutes/2020/monetary-policy-
        summary-for-the-special-monetary-policy-committee-meeting-on-
        19-march-2020.

Barbrook, Richard, and Andy Cameron. 1996. "The Californian Ideology." *Science as
        Culture* 6 (1): 44–72. https://doi.org/10.1080/09505439609526455.

Barry, Andrew, Georgina Born, and Gisa Weszkalnys. 2008. "Logics of Interdisciplin-
        arity." *Economy and Society* 37 (1): 20–49.

Baumol, William J. 1990. "Entrepreneurship: Productive, Unproductive, and Destruc-
        tive." *Journal of Political Economy* 98 (5): 893–921.

Beck, E. 2002. "P for Political: Participation Is Not Enough." *Scandinavian Journal of
        Information Systems* 14 (1): 77–92.

Beckert, Jens. 2016. *Imagined Futures: Fictional Expectations and Capitalist Dynamics.*
        Cambridge, MA: Harvard University Press.

Beisel, Uli, and Tillmann Schneider. 2012. "Provincialising Waste: The Transformation
        of Ambulance Car 7/83–2 to Tro-Tro Dr. JESUS." *Environment and Planning
        D: Society and Space* 30:639–54.

Berardi, Franco Bifo. 2008. *Félix Guattari: Thought, Friendship, and Visionary Cartog-
        raphy.* Basingstoke, UK: Palgrave Macmillan.

Bernanke, Ben. 2020. "The New Tools of Monetary Policy." *American Economic Review*
        110 (4): 943–83.

Bernanke, Ben, Thomas Luabach, Fredric S. Mishkin, and Adam S. Posen, eds. 1999.
        Inflation Targeting: Lessons from the International Experience. Princeton, NJ:
        Princeton University Press.

Berry, Thomas. 1998. *The Dream of the Earth.* San Francisco: Sierra Club.

Birla, Ritu. 2009. *Stages of Capital: Law, Culture, and Market Governance in Late Colo-
        nial India.* Durham, NC: Duke University Press.

Bishop, Claire. 2012. *Artificial Hells: Participatory Art and the Politics of Spectatorship.*
        London: Verso.

Blinder, Alan S. 2004. *The Quiet Revolution.* New Haven, CT: Yale University Press.

Blinder, Alan S., and Ricardo Reis. 2005. "The Greenspan Standard." Paper presented
        at the Federal Reserve Bank of Kansas City Symposium, Jackson Hole, WY,
        August 25–27.

Blomberg, Jeanette, Lucy Suchman, and Randall Trigg. 1996. "Reflections on a Work-
        Oriented Design Project." *Human-Computer Interaction* 11:237–65.

Bollier, David, and Silke Helfrich. 2019. *Free, Fair and Alive: The Insurgent Power of the
        Commons.* Gabriola Island, BC: New Society.

Bornstein, Erica. 2009. "The Impulse of Philanthropy." *Cultural Anthropology* 24 (4):
        622–51.

Bornstein, Erica, and Redfield, Peter. 2011. "Introduction to the Anthropology of Humanitarianism." In *Forces of Compassion: Humanitarianism between Ethics and Politics*, edited by Erica Bornstein and Peter Redfield, 3–30. Santa Fe, NM: School for Advanced Research Press.

Bowie, Katherine A. 1998. "The Alchemy of Charity: Of Class and Buddhism in Northern Thailand," *American Anthropologist* 100 (2): 469–81.

Bowker, Geof. 2005. *Memory Practices in the Sciences*. Cambridge, MA: MIT Press.

Bristol, Katharine G. 1991. "The Pruitt-Igoe Myth." *Journal of Architectural Education* 44 (3): 163–171.

Bronk, Richard. 2009. *The Romantic Economist: Imagination in Economics*. Cambridge: Cambridge University Press.

Brown, Tim, and Jocelyn Wyatt. 2010. "Design Thinking for Social Innovation." *Stanford Social Innovation Review* (Winter): 29–35.

Brown, Tom. 2009. *Change by Design: How Design Thinking Transforms Organizations and Inspires Innovation*. New York: HarperCollins.

Building on Success. 2010. *Building on Success: New Directions in Global Health: Hearing before the Committee on Foreign Relations, United States Senate, 111th Cong*. Accessed March 7, 2021. http://purl.fdlp.gov/GPO/gp0423.

Bunzl, Matti. 2004. "Boas, Foucault, and the 'Native Anthropologist': Notes toward a Neo-Boasian Anthropology." *American Anthropologist* 106 (3): 434–42.

Callon, Michel. 2007. "Performative Economics." In *Do Economists Make Markets? On the Performativity of Economics*, edited by Donald MacKenzie, Fabian Muniesa, and Lucia Siu, 311–57. Princeton, NJ: Princeton University Press.

Campbell, Angus D. 2017. "Lay Designers: Grassroots Innovation for Appropriate Change. *Design Issues* 33 (111): 30–47.

Cantarella, Luke, Christine Hegel, and George E. Marcus 2015. "A Week in Pasadena: Collaborations toward a Design Modality for Ethnographic Research." *FIELD: A Journal of Socially Engaged Art Criticism* 1 (Spring): 53–94.

———. 2019. *Ethnography by Design: Scenographic Experiments in Fieldwork*. London: Bloomsbury.

Carney, Mark. 2014. "One Mission. One Bank. Promoting the Good of the People of the United Kingdom." Mais Lecture at Cass Business School, City University, London, March 18, 2014.

———. 2018. "Bank of England Speech: Guidance, Contingencies and Brexit." Society of Professional Economists. May 24. https://www.bis.org/review/r180528a.pdf.

Carrillo, Jesús. 2009. "Lavapiés-Atocha, arte público y política municipal." In *Arte en el espacio público: barrios artísticos y revitalización urbana*, edited by Blanca Fernández Quesada and Jesús-Pedro Lorente, 193–211. Zaragoza: Prensas de la Universidad de Zaragoza.

Casas-Cortés, Maribel. 2014. "A Genealogy of Precarity: A Toolbox for Rearticulating Fragmented Social Realities in and out of the Workplace." *Rethinking Marxism* 26 (2): 206–26. https://doi.org/10.1080/08935696.2014.888849.

Castells, Manuel. 1983. *The City and the Grassroots: A Cross-Cultural Theory of Urban Social Movements*. Berkeley: University of California Press.

Castoriadis, Cornelius. 1987. *The Imaginary Institution of Society*. Cambridge, UK: Polity Press.

Catanese, Lynne. 2012. "Thomas Lamb, Marc Harrison, Richard Hollerith, and the Origins of Universal Design." *Journal of Design History* 25 (2): 206–17.

Chadha, Radhika. 2009. "The Limitations of 'Jugaad.'" *Hindu BusinessLine*. Updated January 27, 2011. http://www.thehindubusinessline.com/todays-paper/tp-brandline/the-limitations-of-jugaad/article1083738.ece.

Chakrabarty, Dipesh. 2000. *Provincializing Europe: Postcolonial Thought and Historical Difference*. Princeton, NJ: Princeton University Press.

Chakravartty, Paula, and Sreela Sarkar. 2013. "Entrepreneurial Justice: The New Spirit of Capitalism in Emergent India." *Popular Communication* 11:58–75.

Chan, Anita Say. 2013. *Networking Peripheries: Technological Futures and the Myth of Digital Universalism*. Cambridge, MA: MIT Press.

Chan, Jeffrey K. H. 2017. "Design Ethics: Reflecting on the Ethical Dimensions of Technology, Sustainability, and Responsibility in the Anthropocene." *Design Studies* 54:184–200.

Charnock, Greig, Thomas Purcell, and Ramón Ribera-Fumaz. 2014. *The Limits to Capital in Spain: Crisis and Revolt in the European South*. London: Palgrave Macmillan.

Chumley, Lily. H. 2013. "Evaluation Regimes and the Qualia of Quality. *Anthropological Theory*, 13 (1–2): 169–83.

Clarke, Alison J. 2010. *Design Anthropology: Object Culture in the 21st Century*. New York: Springer.

———. 2013. "Actions Speak Louder." *Design and Culture* 5 (2): 151–68.

———. 2017a. "The Anthropological Object in Design: From Victor Papanek to Superstudio." In *Design Anthropology: Object Culture in Transition*, edited by A. J. Clarke, 37–52. London: Bloomsbury.

———, ed. 2017b. *Design Anthropology: Object Cultures in Transition*. New York: Bloomsbury.

Clinton, H. R. 2010. "Leading through Civilian Power: Redefining American Diplomacy and

Coleman, E. Gabriella. 2012. *Coding Freedom: The Ethics and Aesthetics of Hacking*. Princeton, NJ: Princeton University Press.

Collettivo A/traverso. 1977. *Alice è Il Diavolo*. Milano: Edizioni L'Erba Voglio.

———. 1981. *Alicia Es El Diablo. Radio Libre*. Translated by Paco Quintana. Barcelona: Ed. Ricou (Hacer).

Corbridge, S., and J. Harriss. 2000. *Reinventing India: Liberalization, Hindu Nationalism and Popular Democracy*. Cambridge, UK: Polity.

Cornwall, Andrea. 2000. *Benefciary, Consumer, Citizen: Perspectives on Participation for Poverty Reduction*. Sida Studies, no. 2. Swedish International Development Corporation Agency.

Corsín Jiménez, Alberto. 2007. "Cooperación y Procomún: Relaciones Antropológicas." *Archipiélago: Cuadernos de Crítica de La Cultura* 77–78: 27–32.

———. 2014. "Introduction. The Prototype: More Than Many and Less Than One." *Journal of Cultural Economy* 7 (4): 381–98. https://doi.org/10.1080/17530350.2013.858059.

Corsín Jiménez, Alberto, and Adolfo Estalella. 2016. "Ecologies in Beta: The City as Infrastructure of Apprenticeships." In *Infrastructures and Social Complexity: A Companion*, edited by Penny Harvey, Casper Bruun Jensen, and Atsuro Morita, 141–56. London: Routledge.

———. 2017. "Ethnography: A Prototype." *Ethnos* 82 (5): 846–66. https://doi.org/10.1080/00141844.2015.1133688.

Cortés-Rico, Laura, and Tania Pérez-Bustos. 2019. "The Art of Fieldworking Together." *Interactions* 26 (6): 80–82.

Cross, Jamie. 2014. *Dream Zones: Anticipating Capitalism and Development*. London: Pluto Press.

Cross, Nigel. 2007. *Designerly Ways of Knowing*. New York: Springer.

Cummings, Neil, and Marysia Lewandowska. 2001. *Capital. A Project*. Tate Modern.

Cuninghame, Patrick. 2013. "Autonomia in the 1970s: The Refusal of Work, the Party, and Power." *Cultural Studies Review* 11 (2): 77–94. https://doi.org/10.5130/csr.v11i2.3660.

D'Anjou, Philippe. 2010. "Beyond Duty and Virtue in Design Ethics." *Design Issues* 26 (1): 95–105.

Das, Veena. 2015. "What Does Ordinary Ethics Look Like?" In *Four Lectures on Ethics: Anthropological Perspectives*, edited by W. K. Michael Lambek, Veena Das, and Didier Fassin. Chicago: Hau.

de la Cueva, Javier. 2004. "Re: Competencias de las entidades de gestión." Copyleft. June 2004. https://listas.sindominio.net/mailman/private/copyleft/2004-June/001472.html.

de Laet, Marianne, and Annemarie Mol. 2000. "The Zimbabwe Bush Pump: Mechanics of a Fluid Technology." *Social Studies of Science* 30:225–263.

Desan, Christin, 2014. *Making Money: Coin, Currency, and the Coming of Capitalism*. Oxford: Oxford University Press.

Design Studio for Social Intervention (DS4SI). 2020. *Ideas, Arrangements, Effects: Systems Design and Social Justice*. New York: Minor Compositions.

Dewey, John. (1927) 1991. *The Public and Its Problems*. Athens, OH: Swallow Press.

Dilnot, Clive. 1984. "The State of Design History, Part I: Mapping the Field." *Design Issues* 1 (1): 4.

———. "The Artificial and What It Opens Towards." *Design and the Question of History*, edited by T. Fry, C. Dilnot, and S. Stewart, 165–203. London: Bloomsbury.

Doctor Roncero, Rafael, ed. 2003. *Nuevas Cartografías de Madrid*. Madrid: La Casa Encendida y Casa de América.

Domínguez, Carlos V. 2012. "Fragmentación, Red, Autonomía." In *Tomar y hacer en vez de pedir y esperar. Autonomía y movimientos sociales. Madrid, 1985–2011*, edited by Francisco Salamanca and Gonzalo Wilhelmi Casanova, 51–71. Madrid: Solidaridad Obrera.

Domínguez, Carlos V., and Margarita Padilla. 2008. "Okupar el Vacío desde el Vacío." In *Autonomía y Metrópolis. Del movimiento okupa a los centros sociales de segunda generación*, edited by Javier Toret, Nicolás Sguiglia, Santiago Fernández Patón, and Mónica Lama, 53–56. Málaga: CEDMA.

Dong, Andy. 2008. "The Policy of Design: A Capabilities Approach." *Design Issues* 24 (4): 76–87.

Eames, Charles, and Ray Eames. 1959. *A Communications Primer*. Los Angeles: Classroom Film Distributors.

Ehn, Pelle. 1988. *Work-Oriented Design of Computer Artifacts*. 2nd ed. Stockholm: Arbetslivscentrum.

Eichengreen, Barry. 2008. *Globalizing Capital: A History of the International Monetary System*. 2nd ed. Princeton, NJ: Princeton University Press.

Elam, Mark. 1994. "Puzzling Out the Post-Fordist Debate: Technology, Markets and Institutions." In *Post-Fordist Reader*, edited by Ash Amin, 43–70. London: Blackwell.

Elyachar, Julia. 2010. "Phatic Labor, Infrastructure, and the Question of Empowerment in Cairo." *American Ethnologist* 37 (3): 452–64.

———. 2012. "Next Practices: Knowledge, Infrastructure, and Public Goods at the Bottom of the Pyramid." *Public Culture* 24, no. 1 (66): 109–29.

Erie, Matthew S. 2016. "Sharia, Charity, and Minjian Autonomy in Musilm China: Gift Giving in a Plural World." *American Ethnologist* 43 (2): 311–24.

Escobar, Arturo. 1991. "Anthropology and the Development Encounter: The Making and Marketing of Development Anthropology." *American Ethnologist* 18 (4): 658–82.

———. 2017. "Stirring the Anthropological Imagination: Ontological Design in Spaces of Transition." In *Design Anthropology: Object Culture in Transition*, edited by A. J. Clarke, 201–16. London: Bloomsbury.

———. 2018a. "Autonomous Design and the Emergent Transnational Critical Design Studies Field." *Strategic Design Research Journal* 11 (2): 139–46.

———. 2018b. *Designs for the Pluriverse: Radical Interdependence, Autonomy, and the Making of Worlds*. Durham, NC: Duke University Press.

———. 2020. *Pluriversal Politics: The Real and the Possible*. Durham, NC: Duke University Press.

———. 2020b. "Designing as a Futural Praxis for the Healing of the Web of Life." In *Design in Crisis: New Worlds, Philosophies and Practices*, edited by T. Fry and A. Nocek, 25–42. London: Routlege.

———. 2020c. "El pensamiento en tiempos de pos/pandemia." In *Pandemia al Sur*, edited by Olver Quijano, 31–54. Buenos Aires: Prometeo Libros.

Escobar, Arturo, Michal Osterweil, and Kriti Sharma. Forthcoming. *Designing Relationally: Making and Restor(y)ing Life*. London: Bloombury.

Esser, Josef, and Joachim Hirsch. 1994. "The Crisis of Fordism and the Dimensions of a

'Post- Fordist' Regional and Urban Structure." In *Post-Fordist Reader*, edited by Ash Amin, 71-97. London: Blackwell.

Estalella Fernández, Adolfo, Jara Rocha, and Antonio Lafuente. 2013. "Laboratorios de Procomún: Experimentación, Recursividad y Activismo." *Teknokultura. Revista de Cultura Digital y Movimientos Sociales* 10 (1): 21-48.

Estalella, Adolfo, and Tomas Sanchez Criado, eds. 2018. *Experimental Collaborations: Ethnography through Fieldwork Devices*. London: Berghahn.

Esteva, Gustavo. 2020. "El día después." In *Pandemia al Sur*, edited by Olver Quijano, 55-67. Buenos Aires: Prometeo Libros.

Fabian, Johannes. 1983. *Time and the Other: How Anthropology Makes Its Object*. New York: Columbia University Press.

———. 2008. *Ethnography as Commentary: Writing from the Virtual Archive*. Durham, NC: Duke University Press.

Fassin, Didier. 2008. "Beyond Good and Evil?" *Anthropological Theory* 8 (4): 333-44.

Faubion, James D. 2011. *An Anthropology of Ethics*. Cambridge: Cambridge University Press.

Fehérváry, Krisztina. 2013. *Politics in Color and Concrete: Socialist Materialities and the Middle Class in Hungary*. Bloomington: Indiana University Press.

Fennell, Catherine. 2015. *Last Project Standing: Civics and Sympathy in Post-Welfare Chicago*. Minneapolis: University of Minnesota Press.

Ferguson, James. 1994. *The Anti-Politics Machine: "Development," Depoliticization, and Bureaucratic Power in Lesotho*. Minneapolis: University of Minnesota Press.

Findeli, Alain. 1994. "Ethics, Aesthetics, and Design." *Design Issues* 10 (2): 49-68.

Fineder, Martina, and Thomas Geisler. 2010. "Design Criticism and Critical Design in the Writings of Victor Papanek (1923-1998)." *Journal of Design History* 23, no. 1 (March 1): 99-106. https://doi-org.ezproxy.lancs.ac.uk/10.1093/jdh/epp067.

Fischer, Stanley. 2016. Remarks by Stanley Fischer Vice Chairman Board of Governors of the Federal Reserve System at "A Conference in Honor of Michael Woodford's Contributions to Economics," cosponsored by the Federal Reserve Bank of New York, Columbia University Program for Economic Research, and Columbia University Department of Economics New York, New York, May 19.

Friedman, Batya, and Peter H. Kahn, Jr. 2003. "Human Values, Ethics, and Design." In *The Human-Computer Interaction Handbook: Fundamentals, Evolving Technologies and Emerging Applications*, edited by J. A. Jacko and A. Sears, 1177-209. Hillsdale, NJ: L. Erlbaum Associates.

Friedman, Milton. 1948. "A Monetary and Fiscal Framework for Economic Stability." *American Economic Review* 38 (3): 245-64.

———. 1970. "The Counter-Revolution in Monetary Theory: First Wincott Memorial Lecture." Delivered at the Senate House, University of London, London, September 16.

Fry, Tony. 2009. *Design Futuring: Sustainability, Ethics and New Practice*. Oxford: Berg.

———. 2011. *Design as Politics*. Oxford: Berg.

———. 2012. *Becoming Human by Design*. Oxford: Berg

———. (1999) 2020. *Defuturing. A New Design Philosophy*. London: Bloomsbury.

Gabor, Daniela, and Bob Jessop. 2015. "Mark My Words: Discursive Central Banking in Crisis." In *Financial Cultures and Crisis Dynamics*, edited by Bob Jessop, Brigitte Young, and Christoph Scherrer, 294–315. London: Routledge.

Gago, Verónica. 2015. *La razón neoliberal*. Buenos Aires: Tinta Limón.

Gatt, Caroline, and Tim Ingold. 2013. "From Description to Correspondence: Anthropology in Real Time." In *Design Anthropology: Theory and Practice*, edited by Wendy Gunn, Ton Otto, and Rachel Charlotte Smith,139–58. Milton Park, UK: Taylor & Francis.

Geertz, Clifford. 1973. "Deep Play: Notes on the Balinese Cockfight." In *The Interpretation of Cultures*, 412–53. New York: Basic Books.

Gell, Alfred. 1992. "The Technology of Enchantment and the Enchantment of Technology." *Anthropology, Art, and Aesthetics*, edited by J. Coote and A. Shelton, 40–63. Oxford: Clarendon Press.

Goethe, Johan Wolfgang von. 1978. *Elective Affinities*. New York: Penguin.

Goh, D. P. S. 2006. "States of Ethnography: Colonialism, Resistance, and Cultural Transcription in Malaya and the Philippines, 1890s–1930s." *Comparative Studies in Society and History* 49 (1): 109–42.

Goldman, M. 2006. *Imperial Nature: The World Bank and Struggles for Social Justice in the Age of Globalization*. New Haven, CT: Yale University Press.

Goodman, Elizabeth, Erik Stolterman, and Ron Wakkary. 2011. "Understanding Interaction Design Practices." *CHI '11: Proceedings of the SIGCHI Conference on Human Factors in Computing Systems* (May): 1061–70. http://doi.org/10.1145/1978942.1979100.

Goodwin, Brian. 2007. *Nature's Due: Healing Our Fragmented Culture*. Edinburgh: Floris Books.

Goodwin, Charles. 1994. "Professional Vision." *American Anthropologist* 96 (3): 606–33.

Graeber, David. 2004. *Fragments of an Anarchist Anthropology*. Chicago: Prickly Paradigm Press.

Graffam, Gray. 2010. "Design Anthropology Meets Marketing." *Anthropologica* 52 (1): 155–64.

Greenbaum, Joan, and Morten Kyng, eds. 1991. *Design at Work: Cooperative Design of Computer Systems*. Hillsdale, NJ: L. Erlbaum Associates.

Greenhalgh, Susan. 2003. "Planned Births, Unplanned Persons: 'Population' in the Making of Chinese Modernity." *American Ethnologist* 30 (2): 196–215.

Guattari, Félix. 1984. *Molecular Revolution: Psychiatry and Politics*. Translated by Rosemary Sheed. Hardmondsworth, UK: Penguin Books.

Gunn, Wendy, and Jared Donovan, eds. 2012. *Design and Anthropology*. London: Ashgate.

Gunn, Wendy, Ton Otto, and Rachel Charlotte Smith, eds. 2013. *Design Anthropology: Theory and Practice*. London: Bloomsbury.

Gupta, Akhil, and James Ferguson. 1997. "Discipline and Practice: 'The Field' as Site, Method and Location in Anthropology." In *Anthropological Locations: Boundaries and Grounds of a Field Science*, edited by Akhil Gupta and James Ferguson, 1–46. Berkeley: University of California Press.

Gutiérrez, Alfredo. 2017. *Diseños otros y para un mundo en curso de ser otros*. Universidad de Caldas. ISEA 2017.

Gutiérrez Aguilar, Raquel. 2008. *Los ritmos del Pachakuti. Movilización y levantamiento indígena-popular en Bolivia*. Buenos Aires: Tinta Limón.

———. 2017. *Horizontes comunitario-populares*. Madrid: Traficante de Sueños.

———, ed. 2018. *Comunalidad, tramas comunitarias y producción de lo común*. Oaxaca: Colectivo Editorial Pez en el Árbol.

Hallam, Elizabeth, and Tim Ingold, eds. 2016. *Making and Growing: Anthropological Studies of Organisms and Artefacts*. London: Routledge.

Hamdy, Sherine. 2012. *Our Bodies Belong to God: Organ Transplants, Islam, and the Struggle for Human Dignity in Egypt*. Berkeley: University of California Press.

Hamdy, Sherine, Coleman Nye, Sarulla Bao, and Caroline Brewer. 2018. *Lissa: A Story About Medical Promise, Friendship, and Revolution*. Toronto: University of Toronto Press.

Hamraie, Aimi. 2017. *Building Access: Universal Design and the Politics of Disability*. Minneapolis: University of Minnesota Press.

Hardt, Michael, and Antonio Negri. 2005. *Multitude: War and Democracy in the Age of Empire*. New York: Penguin.

———. 2009. *Commonwealth*. Cambridge, MA: Belknap Press.

Harrison, S., P. Sengers, and D. Tatar. 2011. "Making Epistemological Trouble: Third-Paradigm HCI as Successor Science." *Interacting with Computers* 23 (5): 385–92.

Hartblay, Cassandra. 2017. "Good Ramps, Bad Ramps: Centralized Design Standards and Disability Access in Urban Russian Infrastructure." *American Ethnologist* 44 (1): 9–22.

Hartman, Saidiya. 2019. *Wayward Lives, Beautiful Experiments. Intimate Histories of Social Upheaval*. New York: W. W. Norton.

Harvey, David. 1990. *The Condition of Postmodernity: An Inquiry into the Origins of Cultural Change*. London: Wiley.

Hayward, Stephen. 1998. "'Good Design Is Largely a Matter of Common Sense': Questioning the Meaning and Ownership of a Twentieth-Century Orthodoxy." *Journal of Design History* 11 (3): 217–33.

Herrmann, Gretchen M. 1997. "Gift or Commodity: What Changes Hands in the U.S. Garage Sale?" *American Ethnologist* 24 (4): 910–30.

Hickey, Sam, and Giles Mohan. 2005. "Relocating Participation within a Radical Politics of Development." *Development and Change* 36, no. 2 (March 1): 237–62. https://doi.org/10.1111/j.0012-155X.2005.00410.x.

Ho, Karen. 2009. *Liquidated: An Ethnography of Wall Street*. Durham, NC: Duke University Press.

Holmes, Douglas R. 2014a. *Economy of Words: Communicative Imperatives in Central Banks*. Chicago: University of Chicago Press.

———. 2014b. "Communicative Imperatives in Central Banks." *Cornell International Law Journal*. 47 (1): 15–61.

———. 2016. "Central Bank Capitalism: Visible Hands, Audible Voices." *Anthropology Today*. 32 (6): 3–7.

———. 2018. "A Tractable Future: Central Banks in Conversation with their Publics." In *Uncertain Futures: Imaginaries, Narratives and Calculation in the Economy*, edited by Jens Beckert and Richard Bronk, 173–93. Oxford: Oxford University Press.

Holmes, Douglas R., and George E. Marcus. 2006. "Fast-Capitalism: Para-Ethnography and the Rise of the Symbolic Analyst." In *Frontiers of Capital: Ethnographic Reflections on the 15 New Economy*, edited by Melissa S. Fisher and Greg Downey, 33–57. Durham, NC: Duke University Press.

———. 2012. "Collaborative Imperatives: A Manifesto, of Sorts, for the Reimagination of the Classic Scene of Fieldwork Encounter." In *Collaborators Collaborating: Counterparts in Anthropological Knowledge and International Research Relations*, edited by Monica Konrad, 127–43. Oxford: Berghahn Books.

———. 2021. "How Do We Collaborate: An Updated Manifesto." In *Anthropology Today: A Collection of Exceptions*, edited by Dominic Boyer and George Marcus. Ithaca, NY: Cornell University Press.

Holston, James. 1989. *The Modernist City: An Anthropological Critique of Brasilia*. Chicago: University of Chicago Press.

Howe, Richard H. 1978. "Max Weber's Elective Affinities: Sociology within the Bounds of Pure Reason." *American Journal of Sociology*, 84 (2): 366–85.

Howell, Signe, ed. 1997. *The Ethnography of Moralities*. London: Routledge.

IDEO. 2011. *Human-Centered Design Toolkit*. 2nd edition. Palo Alto, CA: IDEO.

Ignatova, Jacqueline A. 2017. "The 'Philanthropic' Gene: Biocapital and the New Green Revolution in Africa." *Third World Quarterly* 38 (10): 2258–75.

Ingold, Tim. 2008. "Anthropology Is Not Ethnography." *Proceedings of the British Academy* 154: 69–92.

———. 2010. *Bringing Things to Life: Creative Entanglements in a World of Materials*. Realities Working Paper No. 15 (Vol. 44). University of Manchester, Manchester, UK.

———. 2011. *Being Alive: Essays on Movement, Knowledge and Description*. London: Routledge.

———. 2012. "Toward an Ecology of Materials." *Annual Review of Anthropology* 41 (1): 427–42.

———. 2013. *Making: Anthropology, Archaeology, Art and Architecture*. New York: Routledge.

Instituto Nacional de Estadística. 1995. "Anuario Estadístico de España. Año 1995." Madrid. http://www.ine.es/inebaseweb/treeNavigation.do?tn=151078.

Irani, Lilly. 2018. "'Design Thinking': Defending Silicon Valley at the Apex of Global Labor Hierarchies." *Catalyst: Feminism, Theory, Technoscience* 4 (1): 1–19. https://doi.org/10.28968/cftt.v4i1.243.

———. 2019. *Chasing Innovation: Making Entrepreneurial Citizens in Modern India*. Princeton, NJ: Princeton University Press.

Jain, S. S. Lochlann. 2004. "'Dangerous Instrumentality': The Bystander as Subject in Automobility." *Cultural Anthropology* 19 (1): 61–94.

———. 2006. *Injury: The Politics of Product Design and Safety Law in the United States*. Princeton, NJ: Princeton University Press.

Jayal, Niraja Gopal. 2013. *Citizenship and Its Discontents*. Cambridge, MA: Harvard University Press.

Joerges, Bernward. 1999. "Do Politics Have Artefacts?" *Social Studies of Science* 29 (3): 411–31.

Juris, Jeffrey S. 2008. *Networking Futures: The Movements against Corporate Globalization*. Durham, NC: Duke University Press.

Kaur, R., 2016. "The Innovative Indian: Common Man and the Politics of Jugaad Culture." *Contemporary South Asia* 24 (3): 313–27.

Keane, Webb. 2016. *Ethical Life: Its Natural and Social Histories*. Princeton, NJ: Princeton University Press.

Kelty, Christopher M. 2008. *Two Bits: The Cultural Significance of Free Software*. Durham, NC: Duke University Press.

———. 2019. *The Participant: A Century of Participation in Four Stories*. Chicago: University of Chicago Press.

Knorr-Cetina, Karin. 1999. *Epistemic Cultures: How the Sciences Make Knowledge*. Cambridge, MA: Harvard University Press.

Kolb, Lucie, and Gabriel Flückiger. 2013. "New Institutionalism Revisited." *On Curating* Special Issue on (New) Institution (Alism) (December).

Kohli, Atul. 2006. "Politics of Economic Growth in India, 1980–2005: Part II: The 1990s and Beyond." *Economic and Political Weekly* 41 (14): 1361–70.

Kondo, Dorinne. 1996. "Shades of Twilight: Anna Deveare Smith and Twilight: Los Angeles 1992." In *Connected: Engagements With Media*, Late Editions 3, edited by George E. Marcus, 313–46. Chicago: University of Chicago Press.

Koskinen, Ilpo. 2016. "Agonistic, Convivial, and Conceptual Aesthetics in New Social Design." *Design Issues* 32 (3): 18–29.

Krugman, Paul. 1999. "Thinking about the Liquidity Trap." December. http://web.mit.edu/krugman/www/trioshrt.html.

Lafuente, Antonio. 2005. "El museo como casa de los comunes." *Claves de razón práctica* 157:24–31.

Laidlaw, James. 2013. *The Subject of Virtue: An Anthropology of Ethics and Freedom*. Cambridge: Cambridge University Press.

Lambek, Michael. 2010. Introduction to *Ordinary Ethics: Anthropology, Language, and Action*, edited by Michael Lambek, 1–36. New York: Fordham University Press.

Larkin, Brian. 2013. "The Politics and Poetics of Infrastructure." *Annual Review of Anthropology* 42 (1): 327–43.

Latour, Bruno. 1992. "Where Are the Missing Masses? The Sociology of a Few Mundane Artifacts." In *Shaping Technology/Building Society: Studies in Sociotechnical Change*, edited by W. Bijker and J. Law, 225–58. Cambridge, MA: MIT Press.

———. 1994. *We Have Never Been Modern*. Cambridge, MA: Harvard University Press.

———. 2007. *Reassembling the Social: An Introduction to Actor-Network-Theory*. Oxford: Oxford University Press.

Law, John. 2004. *After Method: Mess in Social Science Research*. London and New York: Routledge.

Lefebvre, Henri. 2009. "Theoretical Problems of Autogestion." In *State, Space, World: Selected Essays*, edited by Neil Brenner and Stuart Elden, 138–52. Minneapolis: University of Minnesota Press.

Leff, Enrique. 2014. *La apuesta por la vida*. México: Siglo 000I.

Lévi-Strauss, Claude. 1966. *The Savage Mind*. Chicago: University of Chicago Press.

———. 1969. *The Elementary Structures of Kinship*. Boston: Beacon Press.

Levine, Caroline. 2015. *Forms: Wholes, Rhythm, Hierarchy, Network*. Princeton, NJ: Princeton University Press.

Li, Tania Murray. 2007. *The Will to Improve: Governmentality, Development, and the Practice of Politics*. Durham, NC: Duke University Press.

Lippmann, Walter. (1927) 2002. *The Phantom Public*. New Brunswick, NJ: Transaction.

Low, Setha. 2003. *Behind the Gates: Life, Security and the Pursuit of Happiness in Fortress America*. New York: Routledge.

Lozano, Betty Ruth. 2019. *Aportes a un feminismo negro decolonial*. Quito: Abya Yala.

Luisetti, Federico, John Pickles, and Wilson Kaiser, eds. 2015. *The Anomie of the Earth: Philosophy, Politics, and Autonomy in Europe and the Americas*. Durham, NC: Duke University Press.

Luvaas, Brent. 2012. *DIY Style: Fashion, Music, and Global Digital Cultures*. London: Bloomsbury.

MacKenzie, Donald. 2006. *An Engine, Not a Camera: How Financial Models Shape Markets*. Cambridge, MA: MIT Press.

MacKenzie, Donald, Fabian Muniesa, and Lucia Siu. 2007. Introduction to *Do Economists Make Markets? On the Performativity of Economics*, edited by Donald MacKenzie, Fabian Muniesa, and Lucia Siu, 1–19. Princeton, NJ: Princeton University Press.

Malinowski, Bronislaw. 1922. *Argonauts of the Western Pacific: An Account of Native Enterprise and Adventure in the Archipelagoes of Melanesian New Guinea*. Boston: E. P. Dutton.

Mamdani, M. 1996. *Citizen and Subject: Contemporary Africa and the Legacy of Late Colonialism*. Princeton, NJ: Princeton University Press.

Manzini, Ezio. 1992. "Prometheus of the Everyday: The Ecology of the Artificial and the Designer's Responsibility." *Design Issues* 9 (1): 5–20.

———. 2015. *Design, When Everybody Designs: An Introduction to Design for Social Innovation.* Cambridge, MA: MIT Press.

———. 2019. *Politics of the Everyday.* London: Bloomsbury.

Maranhao, Tullio (ed.). 1990. *The Interpretation of Dialogue.* University of Chicago Press.

Marcos, Subcomandante. 1997. "El EZLN acude al Encuentro Intercontinental por la Humanidad y contra el Neoliberalismo a presentar la imagen del otro México, el México indígena, el México rebelde y digno." *Enlace Zapatista* (blog). July 18, 1997. http://enlacezapatista.ezln.org.mx/1997/07/17/el-ezln-acude-al-encuentro-intercontinental-por-la-humanidad-y-contra-el-neoliberalismo-a-presentar-la-imagen-del-otro-mexico-el-mexico-indigena-el-mexico-rebelde-y-digno/.

Marcus. George E. 1995. "Ethnography in/of the World System: The Emergence of Multi-Sited Ethnography." *Annual Review of Anthropology* 24: 95–117.

———. 1997. "The Uses of Complicity in the Changing Mise-en-Scene of Anthropological Fieldwork." *Representations* 59:85–108.

———, ed. 1999. *Critical Anthropology Now: Unexpected Contexts, Shifting Constituencies, Changing Agendas.* Santa Fe, NM: School of American Research.

———. 2003. "On the Unbearable Slowness of Being an Anthropologist Now: Notes on a Contemporary Anxiety in the Making of Ethnography." *Xcp* 12:7–20.

———. 2014. "Prototyping and Contemporary Anthropological Experiments with Ethnographic Method." *Journal of Cultural Economy* 7 (4): 399–410.

———. 2015. "Ethnography between the Virtue of Patience and the Anxiety of Belatedness Once Coevalness Is Embraced." In *Time and the Field*, edited by Steffen Dalsgaard and Morten Nielsen, 14–55. London: Berghahn.

———. 2016a. "A Chronicle of Art and Anthropology at the World Trade Organization . . . in Five Not So Easy Pieces." *FIELD* 3 (Winter): 39–71.

———. 2016b. "Jostling Ethnography between Design and Participatory Art Practices . . . and the Collaborative Relations That It Engenders." In *Design Anthropological Futures*, edited by Rachel C. Smith, Kasper Tang Vangkilde, Mette Gislev Kjaersgaard, Ton Otto, Joachim Halse, and Thomas Binder, 105–20. London: Bloomsbury Press.

Marcus, George, and Michael Fischer. 1986. *Anthropology as Cultural Critique: An Experimental Moment in the Human Sciences.* Chicago: University of Chicago Press.

Margolin, Victor. 2002. *The Politics of the Artificial: Essays on Design and Design Studies.* Chicago: University of Chicago Press.

———. 2015. *World History of Design.* London: Bloomsbury Academic.

Margulis, Lynn. 1998. *Symbiotic Planet. A New Look at Evolution.* New York: Basic Books.

Martínez López, Miguel Ángel, and Ángela García Bernardos, eds. 2014. *Okupa*

Madrid (1985–2011): Memoria, reflexión, debate y autogestión colectiva del conocimiento. Madrid: Seminario de Historia Política y Social de las Okupaciones en Madrid-Metrópolis.

Mauss, Marcel. 2000. *The Gift: The Form and Reason for Exchange in Archaic Societies*. New York: W. W. Norton.

McClaurin, Irma. 2020. "COVID-19 Is a Game Changer for Grad Schools and Anthropology." *Anthropology News*, June 3, 2020. https://www.anthropology-news.org/index.php/2020/06/03/a-game-changer-for-grad-schools-and-anthropology/.

McCloskey, Deidre. 1985. *The Rhetoric of Economics*. Madison: University of Wisconsin Press.

McGoey, L. 2015. *No Such Thing as a Free Gift: The Gates Foundation and the Price of Philanthropy*. London: Verso.

McKinnon, Ronald I. 1973. *Money and Capital in Economic Development*. Washington, DC: Brookings Institution.

Medina, Eden, Ivan da Costa Marques, and Christina Holmes, eds. 2014. *Beyond Imported Magic: Science, Technology and Society in Latin America*. Cambridge, MA: MIT Press.

Mehrotra, N. N. 1987. "Indian Patents Act, Paris Convention and Self-Reliance." *Economic and Political Weekly* 22 (34): 1461–65.

Mellow, James R. 1972. "Mr. Nader, Have You Met Mr. Papanek?" *New York Times*, February 27, D21.

Membretti, Andrea, and Pierpaolo Mudu. 2013. "Where Global Meets Local: Italian Social Centres and the Alterglobalization Movement." In *Understanding European Movements: New Social Movements, Global Justice Struggles, Anti-Austerity Protest*, edited by Cristina Flesher Fominaya and Laurence Cox, 76–93. Oxford: Routledge.

Merton, Robert K. 1936. "The Unanticipated Consequences of Purposive Social Action." *American Sociological Review* 1 (6): 894–904.

———. 1948. "The Self-Fulfilling Prophecy." *Antioch Review* 8 (2): 193–210.

Mignolo, Walter. 2012. *Local Histories/Global Designs: Coloniality, Subaltern Knowledges and Border Thinking*. Princeton, NJ: Princeton University Press.

Morgan, Mary S. 2012. *The World in the Model: How Economists Work and Think*. Cambridge: Cambridge University Press.

Mosse, David. 2011. "Social Analysis as Corporate Product: Non-economists/Anthropologists at Work in the World Bank in Washington DC." In *Adventures in Aidland: The Anthropology of Professionals in International Development*, edited by David Mosse, 81–102, Oxford: Berghahn.

Moulds, Josephine. 2020. "How Is the World Health Organization Funded?" *World Economic Forum*, April 15. https://www.weforum.org/agenda/2020/04/who-funds-world-health-organization-un-coronavirus-pandemic-covid-trump/.

Muehlebach, Andrea. 2012. *The Moral Neoliberal: Welfare and Citizenship in Italy*. Chicago: University of Chicago Press.

Muehlebach, Andrea, and Nitzan Shoshan. 2012. "Introduction." *Anthropological Quarterly* 85 (2): 317–44.

Murphy, Keith M. 2015. *Swedish Design: An Ethnography.* Ithaca, NY: Cornell University Press.

———. 2016a. "The Aesthetics of Governance: Thoughts on Designing (and) Politics." *Journal of Design Strategies* 8 (1): 23–28.

———. 2016b. "Design and Anthropology." *Annual Review of Anthropology* 45:433–49.

Murphy, Keith M. 2017. "Art, Design, and Ethical Forms of Intervention." In *Between Matter and Method: Encounters in Anthropology and Art*, edited by Gretchen Bakke and Marina Peterson, 97–116. London: Bloomsbury

Murphy, Keith M., and George E. Marcus. 2013. "Epilogue: Ethnography and Design, Ethnography in Design . . . Ethnography by Design." In *Design Anthropology: Theory and Practice*, edited by W. Gunn, T. Otto, and Rachel Charlotte Smith, 251–68. London.

Nakassis, Constantine V. 2012. "Brand, Citationality, Performativity." *American Anthropologist*, 114 (4): 624–38.

Nelson, Sara, and Bruce Braun. 2017. "Autonomia in the Anthropocene: New Challenges to Radical Politics." *South Atlantic Quarterly* 116 (2): 223–35. https://doi.org/10.1215/00382876-3829368.

Noguera, Ana Patricia. 2020. "Ethos—cuerpo—tierra. Diseños-otros en tiempos de transición civilizatoria." In *Polifonías geo-ético-poéticas del habitar-sur*, edited by Ana Patricia Noguera, 271–300. Manizales: Universidad Nacional.

Narotzky, Susana. 2016. "On Waging the Ideological War: Against the Hegemony of Form." *Anthropological Theory* 16 (2–3): 263–84.

Obama, Barack. 2009. "President Obama's Speech in Cairo: A New Beginning." http://www.state.gov/p/nea/rls/rm/2009/124342.htm.

Olson, Valerie. 2018. *Into the Extreme: U.S. Environmental Systems and Politics beyond Earth.* Minneapolis: University of Minnesota Press.

Oosterlaken, Ilse. 2009. "Design for Development: A Capability Approach." *Design Issues* 25 (4): 91–102.

Oosterlaken, Ilse, and Jeroen van den Hoven. eds. 2012. *The Capability Approach, Technology and Design.* New York: Springer.

Ott, Katherine. 2014. "Disability Things: Material Culture and American Disability History, 1700–2010." In *Disability Histories*, edited by S. Burch and M. Rembis, 119–35. Urbana: University of Illinois Press.

Palacios Córdoba, Elba Mercedes. 2019. "Sentipensar la paz en Colombia: Oyendo las reexistentes voces pacíficas de mujeres Negras Afrodescendientes." *Memorias: Revista Digital de Historia y Arqueología desde el Caribe colombiano* 38 (May–August): 131–61.

Papanek, Victor. 1972. *Design for the Real World: Human Ecology and Social Change.* New York: Pantheon Books.

———. 1984. *Design for the Real World: Human Ecology and Social Change.* 2nd ed. New York: Pantheon.

Paredes, Julieta. 2012. *Hilando fino desde el feminismo comunitario.* La Paz: DED.

Parry, Jonathan. 1986. "The Gift, the Indian Gift and the 'Indian Gift.'" *Man, New Series* 21 (3): 453–73.

Partners for a New Beginning. 2010. Cision PR Newswire, September 22, 2010. http://www.prnewswire.com/news-releases/partners-for-a-new-beginning-announces-full-steering-committee-and-clinton-global-initiative-commitments-103521374.html.

Patnaik, Dev, and Peter Mortenson. 2009. *Wired to Care: How Companies Prosper When They Create Widespread Empathy.* Upper Saddle River, NJ: FT Press.

Pérez-Bustos, Tania. 2016. "El tejido como conocimiento, el conocimiento como tejido: Reflexiones feministas en torno a la agencia de las materialidades" (Weaving as knowledge, knowledge as weaving: Feminist reflections on the agency of materialities) *Revista Colombiana de Sociología* 39 (2): 163–82.

———. 2017. "Thinking with Care: Unraveling and Mending in an Ethnography of Craft Embroidery and Technology." *Revue d'anthropologie des connaissance* 11 (1): a–u.

Pérez-Bustos, Tania, Eliana Sánchez-Aldana, and Alexandra Chocotá-Piraquive. 2019. "Textile Material Metaphors to Describe Feminist Textile Activisms: From Threading Yarn, to Knitting, to Weaving Politics." *Textile: Cloth and Culture* 17 (4): 368–77.

Peters, Tom, and Robert Waterman, Jr. 1982. *In Search of Excellence: Lessons from America's Best-Run Companies.* New York: HarperCollins.

Philip, Kavita. 2004. *Civilizing Natures: Race, Resources, and Modernity in Colonial South India.* New Brunswick, NJ: Rutgers University Press.

———. 2005. "What Is a Technological Author? The Pirate Function and Intellectual Property." *Postcolonial Studies* 8 (2): 199–218.

Philip, Kavita, Lilly Irani, and Paul Dourish. 2010. "Postcolonial Computing: A Tactical Survey." *Science, Technology, and Human Values* 37 (1): 1–27.

Polanyi, Karl. 1944. *The Great Transformation: The Political and Economic Origins of Our Time.* Boston: Beacon Press.

Postigo, Hector. 2012. *The Digital Rights Movement: The Role of Technology in Subverting Digital Copyright.* Cambridge, MA: MIT Press.

Postma, Carolien, Kristina Lauche, and Pieter Jan Stappers. 2012. "Social Theory as a Thinking Tool for Empathic Design." *Design Issues* 28 (1): 30–49.

Prashad, V. 2012. *The Poorer Nations: A Possible History of the Global South.* New York: Verso.

Puig de la Bellacasa, María. 2017. *Matters of Care. Speculative Ethics in More Than Human Worlds.* Minneapolis: University of Minnesota Press.

Pullin, Graham. 2009. *Design Meets Disability.* Cambridge, MA: MIT Press.

Quijano, Olver. 2012. *Ecosimías. Visiones y prácticas de diferencia autonómica/cultural en contextos de multiplicidad.* Popayán: Editorial Universidad del Cauca.

Rabinow, Paul, George E. Marcus, James D. Fabion, and Tobias Rees. 2008. *Designs for an Anthropology of the Contemporary.* Durham, NC: Duke University Press.

Rajagopal, Arvind. 2011. "The Emergency as Prehistory of the New Indian Middle Class." *Modern Asian Studies* 45 (5): 1003–49.

Ramanna, Anitha. 2002. "Policy Implications of India's Patent Reforms: Patent Applications in the Post-1995 Era." *Economic and Political Weekly* 37 (21): 2065–75.

Rattray, Nicholas. 2007. "Evaluating Universal Design: Low- and High-Tech Methods for Mapping Accessible Space." *Practicing Anthropology* 29 (4): 24–28.

Redfield, Peter. 2016. "Fluid Technologies: The Bush Pump, the LifeStraw® and Micro-worlds of Humanitarian Design." *Social Studies of Science* 46 (2):159–83.

Rees, Tobias. 2008. "Afterwards." In *Designs for an Anthropology of the Contemporary*, edited by Rabinow, Paul, George E. Marcus, James D. Fabion, and Tobias Rees, 115–121. Durham, NC: Duke University Press.

Riechmann, Jorge, Adrian Almazan, and 300 other signatures. "La necesidad de luchar contra un mundo 'virtual.'" CTXT, March 5, 2020. https://ctxt.es/es/20200501/Firmas/32143/riechmann-yayo-herrero-digitalizacion-corona-virus-teletrabajo-brecha-digital-covid-trazado-contactos.htm.

Riles, Annelise. 2018. *Financial Citizenship: Experts, Publics, and the Politics of Central Banking*. Cornell Global Perspectives. Ithaca, NY: Cornell University Press.

Rivera Cusicanqui, Silvia. 2018. *Un mundo ch'ixi es posible*. Buenos Aires: Tinta Limón.

Robbins, Joel. 2013. "Beyond the Suffering Slot: Toward an Anthropology of the Good." *Journal of the Royal Anthropological Institute* 19:447–62.

Roper, C. 2013. "The Human Element: Melinda Gates and Paul Farmer on Designing Global Health." *WIRED* 21, no. 12 (November 12). http://www.wired.com/2013/11/2112gatefarmers/.

Roy, Ananya. 2010. *Poverty Capital: Microfinance and the Making of Development*. Routledge.

Roy, Srirupa. 2007. *Beyond Belief: India and the Politics of Postcolonial Nationalism*. Politics, History, and Culture. Durham, NC: Duke University Press.

Rubin, Gayle. 1975. "The Traffic in Women: Notes on the 'Political Economy' of Sex." In *Toward an Anthropology of Women*, edited by R. R. Reiter, 157–210. New York: Monthly Review Press.

Rubio-Pueyo, Vicente. 2016. "Laboratorios de La Historia. Los Centros Sociales Como Productores de Cultura Política En La España Contemporánea (1997–2015)." *Journal of Spanish Cultural Studies* 17 (4): 385–403. https://doi.org/10.1080/14636204.2016.1240438.

Rudnyckyj, Daromir. 2014. "Economy in Practice: Finance and the Problem of Market Reason." *American Ethnologist* 41 (1): 110–27.

———. 2019. *Beyond Debt: Islamic Experiments in Global Finance*. Chicago: University of Chicago Press.

Sádaba Rodríguez, Igor, and Gustavo Roig Domínguez. 2004. "El Movimiento de Okupación Ante Las Nuevas Tecnologías: Okupas En Las Redes." In *¿Dónde están las llaves? El movimiento okupa: Prácticas y contextos sociales*, edited by Ramón Adell Argilés and Miguel Ángel Martínez López, 267–91. Madrid: Los Libros de la Catarata.

Sahlins, Marshall. 1972. *Stone Age Economics*. New York: Routledge.

Salvador, Tony, Genevieve Bell, and Ken Anderson. 1999. "Design Ethnography." *Design Management Journal* 10 (4): 35–41.

Sanjek, Roger, ed. 1990. *Fieldnotes: The Makings of Anthropology*. Ithaca, NY: Cornell University Press.

Sanjek, Roger, and Susan W. Tratner. 2016. *eFieldnotes: The Makings of Anthropology in the Digital World*. Philadelphia: University of Pennsylvania Press.

Schüll, Natasha Dow. 2012. *Addiction by Design: Machine Gambling in Las Vegas*. Princeton, NJ: Princeton University Press.

Schumpeter, A. 1934. *The Theory of Economic Development: An Inquiry into Profits, Capital, Credit, Interest, and the Business Cycle*. New Brunswick, NJ: Transaction Books.

Schwittay, Anke. 2014. "Designing Development: Humanitarian Design in the Financial Inclusion Assemblage." *PoLAR: Political and Legal Anthropology Review* 37 (1): 29–47.

Scott, James C. 1998. *Seeing like a State: How Certain Schemes to Improve the Human Condition Have Failed*. New Haven, CT: Yale University Press.

Searle, John. 1969. *Speech Acts: An Essay in the Philosophy of Language*. Cambridge: Cambridge University Press.

Segal, L. D., and J. F. Suri. 1997. "The Empathic Practitioner: Measurement and Interpretation of User Experience." In *Proceedings of the Human Factors and Ergonomics Society . . . Annual Meeting* 1:451. Human Factors and Ergonomics Society. http://search.proquest.com/openview/b70abb11b9072b3d5623a58 88104305a/1?pq-origsite=gscholar.

Segato, Rita Laura. 2016. *La guerra contra las mujeres*. Madrid: Traficantes de Sueños.

———. 2018. *Contra-pedagogías de la crueldad*. Buenos Aires: Prometeo.

Shankar, Shalini. 2015. *Advertising Diversity: Ad Agencies and the Creation of Asian American Consumers*. Durham, NC: Duke University Press.

Shaw, Edward 1973. *Financial Deepening in Economic Development*. New York: Oxford University Press,

Shead, Sam. 2017. "Amazon now has 45,000 robots in its warehouses." *Business Insider*, January 3. http://www.businessinsider.com/amazons-robot-army-has-grown-by-50-2017-1.

Shohet, Merav. 2013. "Everyday Sacrifice and Language Socialization in Vietnam: The Power of a Respect Particle." *American Anthropologist* 115 (2): 203–17.

Simon, Herbert A. 1996. *Sciences of the Artificial*. 3rd ed. Cambridge, MA: MIT Press.

Simonsen, Jesper, and Toni Robertson, eds. 2012. *Routledge International Handbook of Participatory Design*. London and New York: Routledge.

sinDominio.net. 2004. "Preguntas Frecuentes Sobre El Proyecto SinDominio.Net." 2004. http://sindominio.net/article.php3?id_article=31.

Singleton, John, with Arthur Grimes, Gary Hawke, and Frank Holmes. 2006.

Innovation and Independence: The Reserve Bank of New Zealand. Auckland, NZ: Auckland University Press.

Slaughter, Anne-Marie. 2009. "America's Edge: Power in the Networked Century." *Foreign Affairs* 88 (1): 94–113.

Smith, Rachel Charlotte, Kasper Tang Vangkilde, Mette Gislev Kjærsgaard, Ton Otto, Joachim Halse, and Thomas Binder, eds. 2016. *Design Anthropological Futures.* New York: Bloomsbury.

Spelman, Elizabeth V. 2002. *Repair: The Impulse to Restore in a Fragile World.* Boston: Beacon Press.

Stairs, David. 2005. "Altruism as Design Methodology." *Design Issues* 21 (2): 3–12.

Stengers, Isabelle. 2017. "Autonomy and the Intrusion of Gaia." *South Atlantic Quarterly* 116 (2): 381–400. https://doi.org/10.1215/00382876-3829467.

Strathern, Marilyn. 1987. "An Awkward Relationship: The Case of Feminism and Anthropology," *Signs* 12 (2): 276–92.

———. 1988. *The Gender of the Gift: Problems with Women and Problems with Society in Melanesia.* Berkeley: University of California Press.

———. 1995. *Shifting Contexts: Transformations in Anthropological Knowledge.* New York: Routledge.

———. 2004. *Commons and Borderlands: Working Papers on Interdisciplinarity, Accountability and the Flow of Knowledge.* Herefordshire, UK: Sean Kingston.

Subramanian, Arvind. 2014. "Arvind Subramanian Keynote at India Innovation Conference." PennGlobal. Published on January 2, 2014. YouTube video. https://www.youtube.com/watch?v=P_geC7UryLY.

Suchman, Lucy. 1987. *Plans and Situated Actions: The Problem of Human-Machine Communication.* New York: Cambridge University Press.

———. 2002. "Practice-Based Design: Notes from the Hyper-Developed World." *Information Society* 18 (2): 139–44.

———. 2007. *Human-Machine Reconfigurations.* New York: Cambridge University Press.

———. 2011. "Anthropological Relocations and the Limits of Design." *Annual Review of Anthropology* 40 (1): 1–18.

———. 2013. "Consuming Anthropology." In *Interdisciplinarity: Reconfigurations of the Social and Natural Sciences*, edited by A. Barry and G. Born, 141–60. London: Routledge.

Suchman, Lucy, Randall Trigg, and Jeanette Blomberg. 2002. "Working Artefacts: Ethnomethods of the Prototype." *British Journal of Sociology* 53 (2): 163–79.

Sunder, Madhavi. 2006. "IP³." *Stanford Law Review* 59 (2): 257–332.

Suri, J. F. 2001. "The Next 50 Years: Future Challenges and Opportunities for Empathy in Our Science." *Ergonomics* 44 (14): 1278–89.

Suzuki, S. 1970. *Zen Mind, Beginner's Mind.* Edited by T. Dixon. New York: Walker/Weatherhill.

Svampa, Maristella. 2020. "Reflexiones para un mundo pos-Coronavirus." In *La fiebre. Pensamiento contemporáneo en tiempo de pandemias*, edited by Pablo Amadeo, 17–38. Buenos Aires: Editorial ASPO.

Taylor, Alex S. 2011. "Out There." In *Proceedings of the SIGCHI Conference on Human Factors in Computing Systems*, 685–94, CHI '11. New York: Association for Computing Machinery.

Thorpe, Ann. 2010. "Design's Role in Sustainable Consumption." *Design Issues* 26 (2): 3–16.

Throop, C. Jason. 2008. "On the Problem of Empathy: The Case of Yap, Federated States of Micronesia." *Ethos* 36 (4): 402–26.

———. 2010. "Latitudes of Loss: On the Vicissitudes of Empathy." *American Ethnologist* 37 (4): 771–82.

———. 2012a. "Moral Sentiments." In *A Companion to Moral Anthropology*, edited by D. Fassin, 150–68. Oxford: John Wiley and Sons.

———. 2012b. "On the Varieties of Empathic Experience: Tactility, Mental Opacity, and Pain in Yap." *Medical Anthropology Quarterly* 26 (3): 408–30.

TILT Collective. 2013. *Codesigning Space: A Primer*. Artifice Books.

Trigg, Randall, Jeanette Blomberg, and Lucy Suchman. 1999. "Moving Document Collections Online." *Proceedings of the Sixth European Conference on Computer-Supported Cooperative Work (ECSCW), Copenhagen, Denmark* (September 12–16): 331–50.

Truffaut, Francois. 1985. *Hitchcock: Interviews with Francois Truffaut*. Rev. ed. New York: Simon and Schuster.

Tsing, Anna Lowenhaupt. 2005. *Friction: An Ethnography of Global Connection*. Princeton, NJ: Princeton University Press.

Tsing, Anna Lowenhapt. 2015. *The Mushroom at the End of the World: On the Possibility of Life in Capitalist Ruins*. Princeton, NJ: Princeton University Press.

Tuckett, David, Douglas R. Holmes, Alice Pearson, and Graeme Chaplin. 2020. "Monetary Policy and the Management of Uncertainty: A Narrative Approach." Bank of England Staff Working Paper 870 (June): 1–28.

Tufte, Edward R. 2006. *The Cognitive Style of Powerpoint: Pitching Out Corrupts Within*. Cheshire, CT: Graphics Press.

Tufte, Thomas. 2013. "Towards a Renaissance in Communication for Social Change: Redefining the Discipline and Practice in the Post "ArabSpring" Era." In *Speaking Up and Talking Back? Media, Empowerment and Civic Engagement among East and Southern African outh*, edited by Thomas Tufte, Norbert Wildermuth, Anne-Sofie Hansen-Skovmoes, and Winnie Mitullah, 19–36. Gothenburg: Nordicom.

Tzul Tzul, Gladys. 2018. *Sistemas de gobierno comunal indígena*. México: Instituto Amaq'.

Urban, Greg, and Kyung-Nan Koh. 2013. "Ethnographic Research on Modern Business Corporations." *Annual Review of Anthropology* 42 (1): 139–58.

USAID. 2012. "USAID/India Country Development Cooperation Strategy: 2012–2016."

USAID. https://www.usaid.gov/sites/default/files/documents/1861/India_
    CDCS.pdf.

Vaneigem, Raoul. 1998. *The Movement of the Free Spirit*. New York: Zone Books.

Verbeek, Peter-Paul. 2006. "Materializing Morality: Design Ethics and Technological
    Mediation." *Science Technology and Human Values* 31 (3): 361–80.

———. 2008. "Morality in Design: Design Ethics and the Morality of Technological
    Artifacts." In *Philosophy and Design: From Engineering to Architecture*, edited
    by P. E. Vermaas, P. Kroes, A. Light, and S. A. Moore, 91–104. New York:
    Springer.

Verran, Helen. 1998. "Re-imagining Land Ownership in Australia." *Postcolonial Studies*
    1 (2): 237–54.

Vidal, Miguel. 2003. "[Copyleft] Reunion Casa Encendida." Copyleft. February
    2003. https://listas.sindominio.net/mailman/private/copyleft/2003-Febru-
    ary/000087.html.

———. 2004. "Comentarios a Las FAQ y Estructura." Copyleft. July 2004. https://
    listas.sindominio.net/mailman/private/copyleft/2004-July/001713.html.

Virno, Paolo. 1996. "Virtuosity and Revolution: The Political Theory of Exodus." In
    Radical Thought in Italy: A Potential Politics, edited by Paolo Virno and
    Michael Hardt, 189–210. Minneapolis: University of Minnesota Press.

Vlieghe, Gertjan. 2020. "Monetary Policy and the Bank of England's Balance Sheet,"
    Speech delivered at the Bank of England, London, April 23.

Waal Malefyt, Timothy de. 2009. "Understanding the Rise of Consumer Ethnography:
    Branding Technomethodologies in the New Economy." *American Anthro-
    pologist* 111 (2): 101–10.

Wasson, Christina. 2000. "Ethnography in the Field of Design." *Human Organization*
    59 (4): 377–88.

Weber, Max. 2002. *The Protestant Ethic and the Spirit of Capitalism: and Other Writ-
    ings*. New York: Penguin.

Weems, Jason. 2012. "War Furniture Charles and Ray Eames Design for the Wounded
    Body." *Boom: A Journal of California* 2 (1): 46–48.

Weiner, Annette. 1992. *Inalienable Possessions: The Paradox of Keeping While Giving*.
    Berkeley: University of California Press.

Wilf, Eitan Y. 2013. "Toward an Anthropology of Computer-Mediated, Algorithmic
    Forms of Sociality." *Current Anthropology* 54 (6): 716–39.

———. 2014. "Semiotic Dimensions of Creativity." *Annual Review of Anthropology*
    43:397–412.

———. 2015. "Routinized Business Innovation: An Undertheorized Engine of Cul-
    tural Evolution." *American Anthropologist* 117 (4): 679–92.

———. 2016. "The Post-it Note Economy: Understanding Post-Fordist Business Inno-
    vation through One of Its Key Semiotic Technologies." *Current Anthropology*
    57 (6): 732–60.

———. 2019. *Creativity on Demand: The Dilemmas of Innovation in an Accelerated
    Age*. Chicago: University of Chicago Press.

Winner, Langdon. 1980. "Do Artifacts Have Politics?" *Daedalus* 109 (1): 121–36.

Wood, Siri Karlin. 1996. "Approaches to Grassroots AIDS Education in Africa." In *AIDS Education*, edited by Inon I. Schenker, Galia Sabar-Friedman, and Francisco S. Sy, 29–34. Boston: Springer.

Woodford, Michael. 2012. "Methods of Policy Accommodation at the Interest-Rate Lower Bound." Paper presented at "The Changing Policy Landscape," Federal Reserve Bank of Kansas City Symposium, Jackson Hole, WY, August 31–September 1.

World Bank. 2015. *World Development Report 2015: Mind, Society, and Behavior.* Washington, DC: World Bank. h.p://www.worldbank.org/en/publication/wdr2015.

Yarrow, Thomas. 2019. *Architects: Portraits of a Practice.* Ithaca, NY: Cornell University Press.

Yellen, Janet. 2013. "Communications in Monetary Policy." Speech presented at the Society of American Business Editors and Writers 50th Anniversary Conference, Washington, DC, April 4.

Zaloom, Caitlin. 2006. *Out of the Pits: Traders and Technology from Chicago to London.* Chicago: University of Chicago Press.

Zigon, Jarrett. 2008. *Morality: An Anthropological Perspective.* Oxford: Berg.

Participants in the School for Advanced Research Advanced Seminar "Designs and Anthropologies," co-chaired by Keith M. Murphy (not pictured) and Eitan Wilf, February 11–15, 2018. *Front row, left to right*: Alberto Corsín Jiménez, Eitan Wilf, and Lucy Suchman. *Back row, left to right*: Douglas R. Holmes, Lilly Irani, Lochlann Jain, Lily Chumley, and George E. Marcus. Photograph by Garret Vreeland. © School for Advanced Research.

ALBERTO CORSÍN JIMÉNEZ
Department of Social Anthropology, Spanish National Research Council, Madrid

ARTURO ESCOBAR
Department of Anthropology, University of North Carolina, Chapel Hill
Culture, Memory, and Nation Group, Universidad del Valle, Cali
Cultural Studies Groups, Universidad Javeriana, Bogotá

DOUGLAS R. HOLMES
Department of Anthropology, Binghamton University

LILLY IRANI
Departments of Communication, Science Studies, Computer Science, and Critical Gender Studies, Design Lab, University of California, San Diego

GEORGE E. MARCUS
Department of Anthropology, University of California, Irvine

KEITH M. MURPHY
Department of Anthropology, University of California, Irvine

LUCY SUCHMAN
Department of Sociology, Lancaster University

EITAN Y. WILF
Department of Sociology and Anthropology, Hebrew University of Jerusalem

Page numbers in italic text indicate illustrations.

www.ingramcontent.com/pod-product-compliance
Lightning Source LLC
Chambersburg PA
CBHW031129270326
41929CB00011B/1552